OUT OF THE SIEGE OF
SARAJEVO

OUT OF THE SIEGE OF SARAJEVO
MEMOIR OF A FORMER YUGOSLAV

Jasna Levinger-Goy

Pen & Sword
MILITARY
AN IMPRINT OF PEN & SWORD BOOKS LTD.
YORKSHIRE – PHILADELPHIA

First published in Great Britain in 2022 by
PEN & SWORD MILITARY
An imprint of
Pen & Sword Books Ltd
Yorkshire - Philadelphia

Copyright © Jasna Levinger-Goy, 2022

ISBN 978 1 39909 862 5

The right of Jasna Levinger-Goy to be identified as Author of this work has been asserted by her in accordance with the Copyright, Designs and Patents Act 1988.

A CIP catalogue record for this book is available from the British Library

All rights reserved. No part of this book may be reproduced or transmitted in any form or by any means, electronic or mechanical including photocopying, recording or by any information storage and retrieval system, without permission from the Publisher in writing.

Front cover collage © Emanuela Cusin & Unidentified Artists, *Untitled* (2014), courtesy Emanuela Cusin

'Može li čovjek biti Bosanac?' & 'Kratka povijest holokausta kroz dva telefonska imenika' © Miljenko Jergović

Ivo Andrić, PISMO IZ 1920. GODINE / A LETTER FROM 1920 © The Ivo Andrić Foundation, Beograd, SERBIA

'A Letter from 1920', in translation from *The Damned Yard and Other Stories* © Celia Hawkesworth

Quotations in Addendum by permission of:
www.bbc.co.uk/history/worldwars/wwtwo/partisan_fighters_01.shtml © BBC Commercial, Rights and Business Affairs & © Dr Stephen A Hart

Typeset in Ehrhardt MT & 11.5/14
by SJmagic DESIGN SERVICES, India.
Printed and bound in the UK by CPI Group (UK) Ltd.

Pen & Sword Books Ltd incorporates the imprints of Pen & Sword Archaeology, Atlas, Aviation, Battleground, Discovery, Family History, History, Maritime, Military, Naval, Politics, Social History, Transport, True Crime, Claymore Press, Frontline Books, Praetorian Press, Seaforth Publishing and White Owl

For a complete list of Pen & Sword titles please contact

PEN & SWORD BOOKS LTD
47 Church Street, Barnsley, South Yorkshire, S70 2AS, England
E-mail: enquiries@pen-and-sword.co.uk
Website: www.pen-and-sword.co.uk

Or

PEN & SWORD BOOKS
1950 Lawrence Rd, Havertown, PA 19083, USA
E-mail: Uspen-and-sword@casematepublishers.com
Website: www.penandswordbooks.com

For Ned, the one and only, who helped me stay sane

When things go well 'tis easy to be good.
In suffering is it seen who is the hero.[1]

U dobru je lako dobar biti,
Na muci se poznaju junaci.[2]

Contents

About the Author		viii
Acknowledgments		ix
Author's Note		xi
Chapter 1	Prelude to the Events to Come	1
Chapter 2	Blind Denial	15
Chapter 3	Reluctant Recognition	52
Chapter 4	Rude Awakening	66
Chapter 5	Recovery	107
Epilogue		137
Addendum	Yugoslavia in the Second World War	141
Appendix A	2021 Update of Family Members and the People from Sarajevo Mentioned in the Text	144
Appendix B	Excerpt from a Story by Ivo Andrić	149
Endnotes		150

About the Author

Jasna Levinger-Goy was born in Sarajevo, former Yugoslavia. She has a BA in English Language and Literature from Sarajevo University, an MA in Linguistics from Georgetown University, Washington DC, and a PhD, also in Linguistics, from Zagreb University. In the former Yugoslavia she was a university lecturer at Sarajevo University and later at Novi Sad University. In the UK she was a lector in Serbo-Croat at SSEES, University College London and a tutor in interpreting at London Metropolitan University. She has published a number of articles and translations both in Serbo-Croat and in English. While in Sarajevo she translated Emily Dickinson's poetry in cooperation with Marko Vešović, published by Svjetlost Sarajevo in 1989 and by OKF Cetinje in 2014. She moved to the UK during the Bosnian civil war and married Edward Dennis Goy, a Cambridge University Slavist. They worked together on various translations, including translations into English of the Yugoslav novels, *The Fortress* by Meša Selimović and *The Banquet in Blitva* by Miroslav Krleža. In the early 2000s she qualified as an integral psychotherapist and has her own practice in Cambridge.

Acknowledgments

This book traces a difficult personal journey but writing about it gave me much pleasure. I sincerely hope readers will share some of that pleasure or, at least, find the story interesting. However, my pleasure would have been hugely diminished had I not had so many generous and supportive people around me. It is not easy to mention them all, but I would like to mention those who stick out in my mind.

Firstly, many thanks to Emanuela Cusin who kindly gave me permission to use the collage on the front cover which I believe reflects the place I was in during the ten years of my troubled journey. I also owe special gratitude to a group of close friends and family: Dianne, Dodo, Goran, Henika, Jenny, Julia, Nina, Tatjana and Zvonko. Many of them even had the patience to read my first rough draft which was far too dense and raw and definitely not an easy read. They all made pertinent comments which gave me a necessary early impetus to carry on working.

I owe enormous gratitude to another group of friends who helped and supported me in various ways. Deborah Evans gave me the initial push to start writing. She believed in my ability to write this book (rightly or wrongly) more than I did. Patrick Miles was hugely generous with both his time and advice and was there for me whenever I needed him, and it was not seldom. He was my 'guru' and without him this book would likely have never left my computer. Piotr Kuhivchak provided the first specific and very helpful suggestions that radically changed the early shape of the manuscript, and for the better. Bogdan Rakić read the revised version and pointed to a significant underlying thread in the text of which I was unaware and motivated me to further expand on it. Jane Qualtrough supported me the way only a true friend can. Among other things she spent an enormous amount of time and energy not only reading my manuscript, but also editing it thoroughly after I introduced the first post-copyediting amendments. Her understanding of the text and consequently her appropriate suggestions were of immense value.

I would also like to thank Miranda Bethell with whom I have a virtual relationship, not an unusual phenomenon these days. We have never met but, by strange coincidence, she encouraged and supported me online which gave me much-needed additional incentive. My thanks go to Paul Martin who efficiently copyedited an earlier version and without whom this book would have had a very different destiny. He put me in touch with Chris Brown who in turn put me in touch with Pen & Sword Publishers. Chris Brown made negotiating the publishing contract a happy undertaking together with Claire Hopkins, Pen & Sword commissioning editor, who patiently finalized the submission of the manuscript. Claire was helpful and supportive and made several suggestions, among them to include some photos. I had never thought of adding photos, but accepting her suggestion, I believe, made the book more alive. I am grateful to Laura Hirst, production editor, who made sure everything was running smoothly. And last but by no means least, I owe huge gratitude to Chris Cocks, the Pen & Sword copy editor, who meticulously edited the book with a great deal of professionalism, understanding, patience and empathy. He made sure I did my utmost with the text. Lucky for me (but not for him, I am sure) he had experienced similar circumstances and knew exactly what I wanted to say.

They have all helped shape the final version of the book for which I will for ever be grateful.

Author's Note

This book has been long in the making. I was reluctant to write it for a considerable amount of time, in spite of suggestions to do so by a number of people, among them the first and the most important one being Ned, my husband. The experience was just too raw until recently. Now it feels more settled and more objective.

Names of the people I mention in the text, be they my family or others, are presented in the form in which I was accustomed to addressing them. Therefore, I refer to some people by their nicknames, but not all. Yugoslav names usually indicate belonging to a particular ethnic group, so some such associations might be inevitable. However, I have tried to give that the least possible significance. I point to ethnicity only if deemed necessary. I have tried, but I am not sure whether I have succeeded. Still, it might also depend on the reading of the text. My hope, as the author, has been to offer at least a semblance of objectivity. I have also focused more on emotional than factual aspects, since I deem those more pertinent for the narrative of this book. By offering a personal and subjective view I have tried, at the same time, to hint at the universality of human behaviour, reactions and impulses. That has been the basic idea, not easily achievable though. After all, it is a very personal account of very public events. It covers some ten years of my life, starting with 1992 up until about 2002, roughly from my mid-forties to my mid-fifties. The experience of those ten years has enriched me in many respects but it is certainly the kind of wealth one would happily do without.

Quite significant time has elapsed between the events described and the time of writing, but the strength of feelings is still palpable. After all, the text is based on my own experience of the 1992 civil war[1] in Bosnia and Herzegovina,[2] and its aftermath. It is a story about the pain of being forced to leave behind one's home and all that that entails. It also explores the desperate attempts to recreate a kind of replica of that home and to create a new one. Alongside that, it is also a story about the loss of the identity I believed defined me; the identity which abruptly disappeared with the sudden disintegration of the foundations upon which it had been built. That loss inadvertently initiated a search for some sort of backup identity, the 'replacement' identity. It resulted in both the awakening of a dormant identity I had not acknowledged before and a readiness to accept a new one. Hence, there is a fair amount of emphasis on those private aspects, although the wider, social and political ones have been unavoidable.

Admittedly, it is yet one more book about Sarajevo and former Yugoslavia of the 1990s, but it is one with a distinctly personal slant, focusing mostly on actions of the individuals I came into contact with, their behaviour and feelings. It also delves into the predicament of a person forced to flee both *from* and *to* and the dilemmas often accompanying such a situation.

Some facts might appear confusing, especially the political and social references, but it is not surprising for a region in Europe that has been subject to so much turmoil and so many political changes.[3] The turmoil of the country is best illustrated by the (hi)story of a friend's grandmother: she was born in 1904 (of Serbian ethnicity, a fact relevant here due to the particular political changes), she never moved away from her place of birth, a small town in eastern Herzegovina,[4] and yet managed to live in seven states under seven regimes till her death in 1997. So, the summary of her 'movements' reads as follows: she was born in the Ottoman Empire, which was annexed three years later by the Austro-Hungarian Monarchy. In 1918, she found herself living in the Kingdom of Serbs, Croats and Slovenes, which was in 1929 renamed the Kingdom of Yugoslavia (not a substantial change, just relabelling). The substantial, in her case life-threatening, change came in 1941, when the region came under the jurisdiction of the Independent State of Croatia (NDH, a fascist puppet state of Germany and Italy, overtly anti-Serbian). From 1945, she lived in the Communist Yugoslavia (occasionally changing its name, but not the substance), until the 1990s when she briefly lived in the new creation named the Socialist Republic of Bosnia and Herzegovina,[5] to find herself eventually, in 1992, in the Republic of Srpska[6] (an area which in 1992 seceded from Bosnia and Herzegovina), where she died in 1997.

The account of my experiences in this book is based on memory, a rather fallible, often unreliable phenomenon, so some events might not have happened the way I present them and others might not have even been mentioned. Under traumatic circumstances one sometimes remembers the trivial and forgets the extraordinary. As I. D. Yalom says: 'Memoirs ... are far more fictional than we like to think.'[7] Also considering that under such dire conditions one experiences time differently, the timeline of events within the text might not always be correct. Everything described, though, I remember as such and believe to be true. That includes the references to military positions around Sarajevo and military activities as well. All the

Sarajevo events – political, military and personal – roughly cover the period from March 1992 until mid-August 1992, as I recollect them. Chronology is not always followed: sometimes references (often rendered in italics) to both pre-1992 and post-2002 events were deemed revealing and useful. Some explanations might seem redundant, but due to the fact that the book deals with none-too-familiar details, a few explanations felt called for.

And, finally, it was not by chance that I felt the urge to write this book at the end of September 2019, when Brexit 'temperatures' in the UK ran high, when anger, animosities and divisions were palpable, when language became intemperate. It became quite unsettling for me; it was an unpleasant reminder. Any comparison with my previous experience would be inappropriate, but my visceral, adverse reactions became quite understandable.[8] Hence, the sudden urge to write this book.

References to names and concepts in regards to Yugoslavia, explained mostly in endnotes, are mainly taken from the *Encyclopaedia Britannica*[9] and are clearly indicated.

Chapter 1

Prelude to the Events to Come

The Family of Yugoslavs, in Yugoslavia

I, the author and main 'hero' in this book, lived in Sarajevo, the capital of Bosnia and Herzegovina.[1] I was born after the Second World War and lived in Yugoslavia for the greater part of my life. It was a socialist/communist country, with various names, from 1945 until 1992 (when this story starts). The political system, however, was the same and the same person, Tito, was at the helm,[2] both of the government and of the army, for most of my life in Yugoslavia.

Both my parents grew up in typical Jewish middle-class families.[3] They were born and lived with their respective families in Sarajevo until the Second World War. They were both secular Jews, yet secular or not, being Jewish in the Second World War did not offer 'good prospects' of survival, to put it mildly. However, strangely enough, both parents survived the war along their entire immediate families: my mother, fresh out of high school, with her parents and her younger sister; my father, several years older, with his parents, his older sister and her child.[4]

In 1941, not married yet, they fled Sarajevo, as did all the members of their respective families. The reason they had to flee was the fact that Sarajevo became a part of NDH (Independent State of Croatia) i.e. under the *Ustashi*[5] jurisdiction (a clear threat to life for the Jewish population). The two families (in small groups or individually) went to Mostar[6] which was then under Italian jurisdiction and deemed safe (unfortunately not for long). Actually, it was relatively safe until early spring 1943, when all the Jews were gathered and sent to various Adriatic islands and from there to an Italian concentration camp (not an extermination camp) on the island of Rab.[7] So, all the members of both families, including the young child, born as a refugee, eventually ended up in the same concentration camp. (My parents continued seeing each other all the time.)

They were interned there for less than six months – from spring until autumn. The chances of survival during winter were slim, but due to the Italian surrender in September 1943, the inmates were set free before winter and they fled to inland Croatia, a territory held by the Partisans, i.e. the Communist guerrilla force fighting mostly against the Axis powers during the war.[8]

There both families presented themselves to Tito's Partisans and were allocated shelter with various peasant families in ethnically exclusively Serbian villages in the area.[9] There were frequent raids by both Ustashi and German troops and they had to hide in tree trunks, unused wells and neighbouring forests. It was a traumatic time for all of them, especially for Henika,[10] the young daughter of my father's sister Ella. At the end of the war, my parents got married while they were still in Croatia.

Why they were sent to live only in Serbian villages in Croatia was never very clear to me. Maybe because the Serbs (the minority also bearing the brunt of Ustashi animosities in the NDH), equally threatened as the Jews, could empathize and were more ready to offer shelter to those in dire need? My parents never talked much about their war experiences including the time spent in those villages. If they did mention anything, it was always with either a positive or a humorous slant to their stories. They probably wanted to spare me, born after the war, from any remnants of hatred still alive in some people's minds. Moreover, they probably did not want to dwell on the past, on the negative; they wanted to focus on a future which they saw as promising.

So, after the horrors of the Second World War, in 1945, the two families returned to their hometown of Sarajevo in Bosnia and Herzegovina, then part of the newly established communist Socialist Federal People's Republic of Yugoslavia.[11] They found no belongings; their properties had been looted. However, that did not matter much to them, especially to the young couple, my parents. After all, they had survived with their respective families! Both families were small and most stayed in Sarajevo all their lives.[12]

Having lived through the horrors of the war, with religious, ethnic and ideological hatreds raging and threatening their mere existence, it was not surprising that my parents welcomed the new regime. They both believed in the communist ideals. After all, they got married at the very end of the war, in a Partisan registry office, and wanted to believe in a better future. They started building their life, albeit as 'honest intelligentsia' (a derogatory phrase Tito used in referring to intellectuals in his early speeches) and of Jewish extraction as well. They never did, or would, deny their Jewish origin, but they readily embraced the ideology of 'brotherhood and unity' and defined themselves as Yugoslav.

The idea of unity was especially close to their hearts. Due to their war experiences, they instinctively resented any group separation or tribalism in general, but specifically along religious or ethnic lines. They passed all that onto me and I have always felt very comfortable with all those ideals, as well as with Yugoslav identity.

Although somewhat different, especially in the choice of the vocabulary – for instance the use of an occasional German or Yiddish[13] word – I believe we integrated well with the general population; we certainly wanted to. In any case, Jews as a group were not mentioned much, neither in terms of the Holocaust nor the current life. Jews were a rare 'specimen', unfamiliar to most of the Sarajevo population at the time.[14] On top of that, a huge number of Jews perished in the war and it was not an attractive topic to dwell upon; better avoided. As Miljenko Jergović[15] points out: 'In immature and unfulfilled cultures with no awareness of their own past and origin, in small, provincial milieus, it is best to keep quiet about Jews and Holocaust.'[16] The tragic reality was that the Jews were annihilated. Post-war estimates vary, but, according to most, out of about 12,000 Sarajevo Jews at the outset of the Second World War, only 3,000 returned in 1945.

No wonder then that everyone in my family was happy they had all survived and they did not mull over the past. The present seemed appealing and the future more so, particularly to my parents, in spite of the fact that in 1948 my father was taken by the secret police and falsely accused of being a 'political enemy' and the fact that the family suffered the consequences and social stigma (a fact unbeknown to me till adulthood).[17] They must have shared the sentiment Janina Bauman described in post-war Poland when talking about the Communist Party and the promises of the world and the future they were to make: 'the future was all bliss – without hatred or prejudice, race or nation … the only world in which … all my dreams of belonging would come true?'[18]

Also, no wonder then that the communist ideology of the country they then lived in and where several peoples seemed to live happily together was so attractive to them, especially after the devastating Second World War experience. As Hayden points out: 'The country had been premised on the proposition that the Yugoslav peoples were so closely related ('brotherhood') that they could live together in a common state.'[19] The idea of 'brotherhood and unity' was strongly promoted, a captivating prospect for those who wanted to believe in it. There was also an apparent fairness in society: all had access to free education, free health care and full employment. People were allocated accommodation by the authorities, which meant most people had flats[20] to live in, albeit mostly not spacious ones.[21] On the whole there was no private property ownership, but maybe that did not seem such a bad idea.

Having witnessed how ethnic divisions could be a source of evil, my parents readily embraced the idea of Yugoslav identity which felt like a unifying force. Unsurprisingly, I followed suit. I did not question it; I had no need nor desire to. Not being religious, it was easy for them to accept new non-religious secular customs.[22] They accepted new social codes and, inadvertently, so did I. Admittedly, my maternal grandfather whom I adored, was a believer and a Jew rather than a Yugoslav (as all the younger members of his family were), but it was explained away as his 'old age inflexibility', an inability to accept change, 'even for the better'. Whatever the reason was, there was a tacit agreement in the family that religion was 'his thing', and we never talked about it much.

However, strangely enough, the family had kept[23] *his small prayer book and that was a memento my mother chose to take with her in 1992. I still have it displayed proudly on my shelf. I held onto it. Was it a sign the universe gave me indicating that I would eventually end up inhabiting the 'world', albeit not religiously, in which my grandfather had lived all his life?*

So, I started life as a member of a family of Yugoslavs, aware of my Jewish origins, with very few connections with Judaism. (The irony was that, although I did not feel Jewish, it transpired that other people mostly perceived me as a Jew without openly articulating it.) I had a strong sense of belonging to the country. I also saw my place within many a group such as linguists, the English Department, my circle of friends and, above all, my wider family. I was a university lecturer, working at the English Department since the mid-1970s, not hugely political. I was rather loyal in nature. I was open, extrovert and curious; I spoke my mind. I was divorced and living with my parents (with a slim chance of getting a flat of my own).[24] I had lived a sheltered existence, surrounded by love and understanding. I was even sometimes pampered as an only child. We were not a rich family, but we always had enough. Both parents were professionals, both worked and, as a child, I was looked after either by a nanny that we had always had, or by the extended family. We were a typical middle-class family (similar to my grandparents). I mostly had everything I needed; I never actually wanted for anything that mattered. Growing up, I did not have to fight for things. Maybe that was why I was not aggressive: rather I was a slow, patient, methodical achiever. I believed in proving my points rather than fighting for them; I believed in reaching a goal through personal effort and engagement. I was not unscrupulous, but was both persistent and determined, and stubborn too.

After the divorce, I was single for a long time. I took my divorce very badly. I later had some fleeting relationships, but nothing of any significance. Love was my obsession, but I could not find it, or so it felt. I longed for the loving relationship my parents had, but it was not to be. As time went by, it was more and more difficult to find a suitable person to be with. Finally, Nikola, a married colleague, pursued me and I fell for him. Nikola was charming, intelligent and educated; I both respected him and loved him. We were in a secret relationship for around eight years. I was not comfortable about the fact that he was married, but convinced myself that he knew what he was doing; I was not endangering his marriage. Why did I accept such a demeaning position? Denial or desperation? Probably the latter; I desperately wanted to find love; I needed to love and be loved. (Who knows how long the relationship would have lasted, but for the war that separated us. I left Sarajevo in August 1992. He remained there a bit longer.)

Although I was born and bred in Yugoslavia, I had always felt ambivalent about the culture in which I lived, in spite of feeling strongly embedded in it. It was a sort of paradox I probably was not fully aware of. My return from studying in the US,[25] many years before the Bosnian war, shed some light on the ambivalence I sensed regarding the Yugoslav culture. Was I a misfit or what? Some aspects of the culture, some patterns of behaviour, were strange to me. I felt uncomfortable. I would not comply. I used humour as a weapon to defend myself, even clowning occasionally. No wonder people referred to me as 'bonkers'. Even some family members. I was different. Not bonkers, eccentric maybe. In a way that was my way of protecting my integrity.

As I entered adulthood, I started sensing that it was not easy living in a socialist country.[26] For most people, there was a significant discrepancy between personal and public life. Family values frequently did not match the official, public ones. Personal views often had to be kept secret. There were quite a number of people (not all), for instance, who followed religious customs privately and in secret, while at the same time professing allegiance to the Communist Party and advocating against religion. That was not the case in my family, but still our family values were not necessarily the same as those officially prescribed. Individuals had limited freedom, even freedom of thought. Not as bad as in some countries, but that was little comfort. There were strict rules, somewhat intricate, but predictable. In a 'classless' society, middle class was actually not very welcome. Intelligentsia even less so. The common way Tito used to address[27] his early audience was, 'Workers, peasants and honest intelligentsia'. Honest intelligentsia? Did it then mean that workers and peasants were honest by default, and intelligentsia only as an exception? I was both: middle class and intelligentsia. Even my family background was middle class and intelligentsia. On top of that, I later became a university lecturer with a PhD and an open mind, a recipe for those not to be trusted. I had to find the way to be true to myself, without getting into danger. Not easy. For a believer in truth (to the degree of obsession), it was even harder.

I knew all about the secret police but, for some reason or other, I was not afraid. Was it a case of if one had done nothing wrong, there was nothing to be afraid of?[28] Maybe? Be it as it may, I felt that the secret police were omnipresent, but invisible and not much of a threat. Admittedly, their existence was irritating, but it was not too scary, or so I thought. I could manage that. My friends and colleagues would help, as they did on occasions when I publicly, at meetings, said something non-PC, which, in that context, meant literally any comment that seemed not in favour of the political system.[29] I believed I could defend myself one way or another. I would play the 'bonkers card' or rely on my friends, I thought.

And, on one occasion, it worked. When a student reported to the political minders that I favoured the US university exam procedure over the Yugoslav one, it came back to a colleague and friend, the Head of the Linguistic Chair at the time, who only warned me to watch what I was saying. I was both grateful to her and angry with the minders. Why would an innocent comment made in passing be considered the 'action of the enemy from within', as such actions were referred to? The English Department as a whole, I felt, was a safe place though; it felt like a small, harmonious family. I enjoyed the camaraderie, the friendliness.

However, it turned out I was wrong about being safe from the secret police. Sometime in the late 1980s, it became serious. Neither delusion nor denial, nor eccentricity, helped this time. The entire English Department was assigned to teach Serbo-Croat to a group of American students visiting the University of Sarajevo. One day, I had a strange phone call from someone who introduced himself as 'a friend' (apparently code for secret police). He asked me to come to particular offices – I knew what they were – the next day for 'a friendly chat', officially known as 'informative conversation'. He made it clear that it was not optional. I was not best pleased, but I went and was asked to report to the young plain-clothes policeman should I notice that any of the US students were not what they claimed to be – a strange request, and my explanation that I only communicated with them *ex cathedra*, i.e. I taught grammar and did not have a clue as to who was what, did not help.

So, I was asked to attend another 'friendly chat', which I thought I resolved by playing a bit of a fool. I had hoped that would put him off. It did not. And, when he asked me after that to meet again, at a café, I had had enough. I asked Nikola, whom I considered streetwise, for advice as to how to get rid of the policeman. He told me to tell the chap that I felt it smacked of sexual harassment and that I would report him to his bosses. I was horrified; not only that it was not true, but it also seemed pretentious. The chap was much too young to be accused of falling for me, I thought. However, I did as advised and it worked. The policeman told me to forget that he had ever existed and he never contacted me again. I genuinely could never figure out whether that was some sort of a code Nikola was familiar with, or if it just simply scared the policeman off. Whatever the truth was, I was glad and relieved.

Even though I was told never to tell anyone about this encounter, I told my two colleagues and close friends, Zvonko and Omer, and it transpired that they each had 'their own' secret police contacts matching their respective ethnicities; they were only surprised that mine was not Jewish.

Zvonko and his wife were close friends. What we shared was much more than just our professional relationship. They both supported me in all sorts of ways. The same applied to Omer. He and his wife and children were like a second family to me. We would rely on each other through difficult times, but we also shared the happy ones. We spent many holidays and celebrations together. Apart from my childhood friends I would say they were the closest friends I had had.

It must have been around that time, in the late 1980s, when Zvonko and Omer told me 'their policemen' were of their ethnicity and asked whether 'mine' was Jewish that I started thinking about my identity. Although all my life I had considered myself a Yugoslav with a twist,[30] I suddenly started delving deeper into the issue of my identity. I had always been aware of some traits of my Jewishness but, on the whole, I had not dwelled much on the issue and I certainly had not felt very Jewish.

I guess there must have been many reasons why I ignored my Jewish origin. It took a civil war and fleeing home for me to accept Judaism as a part of my identity, albeit gradually and reluctantly. The fact that Judaism appeared overtly in my life was not caused by either rational or emotional reasons. The Jewish 'label' (as it seemed at first) was assigned to me by an official in Belgrade. I did not have a say in the matter. It was purely a practical solution for the officials.

Ultimately, I had to admit to myself that Yugoslav identity must have been an artificial construct that could not withstand the test of time since it disappeared in less than fifty years. As a consequence, I was left without identity and without much choice. However, the realization that I was suddenly deprived of the identity I believed I had, came in stages and insidiously. No alarm bells rang even when I was officially told I was Jewish for the first time. It was in 1992, in my mid-forties, when, as a refugee, I went to register with the local authorities in Belgrade and they refused to register me as Yugoslav stating that Yugoslav identity did not exist anymore. Hence, they decided to put Jewish instead, having realized that the family was receiving financial support from the Jewish Community. Jewishness gradually grew on me. I worked in the Belgrade Jewish Community Centre and felt I fitted in rather well. Later, in London, I volunteered in a Jewish day-care centre, lived in the Jewish area and finally started recognizing and acknowledging parts of my Jewish identity. I suddenly sensed that there was some sort of commonality between me and the many Jewish people I met. The most obvious proof of that for me came later, in my relationship with my mother's hospital consultant, Dr Noimark,[31] whom my mother nicknamed 'little kippah'[32] (because he wore one). We met him by sheer chance when my mother fell ill and he turned out to be a duty doctor. For us a Godsend. He and I clicked immediately; we shared a sense of humour as well as sensibility, I believed. We did not refer much to our Jewish connection, but I felt that it must have been a factor in our unusually open communication.

Admittedly, Judaism had always puzzled me anyway: I wondered whether it was a faith, ethnicity, or what. There had to be something in the collective memory and in the DNA, in shared traits, even among the secular Jews, I concluded. I could not decide how to categorize it. Eventually I decided to define myself as a Traditional Secular Jew. That about described me.

Sometime in 1997, Nikola rang me up at my home in Cambridge and asked about my plans to return to Sarajevo. I told him I had no intention of doing so. He seemed genuinely perplexed. He appealed to my sense of belonging, my roots. I suddenly heard myself quote Michael Ignatieff.[33] I remembered that I had read somewhere a text in which Ignatieff wrote something about Jews not having roots – they had legs and wherever they felt good then that was their home, to paraphrase him. It sounded right to me and I repeated it. Yes, that was another confirmation of my inherent Judaism.

Sarajevo, Bosnia and Herzegovina: My Birthplace

Sarajevo, my birthplace,[34] is the capital of Bosnia and Herzegovina, often known for the 1914 assassination of Archduke Franz Ferdinand[35] and its relationship to the start of the First World War. Various sources often describe it as the place where the cultures of East and West meet. It is quite true about the older central part of the town, but not true about the many of the newer parts built by the socialist government to provide accommodation for people who found employment in the town.

In any case one can safely say that it is an interesting town for various reasons.

It is situated at over 550 metres, or 1,800 feet, above sea level. The climate exhibits four distinct seasons. It is a continental, one could say dynamic, climate of very cold winters with much snow[36] and dry hot summers, with spring and autumn in between, usually humid, yet mild. Sarajevo is located in a valley surrounded by hills and mountains. The central part of the town along the Miljacka River is confined and, since the valley is narrow, the town spreads up into the surrounding hills too, which is why there are many steep streets, some winding and narrow. The residential areas are cramped and densely populated. However, the valley widens significantly downstream of the Miljacka, westward towards the River Bosna into which it flows. The surrounding mountains here are much farther from the river. The main section of the valley used to be called *Sarajevsko polje* (literally the field of Sarajevo), known for its fertile soil and agriculture where sparsely populated settlements were home to farmers growing produce for sale in Sarajevo. The socialist government later expanded the town into this area.

My memories of the town cover the period from my post-Second World War early childhood till 1992, so the descriptions refer to that period only. As I remember, there were no big squares or boulevards, with only a few parks and fountains throughout the town. There were a few small factories in the town, such as a chocolate factory, a cigarette factory and a brewery, all closely surrounded by buildings where people lived. The more recent, newly built parts to the west of the town connect various suburbs and villages with the main body of the town. Although it grew considerably with time, it was still not a very big town. According to records the population of Sarajevo in 1945 was 115,000 and by 1991 it had grown to about 527,000 inhabitants.

It grew steadily since 1945, yet to me it had always felt rather repressive and claustrophobic. The dark mountains covered in thick coniferous forests surrounding the town centre were certainly a contributing factor. The Miljacka, a shallow river, flows through the town with many bridges of differing style over it, with even a small brook flowing into it, but to me it did not feel big enough to bring any relief from the menace the mountains appeared to create. The combination of density of the buildings, the closeness of the mountains and the frequent smog were mostly responsible for creating in me a sense of oppression.

Originally there were only a few tall buildings, especially in the older part of town; for instance, a not-so-tall clocktower next to the big mosque at Baščaršija, and the building known as the JAT[37] 'skyscraper'[38] nearer the city centre. However, later, mostly in the 1970s and 1980s, the socialist government built several high-rises in the central part of town.[39] Among them were the block of flats which housed the popular coffeehouse named Park (since it was near the so-called *Big Park*), the Parliament building[40] and two office towers[41] popularly called 'Momo' and 'Uzeir' symbolizing the aspirations regarding the concept of 'brotherhood and unity', named after the two characters in a popular TV series: Momo was a Serb and Uzeir a Muslim. So, with these new, impressive buildings the town acquired more metropolis-like features.

There were a number of mosques (apparently significantly increased since 1992), as well as a few Catholic and Orthodox churches and one functioning synagogue (all the others having been converted by the town authorities into venues of secular usage). Quite close to the town centre there were several cemeteries which served the different religious groups, including a Jewish cemetery originating from the sixteenth century (the final burials took place in the 1960s when the cemetery became a monument of national interest). The several parks within the city parameter were precious. Nobody was allowed to walk on the grass (at least until 1992). The grassy areas were usually protected by a single strand of wire strung between small wooden posts.

In my childhood, there were park attendants making sure nobody walked on the grass. To us, the children, they were very scary.

As mentioned, Sarajevo was often enveloped in a low grey smog even on sunny days. That was why the Trebević[42] cable car, which opened in 1959, became very popular. People would frequently take it to get up to Trebević Mountain, to *Vidikovac*, the observation platform, at 1,160 metres, or 3,800 feet, above sea level, in order to escape the gloom of the town and enjoy the sunshine while looking down onto the grey 'sea' concealing Sarajevo.

Throughout my lifetime, Sarajevo had been a peaceful, multi-ethnic town, or so it seemed to me. It comprised not only various ethnic groups and combinations of them,[43] but also the four entities, the four main boroughs, as we knew them: Old City, Centre, New Sarajevo and New City (Stari Grad, Centar, Novo Sarajevo and Novi Grad)[44] spreading from east to west. Both empires, the Ottoman[45] and the Austro-Hungarian[46] that had ruled the area and later the socialist regime[47] left a big stamp on the town as a whole. I had always been aware of the distinct features of each entity.

All four boroughs were architecturally different. Farthest east, within the borough of Stari Grad, was the colourful, vibrant sector called Baščaršija that retained all the hallmarks of the Ottoman Empire: the largest mosque from the Ottoman times, a small square with a distinct *sebilj* fountain[48] and small houses with interesting shop fronts, selling a plethora of handicraft items. Walking downstream along the Miljacka, from the Catholic Cathedral, along the high street and westward towards Marindvor, one came to the borough of Centar, the heart of the town originally built during the era of the Austro-Hungarian Empire. Again, architecturally different, more monumental in appearance, with larger buildings and a mixture of styles. Most of the early post-Second World War additions were introduced in the borough of Centar. Those were, among others, the already mentioned JAT skyscraper, the 'New' Railway Station and the 'Eternal Flame', a memorial to the military and civilian victims of the Second World War.

Each of these two sectors had specific institutions, trades and other activities. The buildings varied in size and some also accommodated residents. At Stari Grad, specifically at Baščaršija, one could find all sorts of crafts and trades, from Turkish-style handmade slippers, to coppersmiths and jewellers, goldsmiths and silversmiths as well as small food outlets and more. Main government institutions were predominantly located in Centar, in buildings built during the Austro-Hungarian rule or those built later but in the similar style. The most popular shops and department stores were there too, as well as cinemas and theatres, the main post office and several banks.

The third borough was called Novo Sarajevo. It was actually a mishmash of style and purpose; for instance, a dairy plant and a disused railway station were located among apartment buildings of various sizes. Initially it did not cover a large area as it did not have too many large buildings, but over time it developed and spread out. Since it was further from the heart of the town it also housed various repair shops and garages. New, often impressive and large structures were built there too, especially in the 1970s and 1980s. Among others were a new hotel, The Bristol that replaced the old one, the Elektroprivreda national grid office building, the Energoinvest office building and a few others.

With time Sarajevo expanded down the wider valley and that became the fourth borough, the borough of Novi Grad. Developments sprang up all over Sarajevsko polje as suburbs displaced the farm lands. Ilidža, once a 'faraway' spa dating from Roman times, suddenly 'came closer' and became one a suburb. All these areas evolved into separate entities with their own names. They were built in different eras, primarily to provide housing, with 'modern', mostly concrete buildings, often high-rises, spreading in different directions, as newly created 'dormitory towns'. The initial area of development was called Grbavica, which consisted of boxlike concrete blocks housing the ever-growing population, initially mostly army personnel.

With time and industrialization, village life gradually diminished as people migrated to the towns in ever greater numbers, and more housing developments appeared, including Dobrinja that stretched all the way to the Sarajevo airport. They all differed architecturally. After the earlier crammed boxlike houses, high-rises were built and later even attractive, smaller houses.

People lived in their uniform buildings, in larger or smaller blocks of flats overlooking each other, but it was nothing unusual. By and large it was the typical way of Sarajevo urban living. With not too many parks and trees in the old town, only narrow streets and crammed multistorey houses – that was the way most people lived. However, the majority of traditional Sarajevans did not like the new parts very much. It was partly snobbery and partly because it seemed and possibly was too impersonal, too characterless. Daily activities were mostly restricted to the central parts; people rarely went to the 'modern' areas, unless they lived there or were visiting.

All the boroughs were connected by tramlines, bus lines and trolleybuses. Streets were also jammed with private vehicles. Walking from Baščaršija to Marindvor and beyond, one felt the physical continuity, but not a continuity in style. One could strongly feel the impact that the centuries had left. Yet to most Sarajevo residents, all four districts, even the newly built 'socialist realism' estates, felt like one integrated whole, albeit of many different flavours. One would feel equally at home in all the sectors, or at least that was how I felt.

Three major ethnic groups – Croats, Muslims[49] and Serbs – lived there together and their lives intertwined more or less successfully and peacefully. The Second World War animosities were not talked about and seemingly not overtly present. However, the socio-political fabric of Bosnia and Herzegovina has always been extremely complicated and seems to have remained so.[50]

I actually had felt quite comfortable living in the city and in the country of my birth. Although I found it somewhat difficult to adapt my behaviour to the requirements of the strict dicta of life in a socialist country, I somehow managed that. All in all, it was a fulfilled and a relatively happy life. However, the new dispensation of 1990/1 brought new, unfamiliar and undefined rules and requirements. The politicians were not 'singing from the same hymn sheet' any more. Each was pulling one way or the other but, for me, there were no sides to take. Conflict became a frequent form of communication. Unsettling. Something sinister was in the making. I, personally, was baffled.

Early Signs of the War in the Making

At the end of 1990, the first free general elections were held in Bosnia and Herzegovina. A number of parties put forward their candidates, some only the candidates of a particular ethnic affiliation. Those parties were the Croatian Democratic Union, Party of Democratic Action (Muslim), Serbian Democratic Party, the League of Communists, Alliance of Reformist Forces of Yugoslavia, Democratic Socialist Alliance and a few more. Rather confusing and chaotic. I was desperately trying to ignore the chaos and follow my convictions. I genuinely believed that there were many people of my persuasion, in spite of some telling me otherwise. To my mind they were far too cynical. I considered myself liberal and democratic, even cosmopolitan, yet actually ethnically Yugoslav, so I voted accordingly. (Although at the time of the last census I took part in, in 1991, apparently some officials collecting data refused to recognize

Yugoslavs. They classed Yugoslavs, along with a few other groups, as 'others'. Ours was one of those and thus I became an 'other'.) However, according to most sources, 75 per cent opted for national(ist) parties, which came as a huge shock to me. In disbelief, I found myself wondering what had happened.

The explanation was clear to some, but not to me. Many analysts of the situation of Yugoslavia in the 1980s point out to the decline of country's economy as the cause for later turmoil: the dire economic situation caused public dissatisfaction and revolt within the political system. That became fertile soil for manipulation of nationalist feelings by various politicians who therefore achieved their goal of destabilizing Yugoslav politics. At the same time, there were various theories in circulation, mostly referring to external meddling. In any case, the political muddle gave rise to the emergence of independent political parties in 1989 and consequently multiparty elections, firstly in Slovenia and then in Croatia in 1990. Unsettling feelings increased with those elections and their results. The situation became quite baffling, not only to the Yugoslav peoples involved but, as it seemed to us, to the international community as well. However, the situation in Bosnia and Herzegovina was still wavering. But, in December 1990, new parties representing the three national communities[51] appeared and all won seats in the Assembly; a tripartite coalition government was formed, with the Bosniak[52] politician Alija Izetbegović leading a joint presidency. We watched every news programme available in order to keep well informed, trying to make sense of it all. Events were moving far too fast, changing almost daily and becoming increasingly worrying. The most concerning was the fact that the coalition was not running smoothly. Divisions and animosities within the Parliament became palpable, shouting a daily occurrence, language uncontrolled. 'Growing tensions both inside and outside Bosnia and Herzegovina, however, made cooperation with the Serb Democratic Party, led by Radovan Karadžić, increasingly difficult.'[53] Tensions spilled over into our daily lives and we feared the outcome. The difficult relationship within the Assembly ended with the Serb Democratic Party withdrawing its representatives from the Bosnian Assembly and setting up a Serb National Assembly in Banja Luka.[54] After that, on 3 March 1992, President Izetbegović officially proclaimed the independence of Bosnia and Herzegovina (which was mainly a coalition of Muslims and Croats), while also in 1992 the Republic of Srpska[55] was officially proclaimed. We sensed that nothing good could come of it and our apprehension grew. Division could never be good, especially not in light of previous history. It was too reminiscent of the Second World War.

It became obvious that what made Yugoslavia, especially Bosnia and Herzegovina, complicated was the identity of the nations or peoples who inhabited it. What was specific about the three ethnic groups was their religious affiliation, which had been at the root of the previous conflict, i.e. the Second World War. Miljenko Jergovic[56] articulated it clearly in an interview, stating: 'the Bosnian problem, as well as the problem of South Slavs in general, lies, however, in the fact that our nations almost fully correspond with our religious identity. Hence, all Catholics are Croats, all those of Orthodox religion are Serbs and all Muslim are Bosniaks. And each of our wars in the twentieth century was a religious war.'

In early 1992 the Bosnian civil war was on the horizon. It was to become a fully fledged armed conflict, mostly between the three major ethnic groups. It would start with a murder, then sporadic shooting and would progress to more serious shooting and shelling. At the beginning, I could not fathom the situation. I couldn't even recognize the sounds. I wondered whether it was a car exhaust backfiring or someone beating a rug.[57] Soon, but probably not soon enough, I learned that it was shooting and shelling, that it was a war which had started.

At the very onset of the civil war, while the phone lines were still working, our family[58] from Lošinj[59] suggested we came to them to escape the war and shelter there until it was over. I still did not fully grasp the serious implications of the forthcoming events. Even if I had, we could not have accepted the invitation because there were no hospitals in Lošinj and my father, terminally ill, needed regular monthly check-ups and treatment. That excuse sounded convincing enough to me.

Sida, my mother's sister, also invited us to come and stay with her family in Belgrade. She lived with her daughter, Sanja, the daughter's husband, Branko and their toddler son, Igor. Luckily, they had a big flat, so joining them seemed feasible. I did consider Belgrade as an option, as a last resort, which to my mind was just a remote possibility. Belgrade would be convenient since, as the capital of the country, it had several hospitals. More importantly, the fact that both Sida and Sanja (as well as some other members of the extended family) were medical doctors was a strong argument in favour of Belgrade. My hope was that they would secure medical support for my father. Ours was the culture where 'who you know' was the way to get things done. So, if the transition from one health authority to another (two different countries by then) did not go smoothly, I knew *veza*[60] – connections – would be the only way. Although I did not like corruption, which was not uncommon in the country, and I was very uncomfortable with it, for some unknown reason, I managed to consider *veza* as something different, acceptable. Delusion, denial or just pragmatism? Yet, going to Belgrade, although more feasible, to me seemed still far from necessary.

Chapter 2
Blind Denial

The Onset

'It is all your fault! Had you, our parents, ever told us about your Second World War experiences, we might have been better prepared,' Božo, the husband of my childhood friend, Mima[1] shouted at my parents. He was deeply upset and scared of the situation and his inabilty to grasp it. Would we have been better prepared? Not that we weren't aware of the previous ethnic conflicts, animosities and killings. Nevertheless, I thought, or wanted to believe, that it was all in the past. Unreasonable as it had been in its nature, according to my undoubtedly naïve view, it was resolved, forgotten, gone forever! Never to be repeated. People learn from their mistakes, don't they? Hadn't those same people created a decent present and cherished hope for the future? I just could not, or would not, open my eyes to it.

Would knowing about those experiences have helped us or only poisoned our minds? Would talking about it have served any purpose? Or did our parents not talk about the atrocities and horrors as Hannah Arendt suggested: 'In order to forget more efficiently we rather avoid any allusion to concentration or internment camps.'[2] Unfortunately, if our parents wanted to forget, the current circumstances unmistakably reminded them of those experiences.

For me, and for those like me who did not want to see or believe, it seemed to have all started out of the blue. I, an adult woman, was reduced to the state of a helpless chid. 'Is it true that war is imminent? No, it's impossible. I couldn't cope with it … my father is ill, my mother frail,' I said to a history professor at the university. He said it seemed likely, and looked at me with a puzzled look. He had known me as a reasonable, strong and educated person. What had happened to me?

The atmosphere in the city was weird. There was something in the air. I could not figure out what. Strange unease. People were too animated; there was an unpleasant buzz all over the place. Empty store shelves, more and more talk of shortages, people buying all sorts of things, black markets popping up, illegal markets of foreign currency too.

I usually had a long daily conversation with Marina, a journalist and a writer. We talked about everything and anything, especially about the things that baffled or irritated us. Marina was a close friend, somewhat eccentric, but perceptive and warm. We trusted each other, which meant a lot to both of us. She confided in me that she was scared too. To Marina, it was reminiscent of Poland at the time of political turmoil years back when she was there. People then were buying lavatory rolls in bulk either because there was talk of imminent shortage of it or because that was the only commodity available in shops. They would string them on a long piece of rope and carry them in big 'chains' over their shoulders, she told me. After that, all hell broke loose. It felt like that, Marina said. God help us. However, I still thought that hers was a somewhat exaggerated perspective, something that could only happen elsewhere, not in Sarajevo; after all, our depleted supermarket shelves still had plenty of lavatory rolls! Marina was a writer and it was probably an embellishment produced by her vivid imagination.

However, the reality was proving me wrong. People were stocking up on food – maybe not lavatory rolls so much! Should I buy some food 'just in case'? I did. Some tinned ham, flour and rice. So, what? It meant nothing and one eats those things anyway. Maybe not tinned ham, but still … I felt both guilty and silly. Why was I buying these things if I did not believe in the possibility of civil war? And I did not. I jealously held onto my trust in humanity. Was I hiding behind it? Most likely.

My friend, Stephen, called from the UK. He had been a British lector[3] in Sarajevo in my student days. It was his first job and he was barely older than the students he taught. I was immediately attracted by his erudition, intellect and kindness, and we soon became friends. We stayed in touch all those years. He told me that there were tanks on the roads between Croatia and Serbia. I did not know that. He said there was going to be a civil war.

'There might be, but it has nothing to do with me,' I said. 'It's an ethnic conflict in which I have no part. It has to do with Serbs, Croats and Muslims. I am none of these.'

'There has yet to be a conflict in which Jews are not affected,' he countered.

Maybe, but I convinced myself that, however intelligent and knowledgeable he was, he still did not know what the real situation here was. I lived here – I would know. Would I, I wondered, though.

Nancy, a friend from my Georgetown days,[4] called from the US. Even though we had read different subjects, we became friends. We lived in the same university-owned building and shared many a fun day. She conspicuously asked me how I was. She sounded a bit panicky. What was the matter with these people? Nothing was happening. Nothing would happen. Anyway, Nancy said, she was sending something for us – a parcel. It arrived: coffee, cigarettes, chocolate, dry fruit, dry vegetables. Crazy. Preposterous. The family ate the chocolates and finished off the cigarettes straight away. There was a shortage of coffee, so I shared it with the ward staff at the hospital where my father was being treated. They were all very kind and supportive of my family. They deserved it. My additional motivation must have been to endear myself to them. However, I genuinely felt the need to show my appreciation and what better way than by giving something that there was a shortage of.

Both Stephen and Nancy had planted a seed of doubt in me. It was good to feel cared for, to be thought of, but their comments made it impossible for me to deny the threat. They compelled me to question my judgement, to dwell on the reality, on the scary options. All I actually wanted was to steer clear of such things.

Yet however hard I tried not to pay attention, I could not miss the fact that suddenly blockades and roadblocks were appearing on the streets. Why, what? I drove through one in March on my way to deliver a tray of cakes for the 8 March, International Women's Day, as was customary, to the nurses and doctors who treated my father. Driving through blockades was scary. No, it would not last, I thought. And it did not, but worse was to come.

In early April, mass protests and public gatherings broke out. The father of my friend, Nina,[5] an old communist believer, joined the early protests calling for patriotism. He did not or could not recognize the nationalistic messages behind the slogans. He did not realize the fact that the notion of patriotism had acquired new connotations: one could be a Yugoslav patriot (considered backward and negative) or a Bosnian, Croatian or Serbian patriot (considered progressive and positive). The protests nominally called for ethnic unity. However, in a multi-ethnic country, a unified ideology based on single-ethnic values seemed impossible. It actually seemed to be about ethnic domination and power. The question was only: which ethnic group would win and dominate? Those protests intended as peaceful, ended up with serious clashes, with ambulance and police services attending.

For the first time, I noticed my newly acquired propensity to pay attention to sounds, their meaning and the effect on me. The unusually numerous ambulances and/or police cars with sirens full blast could be heard incessantly, especially during the days of protests. I could not see the main street from our flat, but I could hear them. A very disturbing, unsettling commotion. The sound of sirens was something I associated with Manhattan, not Sarajevo. Nevertheless, I caught myself listening to them, trying to gauge the location and the type of siren, whether it was an ambulance, police car or fire engine.

Or something else. I did not quite know what the significance of differentiating those sounds was, but I just could not stop myself.

Amid all the confusion a memorable scary event was a sonic boom (or something like it) caused by an aircraft. It was both terrifying and mysterious. We found out that it was a plane that created the awful, literally earthshattering sound, but we never actually found out what kind of a plane it was or who flew it. Our flat shook and it made us feel helpless and inconsequential. The invisible, unexplained loud force could easily and genuinely threaten our lives and possibly obliterate us for no obvious reason.

I was flabbergasted to find myself in many an unfamiliar and intimidating situation. I mostly could not figure out the meaning and significance of things. New parties, new rules of the 'game', with the threat not only obvious and present, but unstructured, unpredictable and disorganized, with the consequences mysterious, frightening and often actually life threatening. How to deal with that? Each street, each cellar, seemed to have different rules, a different 'game', different local militia and different sources of hatred. I did not want to hate – my family had banished hatred a long time ago. I did not want to play the 'game', did not want to take sides, but did not want to be punished for it either. I tried to observe, interpret, fathom. And I waited. For what? Who knows.

Although there were rumours of people leaving the town, I managed to convince myself that staying put was the best option for the family. We had an established routine for my father's uninterrupted medical care (he had advanced bone cancer). My mother was too frail and struggling emotionally to be able to cope with the trip if we left. In addition, I just could not see myself leaving behind my books, my profession and my vocation, all the cornerstones of my identity. Therefore, I found every possible justification not to go. I would not allow myself to evaluate the situation clearly. Delusion, denial, or both?

Gliga rang. He was my divorced husband whose real name was Igor, but everybody knew him as Gilga. I had had no contact with him since we split almost twenty years before, yet he rang up all of a sudden to warn me to keep my mouth shut. He said he knew me only too well, that I would speak my mind. Now was not the time! It was too dangerous now, much more than before, he said. He pleaded with me. He also said that he felt for my parents because he knew their world had collapsed. I was both surprised and moved. He was a dear chap, but the two of us were so different, so incompatible. Maybe we met too young and did not, or could not, appreciate each other's qualities.

So, life went on. People talked more and more about imminent street fighting. I learned what a ricochet was. Thank God, we were safe from that at least! We had no windows directly overlooking the street. 'It is all your fault! You should have told us about your Second World War experience!' I remembered Božo's words. Should they have done that? Would that have helped, I wondered.

Teaching still went on as normal. Few students, admittedly, but some did show up. Three or four sometimes at the end of March and the beginning of April. No point in giving lectures to so few. We chatted. The students were much more aware of the approaching threat. They talked about ethnic cleansing. Lists of names of the residents in apartment blocks. Nonsense, I said. What could a name tell anybody? Unlike most people I was actually incapable of telling whether a name was Serbian or Croatian, even Muslim were it not typical. No, various names could belong to any of the ethnicities, I told them. They looked at me with pitiful glances and told me that I was too naïve. But I was twice their age! How could they know better, be savvier? That was the last class I had there, ever. Yes, they did know better; yes, they kept their eyes open. I had always been seen as a weird one. No wonder Marina used to say to me that I was the most patient impatient person and the thickest intelligent person she had ever known.

Our two Sarajevo families could no longer visit each other regularly as had been our habit. We had been very close. Good, bad or indifferent had always been shared by all seven adults.[6] Being out on the streets became unsafe. It felt unnatural and eerie. Henika, my cousin with whom I had been particularly close, would still visit on her way to work, to the nearby hospital. She was a doctor and was involved with the Jewish Community Centre in that capacity. She told us about contingency plans being made there. I could not pretend I did not hear that. Henika made it very clear to me. It unsettled me hugely. However, maybe it was only the hypersensitive and hypervigilant Jews feeling that way, I said to myself. Yes, that surely was the case.

Did I know I was in denial? Did I know I was so scared?

I soon realized I could hear shooting sounds more often and that it was actual weapons and real shooting. I could not carry on denying it. I became quite scared. It was not something I had ever thought would be a part of my life, nor ever imagined I would have to deal with. In panic, I rang up my friend Omer and asked him what all the shooting was about. A silly question, indeed. He told me that it was *them* shooting at *us* from the mountains. He added that the shooting afterwards was *us* showing *them*, that *we* had a horse in the race too. What horse, what race? Who were *we* and who were *they*? This was not the Omer I had known and loved. I could not relate to it. I certainly did not accept and did not want to know about that kind of division. I reluctantly admitted to myself that I was disappointed with him.

Hesitant Acceptance

Things soon got worse in every sense. Unfortunately, it was not only Omer who showed intolerance. Even my cherished English department, which had managed to stay a cohesive unit in spite of differences, displayed cracks where one would not have expected them. Denial did not work anymore; delusions did not help. I had to try to evaluate the situation more reasonably and start contemplating leaving Sarajevo. I still found it a far-fetched idea.

I diligently listened to the radio and television. One had to be informed and ready. Ready for what? I prepared a 'grab bag' with important documents, medication, money and jewellery. Events were rolling out swiftly, matters changing by the hour. The meaning of some concepts changed, such as common sense, safety, even time. The speed with which events occurred was incredible. One week would have at least a normal month's worth of events packed in with innumerable changes of circumstances. Parliamentary sessions, MPs of various parties squabbling. It was difficult to understand what was going on. Just chaos.

I gradually started taking things more seriously and preparing for the inevitable, whatever that 'inevitable' meant for me. I prepared beetroot juice in large quantities (apparently good for blood) for my father. I tried to organize myself better for 'just in case' situations. So much of our lives became determined by 'just in case' – 'just in case' became the way of life. There was very little structure or routine in our lives and I found it difficult to function in the chaos.

I remembered my parents' Second World War stories about villages being safer than cities. After all, villagers saved my parents' lives back then. The anecdotes about my grandmother bartering her diamond ring for some salt or my aunt exchanging aspirin for potatoes in those villages were not examples I could follow. I was not planning to find a village to move to in case of emergency. However, having assumed that farmers who had some food would not be coming into the town any more to sell their produce, I thought that going to them would be a solution. I believed it could somehow be done. Therefore, I gathered all the addresses of the farmers I used to buy poultry, fruit and vegetables and dairy from, planning to visit them to buy what they had. Little did I know then that the city would later be completely cut off from all the surrounding areas, that we would be trapped within the inner-city limits of besieged Sarajevo and restricted to moving only within the immediate neighbourhood, and, moreover, that our problem would not only be food, but water and electricity as well. And one could not buy that anywhere. The diamond ring was ready, but there was nobody to trade with: an entirely new situation.

At the very onset of the conflict each stairwell had an individual or individuals 'in charge'. In charge of what? Security? Loyalty? Supporting the cause? Which cause, which loyalty? Just a threatening presence. One of those individuals 'in charge', a neighbour from the fifth floor, came and asked us for some Deutsche Marks as a contribution for the purchase of a rifle.[7]

'What do we need a rifle for?' I asked and continued to object.

My father called me to their bedroom and told me to take matters seriously, not to ask questions, just to give him the money. What had happened to my father? Actually, I sensed that his reaction was well founded; it must have been based on some previous experience. The Second World War maybe? Maybe things like that were part of the untold stories.

The town grew seriously smaller for us. Those who were living in each part of Sarajevo stayed within that area. No trips to other parts of town. The previous whole had shattered into pieces. The cohesion appeared broken, the world turned upside down. Acceptable became unacceptable, in the most absurd way. The regular currency, the dinar, was not used anymore; it was Deutsche Marks only, if one had any.[8] Former criminals became militia leaders in charge of a few city blocks. In addition, there was competition among them as to who could be more threatening and more punitive. It was all very disturbing and worrying.

By then, it was pretty obvious that the civil war had started and not much could be done to stop it. At the beginning of May, the most terrible, destructive shelling of the town arrived from the hills abruptly and lasted almost all day. Everybody in our stairwell sheltered in the cellar. We quickly cleared some space to put the chairs we had brought down from the flat. It shocked us all. On the way back up to our flats we realized all the window panes were gone. Broken glass, dust and pieces of cement everywhere. A new unknown sound: walking on glass and cement on the stairs and landings. A spine-chilling sensation.

The flat was full of shattered glass and dust too. It was not too cold, but still something had to replace the window panes. Everybody was putting up plastic sheets. I did the same. At night, I could hear the wind buffeting the plastic sheeting: *whoosh, whoosh, whoosh*. In addition, one could hear hungry, abandoned dogs barking and wailing, even neighbours quarrelling. All night long. Sounds became crucial for survival. I had to master the skill of interpreting the sounds; shelling or 'just' snipers, for instance.

We started going regularly to the cellar during the shelling. It had three separate areas of different sizes. There was a small area with an old couch discarded there – prefect for my father – so after the initial confusion we were allocated that area. Mima and Božo and their dog Bennie joined us because other people objected to the dog. Then Minja and Saša (mother and son), the ground-floor neighbours came too. While Mima and Božo were long-standing friends, Minja was a neighbour we knew but with whom we were not particularly close. It was only at the start of the chaos that we became close. Minja suggested, at the beginning of the conflict, that she queued for our bread ration at the store on our street. If I were to go there myself, it would mean leaving my parents on their own for too long, she said. She also shared some vegetables and homemade tomato juice with us. Those were rare and treasured items. It was an extremely generous and kind gesture; however, not unexpected from a person like Minja whom I got to know well. It was obvious she was one of those people for whom thinking of others came naturally – a kind of person one does not often meet, but it is a privilege to know.

We became 'the cellar cohort' and felt comfortable with each other. What held us together was our shared general outlook and views and opinions of the war as well. We all shunned division and animosity and tried to resist the widespread epidemic of hate. That made us all feel safe with each other. The trust we shared was a precious commodity in those days; we appreciated it greatly and supported each other wherever and whenever possible.

However, the cellar itself was the most unpleasant experience. Apart from the humidity, chill and smells, and the lack of facilities, the air of distrust among people was palpable. Prevalent ethnic divisions created an exaggerated sense of ethnic identity versus otherness and the concept of otherness became fertile ground for exhibiting prejudice and intolerance. People, clustered in groups often along ethnic lines, felt justified in openly expressing their hatred for a certain ethnic group while ignoring, either purposely or otherwise, the presence of individuals of that particular ethnic group (who were clearly sharing the same awful predicament). The scared multi-ethnic congregation of mostly ethnically conscious people, forced to find shelter in the cellar, found themselves sharing the battle of survival. However understandable this manner of venting fear might have been, it was extremely unpleasant to be exposed to the loud outbursts of anger, of cursing and swearing.

Anger and antagonism were present everywhere – in the cellar and outside.

By the mid-spring there were three impenetrable 'belts' around wider Sarajevo making sure that nothing and nobody came in or went out. Each 'belt' was held by one of the three ethnic militaries, depending on the area of the town. Real hardship had started. No food to buy, intermittent supplies of water and electricity, allegedly as retaliation among the warring ethnic armies. Restricted movement, confusion, insecurity. Ultimately life threatening. People started thinking of escaping the town, escaping the awful predicament.

However, I was not one of them; escaping was not at the forefront of my mind. Organizing life according to the circumstances was. We still had some food in the freezer. It had to be used. Electricity cuts were too frequent, so there was no point in keeping it. Mima[9] and Božo were coming to us more and more often. Together our two families finished off the stuff we had in our respective fridges. Water was collected in various containers. We had feasts, and even Bennie, their dog did. But not for long.

Life in Sarajevo went from bad to worse. The incessant heavy shelling continued. The windows in my parents' bedroom were safe: I had taken the mattress from my bed and put it against the inside of the windows. I reinforced it with tomes of encyclopaedias, books made of sturdier stuff, which ironically were issued by the *Yugoslav* Institute of Lexicography. As a consequence of such an elaborate 'project' I had no mattress on my bed so I had to sleep on a sofa in the adjoining room. It was also convenient because I was closer to my parents. The space was well protected by the wall. Safety, true or imagined, was important. Fear for one's life became very real as death was getting ever closer.

People started talking openly about sending children away to spare them whatever evil was on its way (in spite of the attempts by all three military authorities to prevent people leaving the town). Something called the Children's Embassy was hurriedly established and those working there were keen to get hold of eligible children as quickly as possible. Time was of the essence. Therefore, they rang up their acquaintances (I was one of them) to inquire if they knew of anyone who might be interested in sending children (unaccompanied) to Italy. Not an easy decision for a parent to send one's child to a foreign country, not knowing much about the organization itself. I rang up three families I knew. One child was too old, not eligible. One family refused and one accepted. Their children soon left for Italy.

The children remained in Italy, although that had not been the intention.

A former student, by then a colleague, also rang me to ask about possible ways of leaving Sarajevo. She had a newborn and could not bear to stay any longer. She actually was asking me, shyly and indirectly, to refer her to the Jewish Community Centre for evacuation, I realized later. I suppose she was not sure I had any connections there because she knew I was not much of a Jew! At the time, the Jewish Community still had airlifts to Belgrade.[10] When I referred her to people I knew there, she only then said that she was, in fact, of Jewish descent (her grandmother apparently was Jewish). This was the first time I noticed the sudden emergence of people of Jewish origin, a phenomenon which became quite widespread further into the war.

By May, we were almost used to things taking a strange turn, were used to the appearance of new rules of the 'game'. We also got used to doing without things, something we would have considered impossible only a month or two before. Soon, another surprise came: the phone lines in our part of town were cut. We suddenly had no way of contacting the outside world. How to let close family know what was going on? Avdo, a close and hugely caring friend of my father, who lived in the sector of the town that still had phone lines, came to offer to phone anybody we wished to contact. We asked him to ring Sida in Belgrade to tell her that we were all right. He rang her and even came back through all the shelling and shooting, covered in sweat, to pass onto us Sida's message.

Sometime later he was killed in Sarajevo, while queueing for water. I heard it from somebody in Belgrade. I never told my father about it.

Sarajevo was well and truly under siege. The three 'belts' around the town were very effective. The Serbian army (considered enemies by the other two ethnic groups) was mostly up on the south-eastern hills, in Grbavica and in several other suburbs. The other two, i.e. predominantly Muslim forces together with some Croatian formations, were within the inner city limits (where we lived), while in Novo Sarajevo and parts of Novi Grad, the majority of Croatian formations were supported by some Muslim groups. The newly formed official Bosnian army was mostly positioned on several south-western hills around Sarajevo. Each ethnic formation had headquarters in town.

Rumours spread like wildfire. There were stories of looting all over the place. Then the worse reports arrived. So-and-so killed, so-and-so imprisoned, so-and-so disappeared. Evildoing all around. One day a radio station reported that the military in the enemy territory were engaged in 'genocide and even looting'. What a hierarchy of evildoing! Utterly confusing and frightening. I had to try to make sense of the situation or else it would insidiously take over my life and change it even more dramatically.

However, how to make sense of nonsensical events and behaviours? It was all rather shocking to me. As a believer in humanity, in the idea of 'brotherhood and unity', I suddenly found human behaviour hard to fathom. How to explain a casual conversation on a street corner, with a colleague I liked and respected, a professor of literary theory, a person usually measured in his reactions. He suddenly started talking about the genetic makeup of a particular ethnic group. He compared them to termites and stated that they had a propensity to expand their territory every now and again. How to understand such an analysis? What were his reasons and motives? What prompted that? Moreover, his wife was of that particular ethnicity. Was that the reason? Did he protest too much? It was all very sad.

The well-guarded and impenetrable 'belts' and military activities of all the forces equally determined the lives of those in the town, more or less, regardless of the ethnicity. The population in town was a mixture of different ethnicities, even within one family. So, paradoxically, shelling from the surrounding mountains by the Serbian army aimed at the town was aimed as much at Serbs as at any other ethnic group. Therefore, my impression was that within the city, life for the Serbs was more difficult than for the rest of the population. They were not only victims of the outside shooting like everybody else, but were also mistrusted and occasionally imprisoned or even murdered by the other two paramilitaries. (By all accounts, life for Muslims, for instance, was similarly difficult in Grbavica.)[11]

The central Bosnian government was forever expecting and talking about military support from the Western powers, but it never happened. They did have moral support though; various attempts at peace-making were made, and various international delegations visited. It even appeared that the shooting and shelling worsened during those visits. Was there any logic to it?

In spite of all the international efforts, it took over three years to reach some sort of peace in the area.

The number and variety of military and paramilitary authorities in town was baffling. Often, within an area of a few blocks, there were different paramilitaries in charge and different commanders, often those who had had some sort of serious brush with the law. They had unlimited authority and power. Nominally they were there to defend us, but they all definitely were a serious threat to us. Random, as they were, they certainly did not engender confidence. We soon learned that some of these groups were referred to by the name of their leader, be it their first name, or a nickname or whatever. That was their 'military designation'. How bizarre. It was very hard to get one's head around the setup. Each of these uniformed men had the right to search people's flats, or make arrests, without a warrant or any written document, or ID for that matter. Their uniforms and weapons gave them the authority. Allegedly they were looking for enemies and/or hidden firearms and one had to let them in without asking any questions. At one point they came into our flat and asked my frail and nearly paralysed father if he had hidden firearms! In the evenings (on rare occasions when we had electricity), they, reinforced by some neighbours, would shout warnings to everybody that the blackout had to be observed. 'No signals to the enemy up on the mountains,' they shouted. An ominous warning.

Sounds were both disturbing and scary. The scariest of them all, of course, was the sound of shelling. By then, the bombs were not only arriving from the hills, but flying out from our immediate neighbourhood too and it was important to learn the difference between the two sounds. Bennie, the dog, seemed able to differentiate them very well, but I also learned to tell them apart: the shell leaving from somewhere near the house going outwards versus the incoming shell flying over the house to land somewhere far away. However, the most frightening and dangerous shells were those aimed at the house itself and the immediate area. Those could not be heard, I was told.

And it happened. Nothing could be heard until the actual impact. The bomb hit the balcony of the next-door flat. Suddenly, shockingly, early at night while my parents and I were in our sitting room. It was dark outside. Looking at the window, we could make out the sparks against the outside blackness. It created a spooky, undecipherable sensation. However strange it might sound, it took us some time to realize that we were all alive.

A day or two later Zora and Bane, husband and wife, my friends, dropped in. Zora was working at the faculty library so, with time, we became close friends. I had known Bane since early childhood and liked him a lot. They were an uncomplicated, friendly, easy-going couple. What you see is what you get. Bane had managed to get us some eggs when everything had just started. Eggs could keep us going for some time, we thought. One day Bane was arrested, but the paramilitaries let him go because 'Chetniks don't wear Italian shoes' (Chetniks[12] were members of the Serbian nationalist guerrilla force during the Second Word War). Bane always wore nice shoes. The reason they decided he was a Chetnik in the first place was simply because, when checking his ID, they saw he was born in Belgrade, in Serbia. That was enough. We laughed. However, it was not funny. He could have lost his life because of his place of birth. Zora and Bane were worried about their nephew and niece who lived nearby. Teenagers did not understand the seriousness of the situation and had plenty of free time since schools were closed. Therefore, we agreed that they should come to me from time to time and I would teach them English and explain the dangers of the current situation. They refused to believe their own family, accusing them of overprotectiveness, so Zora and Bane hoped they might listen to me.

However, it was not only the teenagers who could not grasp the circumstances. Mrs S, a next-door neighbour in her eighties who lived on her own, was totally lost and frightened. She did not know how to adapt to the new rules; she had nothing against obeying them provided she knew which and how. Being of Serbian ethnicity she would listen to a radio station from Pale, the Republic of Srpska radio station, the enemy broadcast. I warned her about the danger of it being overheard. So, a day or two later she came to me, and asked in a whisper about the things that were allowed and that were not. She wanted me to advise her. Did I know, myself? Quite a few things maybe, mostly those that were more obvious. I shared whatever I knew with her.

In fact, for me, the situation leading to the civil war was more difficult to understand; it seemed too complicated. Suddenly, with the war in full swing, things paradoxically turned out to be simpler, one-dimensional, easier to grasp than in the time preceding the war. The world we inhabited was suddenly narrow, limited, binary. Time lost its dimensions; it was mostly reduced to now, but each now was packed full of hazards. Once human existence was downgraded to survival instincts, basic needs took over and there was very little space for nuances, thinking, evaluating. It was all about reacting and acting: do or be done. The world became limited to several dichotomies: us/them, friend/foe, love/hate, good/evil, necessary/redundant.

Yet our cellar cohort, in spite of everything, managed to laugh a lot in those days. Probably the only defence we had. It certainly released tension temporarily. Mima's and Božo's flat on the fifth floor was hit too. The outside wall of a room was half gone. Where were their daughter's 'lucky glass elephants'? We searched the rubble for them as if our lives depended on it. We found them. We laughed again.

Both the daughter and the son were already with the family in Belgrade, in time to avoid this hell.

The shelling from the all sides was regular. We became somewhat desensitized to the threat of shells by the end of May. One evening, we watched shells flying through the sky while we were at Mima's and Božo's flat. Their flat directly faced the hill from which the shells were fired. Against the blackness of the sky, it almost looked pretty, like fireworks, but with the power and intention to kill.

No wonder that many years later it took me a while to stay calm on Guy Fawkes nights.

In spite of everything life went on. No more teaching at the Faculty of Philosophy building, but there was a thing called *radna obaveza* (obligation to work). Those still in work, if not conscripted, had a certificate stating that they were allocated a specific work obligation. One was under suspicion without it. We all, including the English Department, had meetings at the Faculty of Law/Rectorate premises, where we did more or less nothing. I regularly attended those meetings, although getting there was not always easy. As for the exams, we were instructed to give them at home.

Those meetings, my *radna obaveza*, my compulsory non-activity, became more and more weird, pointless and at times unpleasant. A number of our university colleagues of Serbian ethnicity left Sarajevo and joined the

Republic of Srpska in Pale.[13] The rest of the colleagues present at the meetings mostly felt it their duty or need to distance themselves from and, preferably, make adversarial comments about those who had left. Self-righteousness was prevalent. What was the purpose of the meetings after all? It was not too clear to me. Overall, there was a sense of nervousness in the air. One of the professors brought sedatives along to give to those who felt they could benefit from them. I took some and, to my surprise, discovered a quotation from the Qur'an in the packaging. Indoctrination or medication? Or both?

One student came to my home to take her exam, accompanied by a soldier. Not a paramilitary but a member of the official Bosnian army.[14] A different uniform and different behaviour. He took off his bulletproof vest and left it standing in the hall. I was amazed; I had never seen anything like it. An innocent gesture or a warning? He sat with my parents in the sitting room while I examined the student, apparently his friend, in my study. Luckily, the student was well prepared, so the act of examining students under such absurd circumstances made a bit more sense. The soldier turned out to be a very nice guy; he was adjutant to a Bosnian army general. He told us he was of mixed ethnicity. Yet not a Yugoslav, I noticed. Anyway, he offered to take my father to hospital for tests when the time came because he was driving the general's big comfortable car. Much easier and safer. And he did. I went along and was genuinely grateful, because driving to the hospital, though it was close enough, was an ordeal: several checkpoints and presenting one's ID and *radna obaveza* certificate at each, while the shooting went on. His presence and his car also increased my ratings in the neighbourhood!

By then there were several new neighbours in our stairwell. We wondered where they came from and how they had managed to move into the flats that the previous neighbours had vacated. Soon it became clear that some of the previous residents had quietly fled the besieged town and had left the flats unoccupied, so others, as we gathered, close to the new powers in charge, were given permission to move in, often forcing the door. But instead of the nameplate (flats did not go by numbers but by nameplates) on their front door there was a plate with the acronym RŠTO (the Republic's Headquarters of Territorial Defence). That indicated that they were people of special significance and a potential threat to others. Might was on their side.

One of those new neighbours became one of the 'individuals in charge'. That was not too surprising, but his sudden visit to me was. Wearing parts of some sort of a uniform he came to our flat, boots undone and a Kalashnikov on his shoulder, to tell me that he had to requisition petrol from my car. Could he, please, leave some for possible sudden hospital visits, I asked. He 'generously' agreed. However, he made me put a rubber hose into the tank, suck on it and transfer petrol into his canister. I never again went to hospital with that car, and I would also never forget the taste of petrol in my mouth. Petrol burping lasts a long time. No wonder he gave me the task of transferring the fuel. Yet the very same new neighbour offered Minja some antibiotics, should she need them, after his group had looted the former military hospital!

At the time the majority of old neighbours were still in their flats. I often depended on some of them to help me with taking my father to the cellar (or later to Minja's) since my father could hardly walk. We lived on the second floor, so he had to be carried down the stairs. The stairwell was hazardous, with debris and glass shards all over stairs and the landings. I devised a sort of a belt to secure him in an ordinary kitchen chair when the neighbours carried him. I would also prepare some tea in a flask and hot-water bottles for my parents. (I would warm up saved water on a picnic stove using solid fuel tablets.) Going to the cellar was a complicated and unpleasant affair, so we only went down there when it was absolutely necessary, i.e. only when the shells were incessantly targeting our neighbourhood. However, that was not so easy to figure out. It was hard to gauge how close the shelling was and to react in time to get the neighbours to carry my father. If it was too late, the neighbours would already all have gone to the cellar; if it was too early, the family would unnecessarily be in the cellar for too long.

My mother was in a very bad way. She 'officially' announced that she could not be counted on for anything, not even to boil water. The final straw for her was an earlier live radio broadcast of a negotiation with a person who threatened to destroy the Drina[15] River dam and, consequently, kill thousands of people. It sounded very dramatic. The man's sister was pleading with him on live radio, on behalf of the authorities. My mother just could not cope with the idea of so many lives being lost, yet again. After all, this was the second war in her life. However, at the beginning of the Second World War, she was young, but now she was around seventy. After one of our early visits to the cellar, she came out limping and lisping. I was convinced that she had suffered a stroke. The easiest and safest thing I could think of was to take her to a neuropsychiatrist, her pupil (she was a French language teacher) who lived nearby. He examined her, told me that it was stress, and prescribed a sedative. Luckily, I could get it at the Jewish Community Centre pharmacy.

Several unpleasant experiences made us decide not to go to the cellar any more. The rest of our cellar cohort from the small, confined and separated area decided the same. So, almost a month after our first 'trip' to the cellar, it must have been sometime in May, we decided to gather in Minja's flat on the ground floor during the shelling. The ground floor flat was almost equally safe, but far more comfortable. We shared everything: water, food, information. The radio in Minja's sitting room was on most of the time. We gathered up all the batteries we could find for it. Most of us had to attend our *radna obaveza* at various times. Saša, Minja's son, had just graduated in mechanical engineering and luckily managed to find a job. It was a manual job repairing damaged roofs which, due to the circumstances, was in high demand. A rather strange job for a university graduate, but any job, even such an arduous one, is better than none. It was crucial to get a *radna obaveza* certificate to avoid conscription. With snipers active most of the time, it was hugely dangerous, but better than the frontlines.

Occasionally, it would get busy there, in Minja's ground-floor flat. Visitors came. The mother of one of the 'individuals in charge', the neighbour from the fifth floor who had been collecting money for a rifle, started selling cigarettes and she would often visit. Great. Both my parents smoked and so did I. Nicotine addiction does not stop with war. Hunger can be stifled, but not nicotine craving. I knew how to deal with hunger, even with the scarcity of food. Minja taught me how to pick nettles safely and how to recognize basil in nearby parks. Boiled nettles, with some rice and spice, were a semblance of a soup that filled our stomachs. Minja also taught me how to make filo pastry. Admittedly, it was not the thin pastry it should have been, but filled with a basil/nettles mixture and whatever could be found in the kitchen cupboard, or even filled with small, unripe apples, it worked. Soon we would be given food parcels. The local community distributed dehydrated US Army food and other supplies. I also managed to get some food from the Jewish Community Centre: dry pasta, oil, rice. Proper food, good to keep us going for some time.

One day, in late May, a shell hit a bread queue in the town centre. Henika knew that I was supposed to be in that part of town at the time. In addition, to make matters worse, it was all caught by a television camera and broadcast live. Apparently, there was a woman who looked very much like me. Henika immediately wanted to check whether I was among the wounded or dead. She searched all the clinics and mortuaries but could not find me. She eventually found me at home. We cried our eyes out. If ever we needed proof how much we loved each other, this was about the strongest we could get. In these horrendous times when life became ephemeral, the bond between people and affection among them took on a much deeper meaning.

The end of May was usually the most beautiful time of year in town: not too warm, but warm enough for outdoor activities. May 1992 was equally nice, but we did not notice. Outdoor activities were mostly chores, sunshine almost offensive. How could the sun be so warm and pleasant when our lives had no space for pleasure? Pleasure was something that had to be left in the past.

Future was something we could not and would not contemplate. We lived in the here and now and now was the time for suffering and sacrifice.

Then we heard that some food could be bought for Deutsche Marks in our area. Good news! I went to a small shop and bought some squash. The squash was very hard; I had to cut it with a cleaver. And some greens called cow's greens. Better than nettles. The squash was huge, so I shared it with a few people. I kept searching for food and inventing dishes that I thought were edible, or just seemed edible. Most often, either rice or pasta with anything I could think of: basil/nettles, just spices still left over from the good old days or dehydrated crumbled meatball from the donated food packages were all on the menu. Dried mushrooms were a special treat. Mima gave them to me. She had picked them herself the previous year. Hunger does wonders for one's palate!

I took some of the cow's greens to Ella's family. Henika was looking after the parents, providing food and cooking for them. She had moved in with them. Henika's children were abroad at the time and her partner was in Belgrade. She had lost an enormous amount of weight. After her work at the hospital, Henika would go to her flat where the phone lines were still working to talk to her children before returning to her parents' flat in the middle of town. A lot of walking, a dangerous activity.

Tanja, my younger cousin, Henika's sister, disappeared shortly before the shooting started and the family panicked. We did not know what had happened. Only the worst thoughts. Moni, Tanja's father, desperately looked for her all over town in spite of the danger. He went to her place of work, her flat, everywhere. Tanja's daughter, Ivana, was in the US on an exchange programme for high-school kids. She too was understandably very worried about her mother so she put out an appeal via Radio Sarajevo asking her to get in touch.

Ella, Tanja's mother, seemed to be in complete denial or else she was genuinely unable to grasp the situation. Be that as it may, the aunt insisted on having lunch at a specific time every day, the way she was used to, in spite of the fact that they were cooking in the garden, on an open communal fire, which would be started a bit later than the time she demanded. She also complained about the quality of the food. She refused to eat the cow's greens that I brought, saying that she was certainly not a cow! It was not easy for Henika.

I searched town to find powdered milk, a source of calcium, for my father. No luck there. However, I had a frightening experience: I approached a group of young men to ask where the shop was, only to realize that they did not speak Serbo-Croat[16] and had headbands with Arabic letters inscribed on them. Apparently, they were foreign fighters supporting Bosnian Muslim fighters. By then, not much could shock or scare me, but this did, however.

Snipers were shooting all the time. I literally walked between bullets daily. Shells were falling regularly. The rumour was that the presence of a TV crew meant imminent shelling. Whether it was true or not, we tried to avoid being anywhere near cameras. On the whole the choice for me was either to stay at home as much as possible or ignore the shooting and shelling. I chose the latter and I was not hit. Actually, in the context of powerlessness and randomness of it all, the insignificance of human existence became pronounced. So, risking life started to matter less. Strangely enough, I, who used to be scared when a moth flew by me, now had no reaction to the bullets flying around me. Needs must, or what? Maybe I was too thin, not a good target, I joked (by then I weighed less than forty kilos). Was it a joke or desperation? I was too old to believe in invincibility.

However, there were instances when it was impossible to ignore the bullets, when they literally *whizzed* around me. I must have shielded myself by hiding behind the often-used human defence of 'it won't be me', or else why would I step straight into the fire. Once again, when I went in search of powdered milk, I ended up on the street exposed to sniper fire from various high-rises. A bullet flew past me and landed behind me on the pavement. I could just see the expression of horror on the faces of the people in the Merhamet[17] charity shop I was heading to. I did not have time to get frightened. I got no milk either.

Also, sometime in June, I was on my way to the Jewish Community Centre with a young neighbour I wanted to help get on one of the convoys, when a well-known painter and acquaintance of mine, saw me from a bar he was drinking at. He offered me a drink. I went into the bar to have a scotch and, at the very moment, a shell fell right on the spot where I would have been had I not accepted the drink. A new discovery: a drink could save life! A small piece of shrapnel hit the neighbour, who was standing behind me. There was blood on his back, so we returned home and treated his wound.

One of my preoccupations was to bring food and medication for elderly people I knew or vaguely knew in the area. There were a few, but there was one I could not reach until I found out her name. She was a little old lady living across the road who, my father told me, was his playmate when they were kids. My father never knew her married name, so I shouted from my window, asking for her surname in order to find her by the nameplate on her front door. I wanted to take some food to her and I did. In return, she gave me a piece of bread she'd baked herself and told me to tell my father (she also remembered him) that she now baked quality bread. She obviously had a sense of humour. She was a frail little lady who also needed medication, which I got for her at the Jewish Community pharmacy. She told me that she was actually born Jewish, but converted to Catholicism when she married a Catholic before the Second World War. She was lucky then. Would she be as lucky now?

She was. She 'reclaimed' her Judaism, joined one of the convoys and ended up in the Jewish care home in Zagreb. In 1992, she was a year or two shy of eighty. I learned when I inquired after her that she died there much later.

Shelling and shooting became an integral part of our everyday life either the incoming shelling from the hills, or shelling fired from inside the town. All those shells were flying above and around us. On top of that, sniper fire also came from high buildings and other places in town. One almost got used to it and feared it much less. People, including me, buzzed around in pursuit of 'important chores', such as searching for food or medication and visiting friends and relatives. All of it took one's mind off the peril.

I was losing weight and often felt tired. What kept me going was probably adrenaline. I could not sleep at night. I would give my parents sleeping tablets but I had to stay vigilant. Any serious shelling and I had to organize a trip down to Minja's flat. The burden of responsibility was getting too much. However, I tried desperately hard to hide this from my parents. I was slowly turning into a parent to my own parents. A most awkward position. Difficult to accept, but unavoidable.

I carried on walking, going to faculty meetings, in search of food all over the neighbourhood and after a while even further afield to a relatively distant part of town. I went to the Jewish Community Centre to pick up food parcels. I visited my family and various elderly neighbours. I also visited Lala who lived a bit further out, in a rather dangerous area. She was actually my mother's schoolmate and my ex-university lecturer with whom I became close friends. Lala was seriously ill and housebound.

I suddenly noticed my exaggerated need to help, to be useful. The absurdity of life made it the only way of retaining one's integrity and sanity. I was not afraid anymore; I numbed my fear. Fear was paralysing and I needed to act, so I could not afford fear. It was not practical! I only allowed fear to surface when my parents were in danger; for instance, when the shelling started and I had not organized anything for them. But that was rare.

One day at the beginning of summer, I came to Minja's flat and the group behaved strangely all of a sudden. In a rather histrionic manner, they gave me cushions to put behind my back, offered me water (a precious commodity) and even 'minced steaks' (skilfully made with no meat, only bread and spices). They had mischievous expressions on their faces while inquiring whether I considered them my friends. What kind of a joke was this, I wondered.

It transpired that it had been announced on the radio that morning that all the military authorities in town had given their permission for Jewish Community convoys to take Jewish families, together with their friends, out of the besieged Sarajevo.[18] So, were they my friends, they asked, half in jest. Of course, they were, I said, and I truly meant it. However, I did not let on that I wasn't sure I was ready to leave. Laughter again, making light of an impossible situation. Jews had been singled out again, but this time with surprisingly desirable consequences.

Systemic anti-Semitism on the whole had not been overt in the country, at least as far as I was aware.[19] I personally had experienced only a few incidents, mostly at work. More often than not I would confront the perpetrator and that would be the end of the story. However, that did not work with my ex-mother-in-law; she upset me hugely with her virulent anti-Semitism.[20] I was taken aback but said nothing. It did hurt a lot and obviously paralysed me. Otherwise, I knew how to defend myself. Somehow, one expected it if one were Jewish; that seems to be the Jewish lot. However, the cynicism or paradox of this war was the fact that being Jewish had all of a sudden become a very attractive and desirable proposition. There were convoys, a pharmacy, food parcels and a soup kitchen, all organized by the Jewish Community Centre. Anybody could access most of these things but still many felt that being Jewish would give them priority. They might have been right but, it appeared that no one was turned away.

The irony was that the outlook on Jews unexpectedly changed. Unlike in the Second World War, in this war the yellow Star of David had been replaced by the menorah.[21] I realized with both sadness and delight that this symbol of Judaism did not mean death anymore; it meant salvation. Crowds of people, both Jews and non-Jews, rushed to the Jewish Community Centre to try and get evacuated from Sarajevo, or to get desperately needed medication, or to have a meal in the soup kitchen. Humanity in action. Wasn't there a Jewish saying: 'Whosoever saves a single life, saves an entire universe.'?[22]

Although everybody could use most of those services, it still seemed more practical and easier to be a bona fide member of the community. Unfortunately, until 1992, Jews were not the most popular group of people, so a number of them had tried to conceal their Jewish origin for whatever reason[23] and had changed their names to Yugoslav-sounding ones. A great number of Yugoslav surnames of all ethnic groups ended in 'ić' (pronounced 'ych'[24]), so for instance they would change their names from Papo to Papić, or Guttmann to Dobrović.[25] Suddenly now they decided to reclaim their Jewishness. In addition, those who had remote Jewish connections – for example, who were related either by marriage or through distant relatives – insisted on joining the Jewish Community Centre and insisted on being included on the membership list. Why not, after all?

What struck me as greatly ironic or even paradoxical, though, was the fact that Gliga-Igor, my ex-husband, left Sarajevo on a Jewish convoy. I heard about it much later and never discovered how he had managed to do that. What I remembered with great sadness was the fact that his mother tried very hard to prevent him from marrying me. His mother was an overt anti-Semite. He obviously did not share his mother's views. He loved me and I loved him. We did get married. The later divorce had nothing to do with anti-Semitism. His mother's justification, at the time, for trying to marry him off to 'a nice Catholic girl' instead of me was that it was nothing personal; she just could not allow her son to marry a Jew. She told me that she, my future mother-in-law, shared a common and widespread view that Jews were a nasty, unscrupulous lot! In addition, another reason was that she did not want her grandchildren to end up in a concentration camp should there be another war. And there was another war[26] in which, ironically, her son was saved by the very Jews who she was afraid might be the cause of her grandchildren's demise in a possible new war.

My family's attitude towards the daily threat changed again, so by early summer we stopped going down to Minja's flat every time it felt dangerous. We stayed in our flat and hid in our bathroom when the shelling seemed serious. No outside walls there – apparently safe. Safety as a concept became relative. Squeamishness too. There were times when we had to have lunch in the bathroom. I would cover the toilet bowl (full – there was no water) with a big towel. We put a little collapsible table in there, put a damask tablecloth on it, with napkins, cutlery and nice plates, all very respectable. We would eat there seemingly oblivious to the circumstances.

The new phenomenon was that the exchange of advice, recipes (for dishes made of available ingredients), gossip, news, information and alike was very present and welcome. It must have been sometime in mid-summer that I learned through the grapevine that my mother's distant relatives, living nearby, had left Sarajevo together with their daughter and her family. They had a valuable collection of stamps and asked Mima's mother (who lived in the flat above them) to keep it safe. That was next to impossible, so, together with Mima and Božo, we decided something had to be done. The decision was that I would go to the Jewish Community Centre and inquire whether they could help with saving the stamp collection. The inquiry was not warmly received, quite understandably. They were in the business of saving people's lives, not stamps, I was told. However, one of the officials, David, whom I hardly knew, agreed to help. He told me he would come by later and deal with it. Božo, who was a solicitor for the Community Centre, would legalize it. We agreed. So, David, a university professor with his newly acquired police badge, came, took all the albums, put them in suitcases and we all signed the necessary papers and he left.

The stamps were never found. I could not forgive myself for being so naïve and blindly believing, being so gullible. How come I did not somehow make sure David, whom I hardly knew, could be trusted? The fact that he was a university professor turned policeman was no guarantee. Maybe even the contrary. Many years later, when I visited those relatives, living in Israel then, they were very forgiving and understanding. They certainly did not blame me for the loss of the stamps. In addition, ironically and luckily, the most valuable album was left behind by chance, hidden somewhere. It was found and eventually sold for a decent amount of money.

One day, sometime in July, we came to Minja's to learn that Saša, had lost his job fixing roofs, lost his *radna obaveza* and was obliged to join the official Bosnian army which was predominantly Muslim. He was a Serb. Not a good prospect for survival. Even a Muslim neighbour, who frequented our shelter at Minja's flat, was adamant that Saša should not go. He said he believed any soldier serving with Saša would shoot him from behind, because passions were running so high and hatred was so strong. Also, the officially acknowledged notion of 'ethnic cleansing'[27] reached us via the media and although we tried to block it out, it inadvertently entered our consciousness. So actually, it was undeniable that Saša would be in danger. Fixing roofs under sniper fire was bad enough, but this was out of the question.

A day or two later, the small 'council' in Minja's flat debated and came up with the only possible solution. Saša needed to have his leg fractured. But, how to do that? Having a plaster cast put on a healthy leg would not help. It would be X-rayed and the stratagem discovered. The consequences were unthinkable. We could hire somebody who owned a pistol to shoot him in the leg, but how could we trust such a person? Eventually, Minja asked me if I would take Saša to my friend, a surgeon I knew and trusted (crucial under the circumstances), who lived nearby, to ask him if he would be willing to break Saša's leg. I did. However, he could not do it. He quoted the Hippocratic Oath, but said he could show me how to do it safely: wrap the leg in many towels and put two chairs next to each other with some space between them. Saša should then place his leg on both chairs and I would jump on it. Job done, he said. I was horrified. I could not even think of doing it. We both came back and reported to the group. Nobody could do it. We had to think of something else and quite soon, too.

The Big Decision

Things were getting worse and worse. Life became exhausting and makeshift, more often than not. We had makeshift soups lacking sufficient ingredients. We had makeshift showers where one would stand in a big bucket and use a pitcher to pour water over oneself (due to insufficient water supply, reserved water was kept in the bathtub). We had a makeshift cooker using solid fuel tablets and a few more makeshift inventions. Since we often had no electricity supply, I had to learn how to make a makeshift light for the night, because walking in the pitch-dark was not safe, especially for my parents. I would fill a small glass jar with water, pour a tiny bit of oil on top, pull a piece of cord or string through a thin layer of cork, and that became a lamp, as the mother of my close childhood friend, Tatjana,[28] had taught me. It was a flickering, weak light exuding an unpleasant smell, but at least it gave some light.

Days and nights were filled with constant intermittent shooting and shelling. Actually, death, not only as a threat, was ever-present. It became our reality, yet we tried to banish it from our minds. Numbed fear turned into constant tension and vigilance. Permanent hunger turned food into an obsession. I started dreaming of peaches and tomatoes, literally. Summer arrived, with high temperatures and no window panes or blinds to draw, so the heat was getting into the flat early in the day. It would be far too warm most days.

Out there on the streets there was dust everywhere. Asphalt melted in scorching sunshine, with threatening electric cables that had been cut hanging from the sky above our heads, with rubble and broken glass underfoot. It was difficult to walk and even more difficult to breathe. Sarajevo summers could be very dry. This one was, with no rain to wash the dust off the streets, no breeze to cool the burning skin. It was not much better in our flats either. Urban smells mixed with the smells of sweaty human bodies created an unpleasant combination, both outside and in.

I started going regularly to the Jewish Community Centre. The only way to get there was up and down a very steep street. It was a long and dangerous journey. I had to walk all the way through the centre of town and then across a bridge in order to get to the other side of the Miljacka River where the Community Centre was located, next to the only functioning synagogue. Sometimes I dragged heavy bags of food on the way home in the summer heat and I had significant difficulties breathing. My eyes were bulging and I kept losing weight. My mother thought my thyroid was failing. She wanted me to go and have it checked. So, I went to a friend, a hospital doctor, who luckily had some chemicals left over, so he tested me. Of course, it was not thyroid –

my eyes were big anyway – but now, set in a long, thin, emaciated face they appeared bulging, he told me. Losing weight in spite of eating a lot of pasta and rice, all carbohydrates, surprised me. However, I was told that eating a lot of the same kind of food would cause weight loss. So, all was well!

On one of the quieter days, Nikola visited. I was glad to see him; after all, we used to see each other very often. He was wounded, but not seriously. A piece of shrapnel had caught him while he was on his way to his new job. He now had a senior position in the newly formed government. He seemed proud of it, but I did not approve. Not that anybody asked me. Then, more than ever, I despised politics, parties and governments. He had had a decent profession, so why this radical change, I asked. He tried to justify the move, but I was not buying it. I was stubborn, disappointed and disillusioned, probably.

The new tacit code of conduct required women to dress up with full makeup on as a sign of defiance to the enemy and a declaration of belonging to 'us'. A sign of fearlessness and patriotism! How could a 'rebellion' with mascara and lipstick compete with the might of dynamite-fortified fighters on all sides, threatening to annihilate the entirety of a powerless people? Their might was rendering the whole population helpless and impotent. I did not understand; I did not see any point. It seemed like a futile manifestation of allegiance. But allegiance to what? To some sort of cause, nationalism or tribalism? Which one? Based on what? Why? Utter stupidity and superficiality. Friend or foe, brave or cowardly, us or them: it was a new way of dividing people. Dividing those who had been friends, neighbours, colleagues, who had lived comfortably with each other until recently. Or so I wanted to believe. I somehow preferred to differentiate between humane and inhumane, between good, generous and tolerant versus nasty, selfish and hateful. Wrong time, wrong place.

I probably had to rethink my attitude. I probably had to adapt to the new dispensation. However, it was too alien and unpalatable. I always believed, or wanted to believe, that people help each other in adversity. Unfortunately, overall, disappointingly, not many people (apart from close friends) seemed willing to help each other. Not a pleasant realization. Hence, small gestures acquired maybe inappropriate significance and became a measure of humanity. We started looking at people through different lenses. I caught myself being surprised by both the positive and the negative gestures. Yet again, I felt my reasoning occasionally became childlike. The turns life was taking proved to be more and more unfamiliar.

At one point I met an acquaintance, an art professor, carrying a bag with green vegetables sticking out. I asked him where he had managed to get them. He completely blanked me out and carried on walking. That shocked me.

On the other hand, the engineer who maintained our heating system made a special effort to come and tell us about a secret fresh vegetable 'market' in the cellar of one of the nearby high-rises. I was deeply moved. A childhood friend visited and brought some pickled beetroot for my father, yet found it necessary to mention his ethnicity, something I never knew or thought about. Ethnicity had been one of the things that never mattered to me, and I made a conscious effort not to allow it to matter then either. His reaction puzzled me.

Omer, to whom I turned for comfort when the shooting started, changed. Although I was very close to him and his family, I was surprised to see the transformation at the outset of the war. A former communist, he gradually turned into a nationalist and became untrusting and resentful towards many a colleague. He reproached me by saying that 'my people' had killed 'his people' in the Second World War. Who were 'my people' or 'his people'? Absurd. I thought we belonged to the same people. If, by 'my people', he meant Jews in Yugoslavia in the Second World War, well, they were not in the position to kill anybody; they were the ones being killed. What possessed him, I wondered. Was that ideology or fear-induced anger talking?

In spite of that, he later came to my flat, was as friendly as ever and brought some cigarettes and pitta bread. I was pleased to see him. I was hoping that it was a sort of apology for what he had said earlier. Maybe he regretted it? A mystery I never found an answer to. When he visited again later, he asked me to put him and his family on the list for Jewish convoys. I tried. I was referred to Boris, the official in charge of assembling the list, whom I had not met before. He listened to my request and told me that it was not possible. Apparently, one of the conditions of the military authorities of the ethnic group Omer belonged to was not to permit the entire family to leave. He told me that the approval of all three military authorities was necessary for those allowed on each and every convoy. So, either the wife and kids, or him on his own. Neither was an option for them.[29]

Another friend I had met through my ex-husband came through all the shelling and shooting to try to convince me and plead with me to get my family on a Jewish Community convoy, for my sake and the sake of my family, although he and his family could not leave at the time.[30] It was touching. Yet, a faculty librarian told me angrily that I should go to my 'spare' homeland, Israel, that my place was not in Sarajevo. Why would Israel be my spare homeland? I was born and bred in Sarajevo, in Yugoslavia and so were my parents? Was that an anti-Semitic comment? Most likely.

The literary theory professor who talked about genetic code, a seemingly kind man, once when he saw tears rolling down my face at the faculty meeting, looked at me scornfully and told me rather rudely that I should have stayed at home if I was such a coward. That seemed cruel. But, as another colleague commented, he might have been projecting his fear onto me. Be that as it may, I was hurt. Fearing for one's life should not be a crime, nothing to be ashamed of. However, in my case, it was not even that. I cried because I realized that the shelling had started and I had not organized my parents' 'trip' to the cellar. Where had human empathy disappeared to? Ultimately it was all hugely confusing.

The only clear goal was saving our lives and getting hold of whatever food we could. That became the focus of our daily existence. Food especially fresh food, was hard to come by. One day, Zvonko dropped by. He was returning from the nearby market where he had bought a five-kilo bucket of mustard. That was the only food being sold there. We laughed: what could one do with all that mustard? However, it was not funny. Moreover, Zvonko – being Zvonko – was full of anger and fuming at the colleagues and friends on 'the other side', i.e. those considered the enemies, whether they were up at Pale or those who went abroad 'via Pale'.[31]

He was not the only one to drop by. Many people started visiting, even those who were never or seldom guests in our home. It was obvious that people craved human interaction. On top of that we all needed to show solidarity, to exchange 'expert' analyses, swap information and advice, recount various horrifying rumours; we needed to vent frustration, to make the day feel less long and more meaningful and God knows what else.

Information about food supplies was precious. Thanks to Henika I managed to buy, for Deutsche Marks, of course, a small, very expensive piece of beef from her colleague, a hospital consultant, turned 'butcher', who lived nearby and who was selling meat. My father needed protein. We fried it, gave my father the bigger meaty bit while my mother and I ate the tiny fatty bits with some bread. What a feast it was!

I eventually managed to get to the high-rise the heating engineer had told me about. A group of people was gathered there. Glum-looking uniformed individuals kept popping their heads out of the front door, telling people to leave, claiming that 'there is nothing to be got here'. Nobody moved. The sending away was getting more and more aggressive. Eventually, a number of men in camouflage uniform carrying big boxes arrived and went in. These had to be the vegetables the engineer had told us about, I realized. After that the main entrance opened a fraction at a time and selected people were allowed in. Among the first was a colleague of my father's. He was the father of a prominent university professor and a political activist. I thought he would be helpful, but unfortunately, he refused to tell me how to be accepted as a regular there. So, the chosen few got some food while others were persistently told to leave. I and another woman stayed. We decided to force our way in, one way or another, and never come back. And we succeeded. I managed to get some potatoes, for Deutsche Marks, of course.

Persistent I had always been, but thick-skinned not really. I used to be shy, too. I realized I had changed. However, I kept refusing to explore the causes of the change. Above all, I was reluctant to recognize and admit the overwhelming sense of humiliation and helplessness. Yet, I sensed that this denial, this turning a blind eye, had lasted for far too long. It was time to acknowledge what was staring me in the face and accept it. It was reckless not to register the new upside-down world: an elderly neighbour suddenly turned cigarette smuggler, a literature professor a geneticist, a hospital consultant a butcher, a university music professor a policeman. Distrust, hatred, starvation and ultimately the real threat of death were all around us. Was that the world I wanted to inhabit? Denial was not helpful, not reasonable and, eventually, not even possible. Consequently, I started thinking about leaving.

It was very difficult to decide to leave one's life behind. To leave the hometown where the family had lived all their lives. (My parents only left under duress in the Second World War, to save their lives, and returned as soon as possible.) Our friends were there, most of our relatives, familiar streets, familiar vistas and scents – our own world was there. My parents never dreamt of leaving Sarajevo, especially in their advanced age. They had even bought gravesites and paid for the funeral costs in advance. My aunt Ella and uncle Moni did the same. The two couples had gravesites next to each other.

The irony was that each respective couple ended up buried together, but each couple in a different country. My parents, in spite of the fact that they died in two different countries, were buried together, in Belgrade, Serbia; my aunt and uncle together, in London, UK.

I also did not contemplate moving anywhere any time soon. Even when I was in the US, around my mid-twenties, I did not fancy staying there, although I had opportunities to do so. I could not imagine starting a new life from scratch, having established some sort of satisfactory existence in Sarajevo. Moving anywhere else would most likely have meant a change of career. A significant part of my identity was my work, it was my vocation so it was hard to imagine moving anywhere. How could I leave it? My students were almost a substitute for the children I did not have.

Departure

If truth be told, neither of our two Sarajevo families was seriously thinking of leaving yet. Nevertheless, we discussed the possibility and agreed that, if we decided to leave, all of us would leave at about the same time.[32] Irrational maybe, but that was the way we were. Therefore, the two families started pondering, each family nucleus, with respective pros and cons to consider. There were few ways to leave the besieged Sarajevo, especially legitimately and officially. Most accessible to us were the coach convoys organized by the Jewish Community Centre.[33] There were various explanations as to how the convoys had started, but the important thing was that they had and that our family was eligible.

However, we had to wait for Tanja's return. It turned out that she had gone with a friend to their summer house on a mountain outside our 'belt' and could neither get in touch with her parents nor come back. It was almost as difficult to enter through a 'belt' as it was to leave. Henika had to find a way to bring her back to the besieged Sarajevo. It was not easy. She needed many *vezas*, many a string to pull.

It was probably at the end of July when Tanja returned and the decision was finally made: we were leaving Sarajevo. Having been away from Sarajevo for several months, Tanja found the situation in town unbearable. For the rest of the family, it was 'old news' and, in a way, we were used to it by then. Actually, it was Tanja who sped up the process of finalizing the decision to leave. She made preparations, managed to sell Henika's and her cars and quite rightly saw no point in waiting for anything.

The Jewish Community coach convoys went to the Pirovac resort[34] on the Adriatic coast to give people a brief respite before they were expected to decide where to go from there. The plan for my parents and me was to somehow get to Belgrade in order to stay with Sida and her family. (The other half of the extended family would go to Zagreb and then decide where to go from there.) I did not envisage any problems with securing convoy places for us since we were all Jewish and had been members of the Jewish Community for years, plus my parents were old and ill. In the meantime, I secured permission from the new head of my department to escort my parents, so I was eligible too. At the Jewish Community Centre, the official in charge of convoys, Boris, had the job of deciding whether to accept a particular party and include them on the list, or give an explanation why it was not possible. He also held information about the convoy schedules. Most convoys were a mix of Jews and other ethnicities. The story, a rather convincing one, was that a representative from each ethnic army which had to authorize the convoys imposed their own conditions. Allegedly, one of the conditions was to include some of their friends and family. In that culture, and especially under those circumstances, it made sense. The trip itself was long and hard. Apparently, on average, it took over twenty hours and was an arduous and dangerous coach trip.

There was more and more talk of people leaving, which made our decision seem more reasonable. Probably sometime towards the end of July, during one of my regular visits to the Jewish Community Centre, I ran into David again and mentioned that we were planning to leave soon. He inquired about the quality and make of our TV, gramophone, telephone, etc. Strange, I thought. He explained that, once we decided to go, he would come and take them. I did wonder what he wanted those items for as his home had not been destroyed. Those were the days, though, when there was neither space nor time to dwell on such questions. I just heard myself say that the items had served their purpose and that he could come and take them when the time came. God knows what made me say it, but I did. However, he came much before we were due to leave, with an assistant to help him carry the stuff to the car. He did not like the TV set in the sitting room, so he left that. He took the telephone and some other things, including the small TV set my father was watching at the time in his bedroom (we had a temporary supply of electricity then). David just unplugged it and handed it to his helper. I stood there stunned. David said nothing to my bewildered father and left, without even an apology.

In the entire terribly distressful situation, my biggest concern was my father. He was seriously ill, the final stages of terminal bone cancer. Was it safe to stay? Was it too risky to leave? Yet it was he who decided to take a risk. He was determined we should leave. So, on behalf of the half of our extended family, I went to the Jewish Community offices and asked Boris to put my family on the list. He obviously had some knowledge of my family and our circumstances. What he then said was a real shock. He said that my father would die during the long journey, and that my mother and I would have only two choices: to throw his body out of the coach on top of the Vran Mountain[35] for the wolves to devour him, or get out of the coach, remain with his corpse and be eaten by the wolves ourselves. He asked me whether I was sure I wanted us to go. I was horrified, but determined to go because my father assured me that he could survive it and convinced me that to leave was the only alternative for us. Since I was determined to leave, the comments about my father's survival chances and the subsequent options for my mother and me did not deter me, but nevertheless it unsettled me. I just could not get my head around it. Why had he said that? What was he thinking? Anyway, the date was set: mid-August

1992. Ella and Moni were on an earlier convoy list, while Henika and Tanja were on the same one with us.

I also wanted to put Sveto and his wife on one of the convoys. Sveto meant a lot to me. When I joined the Department, it was Sveto who encouraged me to start my PhD; he believed in me. We eventually became quite close. He and his wife visited us often and said that they were thinking of leaving, one way or another. I spoke to Jaki, the Jewish Community Board member, who was a friend from our teenage years. He took me aside and tried to explain why it was not possible. I feared as much: Sveto's brother was a high-ranking politician in the government[36] of the Republic of Srpska and was considered an enemy by the local authorities. Although Sveto stayed out of politics, to include somebody with the surname he shared with his brother, Jaki claimed, was impossible, even had they not been brothers. He reminded me of some infamous Second World War surnames and by putting them in a similar context, he presumably tried to sound more convincing. I had no choice but to accept the argument.

Now the only question that remained was that of the friends from our 'shelter' at Minja's flat. Minja refused to even contemplate going, for whatever reason. Mima and Božo decided to put themselves on the convoy. Božo was the Jewish Community's solicitor and as such was eligible. However, what about Saša? His leg was not broken, his future was bleak. My father thought that he might be able to adopt him and thus make him a member of the family. Alas, that was not possible. Saša was not a minor and one could not adopt an adult. Then an idea occurred to me: being single, I could marry him. We were all ecstatic. The solution was found. Minja could not be happier. The arrangements were made: we went to the registrar's to book a date for the wedding. Mima and Božo would be the witnesses[37] – and problem solved! I found a ring that looked like a wedding band and gave it to Saša to give to me when the time came. I told Saša that once he actually got married and had children, I would not mind the event being mentioned, but did not want any special significance attached to it. I said I would like to be known as *kuma* (a term used to denote a wedding or christening witness) or something similar. If he did that, his children would not have this dark cloud of their father's awful predicament hanging over their heads. Was it the same rationale that might have guided my parents and that Hannah Arendt[38] talked about? Avoiding mentioning the things one would rather forget? I was not sure.

The day came, in the first week of August, with heavy shelling and shooting. We arrived at the registrar's, where there was no electricity. Luckily, that was not a problem. They used old-fashioned books, not computers. The agreement was that Saša would take my surname to make it more obvious that he was a member of a Jewish family and I would take his to make it all the more convincing. We reported to the clerk who told us to wait in a dark, narrow corridor. We were all apprehensive. Pulling a scam did not come naturally to us. Then the same clerk came and asked Saša to come to his office. The three of us – the two witnesses and I, the 'bride' – remained in the corridor. We started panicking. The only reasonable conclusion was that the deceit had been discovered; the officials had realized that it was a bogus marriage and now Saša would end up in prison, maybe the rest of the party as well. Mima whispered that she had an antique gold coin in her dress pocket, 'just in case': we might need to bribe the officials.

We waited and waited for what seemed like eternity. Then the door opened. Saša appeared and we were all summoned in. It was a small room with the national flag in the corner and the registrar sitting at the desk with a big register of marriages in front of her. I, the 'bride', had a small bouquet in my hands, everything to make it look more convincing. Mima had made it: she still had some chrysanthemums and parsley growing on her balcony. The shy (scared) 'bride' was dressed in an embroidered pale pink blouse and trousers. At least the blouse seemed wedding appropriate, so another attempt at making it look real. The blouse, though, was a few sizes too big because I had lost so much weight. I actually looked pathetic. But who cared about such things?

The ceremony was accompanied by loud shelling and shooting. Not the most pleasant ambience. I asked the registrar if they had the register of deaths handy. Gallows humour, but helpful in diffusing the tension. The registrar liked my sense of humour. Little did she know! Finally, another customary gesture to prove that it was a genuine ceremony: I threw the bouquet. Mima's face darkened. 'How could you waste precious parsley that we could have added to rice!' she told me off later. When we came out, away from earshot, we asked Saša why he had been taken into that office before the ceremony. He told us the official asked him, with Saša having agreed to take my surname and add it to his, whether he would be willing to take my double-barrelled surname. (I had my first husband's surname added to mine, hence double-barrelled. I did not know that one had to apply officially for the change of surname after the divorce.) Of course, he agreed. Consequently, he would end up with three surnames.[39] The surname was almost the entire point of the exercise! No wonder that we struggled to sign the register: a total of six surnames, three surnames each – I added his to two of mine. We laughed again. This time it really was funny, but tragic and absurd too.

I had my permission from the university, allowing me to put my *radna obaveza* on hold in order to escort my frail parents out of Sarajevo. Next,

I needed proof of my father's state of health in order to justify the request to have my husband accompany us. I turned to the doctor who treated my father with huge kindness and humanity and who supported the entire family. I had to go to his home. That was an ordeal as he lived on the thirteenth floor: there was no electricity, so I had had to climb thirteen floors to get to his flat. Not only was I not fit enough for it, but I also had to climb all those stairs in pitch-darkness. The whole trip was unpleasant and seemed to last for ever. Being as kind as he was, he did not mind my visit to his home and provided a sort of certificate indicating how serious my father's state of health was and how much support he needed. I found it very embarrassing. However, it was not the time for timidity; it was about saving lives. So, this certificate formally confirmed that the new son-in-law was needed in helping on the journey. Now, I felt I had a legitimate right to ask for Saša, my husband, to be put on the convoy list together with the rest of our family. I took our wedding certificate and went to Ivica, the president of the Jewish Community. I knew him and was quite fond of him. I also trusted him, so I told him the truth about our bogus marriage. He understood. I then went to Boris, who put my husband on the list. Now, most of the loose ends were tied up.

At Ivica's office, a CNN journalist approached me. I was quite upset already and did not appreciate his less-than-appropriate comments. He asked me why I had not got some rich Jews to fly my father to Belgrade. I thought he was talking nonsense. Maybe he wasn't? However, why always mention Jews and wealth in the same breath? I did not like it and felt very frustrated. I knew no rich Jews, was scared of the coach trip and was revolted by it all. I could feel my anger welling up. I pulled down my T-shirt neckline to show him my emaciated, bony shoulders and chest (as far down as was polite!) in the hope that the state I was in might put him to shame. I naïvely hoped to show him how abysmally he grasped the situation around him. I felt that as a professional, seemingly experienced journalist he should have known better. Ivica sensed my anger so he took over and carried on talking to the journalist in his diplomatic way. I left, still angry. The journalist did not give up. He came to our home a few days later to interview the family before the departure. Not something I was happy about, but I could not throw him out.

Prior to our departure, I felt it was the right time to use the remaining petrol in the car and fetch Ella, my father's sister and Moni, her husband, to say their goodbyes. Was I aware then that those would be their final goodbyes? Probably not. I drove them to our flat and back which was a good use of the remaining petrol. The atmosphere at home was strange, difficult to describe. Tense, uneasy, stilted, with a hint of sadness. They tried not to show how they felt, to put on a brave face but they seemed numb. They sat in silence, a heavy, meaningful silence. What were they thinking? I did not know, but I could guess. The sister never saw the brother again.

Time suddenly seemed to fly. Mid-August 1992. Final preparations for the journey. Many things to take care of. We were not a drinking family, but we did like quality booze. Every trip abroad meant bringing some good cognac, gin or whisky home. Some was kept unopened to be gifted to people on appropriate occasions. What better occasion than survival during a civil war? Therefore, I took several bottles and gave a bottle to each of the people I was fond of and who were staying behind. I went and paid the rent for a few months in advance. I did not want our neighbour's nephew, a refugee from Herzegovina, who was going to move in,[40] to have to pay it. I also made sure the car's roadworthiness certificate was up to date. One could not leave unfinished business or debt, God forbid, behind!

I went to the Jewish Community Centre a few days before departure, to check about the exact arrangements for the trip. Ivica promised me a room in the Community Centre where my parents and I would spend the night before departure. Getting there on the morning of departure, due to the state my parents were in, was very risky. Therefore, to be on the safe side, we would arrive in the evening the day before. However, there was a devastating piece of news waiting for me there. Neither Mima and Božo, nor Saša, would be going with us. The convoy had been reduced from three coaches to one because the previous convoy had had problems on the Vran Mountain. An extremist Croatian formation was operating there and had threatened to remove and kill all the non-Jews, primarily Serbs. Horror stories of the incident were circulating. Therefore, in order to avoid problems of that sort, the officials had decided to cut down the number of coaches (of previously planned three, only one remained) and, consequently, the number of passengers, especially non-Jews. Some remained on the list, but some were taken off. One could not and did not question the reasons.

I was in a state of shock, did not know what to do. Saša was there with me. I thought of taking my family off the list this time and maybe wait for another, luckier convoy, but Saša would not have it. In any case, that was not a reasonable solution. (However, reason was anyway in short supply by then.) Ivica helped me decide by promising that Mima and Božo would be allowed on the next convoy in a month or so, while Saša, at his own suggestion, would receive special provision to travel in his car as part of the convoy (as some people did). So, my family stayed on the list. We went home rather upset, yet hopeful. Hope was an essential ingredient in situations like that. On the other hand, it might have been a tool to camouflage denial.

Minja took the news stoically. A new plan for this later date was devised. As Ivica suggested, Saša would follow in his car as a part of the convoy to a certain point and then take a route in a different direction, planning to fetch his girlfriend, Cica, who lived outside the Sarajevo 'belts', which was the main reason he had suggested following the convoy in his own car. It was a very risky undertaking. He would travel through areas held by different ethnic forces. A backup plan to improve his chances was made. Minja would ask her cardiologist friend to issue a referral for hospitalization in a specialized hospital outside Sarajevo (close to where Cica lived). He would show this at the various checkpoints. Since he was of Serbian ethnicity, there was a danger of him being arrested by the Serbian soldiers as either a deserter, a traitor or a spy. Too scary. However, there was not much choice. A number of my university colleagues were high-ranking officials in the seceded Serbian government, so I suggested using me as a bargaining tool. I told him several anecdotes that would prove to those who knew me that he was genuinely my friend (if not husband), hence could be trusted as neither a spy nor a traitor. Naïve maybe, but that was all any of us could do.

My final chore was to find a way for the books and photographs to be taken care of. They could not be carried, or just left behind in the flat. Therefore, I turned to the mother of my friend Tatjana, who lived nearby with her husband, and who had no intention of leaving. The plan was for me to bring the most important books and albums to their house. She certainly did not mind taking a few suitcases for me, but it had to be done discreetly, she said. Right across from their house was the local paramilitary headquarters, stationed in a former children's nursery, so suitcases might arouse suspicion. She told me to pack the suitcases and leave them in the flat and she would arrange to get them over when it was safe.

And she did sometime later, I found out.

In spite of everything, I foolishly believed then that the war would not last long. Winters in Sarajevo were very severe, snowy and cold, so, in my frightened, childlike mind, I assumed nobody would want to fight then, what with the snow and freezing temperatures. Yet one more sign of serious denial. My fantasy was that, having left, I would return in spring, prepare everything for my parents' return, and bring them back before the summer. I told my student days' lecturer, who had become a friend and a colleague, about my plan and she suggested I stayed with her while preparing the flat for my parents' return. She lived in the same area of town and it all sounded very reasonable. I genuinely believed that this was the solution and it seemed she did too. How blinding could the power of desperation be?

I had to start packing. One suitcase per person, Boris told me. Not an easy task. How does one decide what to take and what to leave? One suitcase would be almost full with father's medicines and other items necessary for his care. Just two left for everything else. What to pack and how? I packed only the necessary things, whatever that meant. Absurdly, the only books I packed were several cookery books. My motivation was totally unrealistic: I thought I might earn some money from selling homemade food during, what I imagined would be, our brief stay in Belgrade. Admittedly I loved cooking and starvation probably made me think of cooking. But what on earth made me imagine that I could earn money selling anything? I had no talent or affinity for moneymaking enterprises.

Sadly, mementoes were not a priority. However, I knew my parents had a few of their parents. I told them they could each take one or two items. Was that cruel? I also decided to take our oil paintings out of their frames, to put them in a suitcase while my parents were asleep so as not to upset them. The paintings were, for us, a symbol of beauty, an aspect of our life that was especially important amid all the ugliness around us.[41] Although not too valuable, they could be sold if the worst came to the worst, I thought. I managed to take the smaller ones out of their frames, but the big one, the one I liked very much, I could not. It was a canvas stretched over plywood and, not thinking clearly, as I tried to pull it off, the dry oil paint flaked onto the floor. That did not upset me much. New times, new values. After all, both the canvas and the frame could be used by Minja as cooking fuel. The practical application of artwork! Maybe not meant to be, but so what?

I also decided to leave my car to Minja. I gave her the car licence, the keys, the garage keys and told her to sell it and buy some food at the black market. Good deeds were the only way to neutralize evil, as I realized later. That actually was a part of my rebellion. Minja, though, never sold the car. She also adhered to the 'good deeds philosophy'.

And then the fateful day came. My mother and I cleaned the flat. One cannot leave one's dirt behind! Paintings used as fuel, rates paid well in advance for the flat to be abandoned and the same flat cleaned thoroughly! Upside-down values. Cleaning was a hard task. I don't know where we got the energy. Human behaviour seemed so unpredictable: how many absurd situations we created for ourselves within an absurd set of circumstances.

By early evening, we were ready. Bane the 'Chetnik' arrived to give us a lift. The small group from Minja's flat helped us. Some of the new neighbours were there. One of those new nameless RŠTO neighbours expressed her bitterness and envy when she saw the family getting ready to leave. Her comment was that Jews were always the lucky ones. Were they? Really? Was she not aware of the irony of such a statement?

We arrived safely at the Community Centre. Bane handed us a small parcel that Minja had asked him to give us. It contained a few real steaks that Minja had cooked for us. She had managed to buy some black-market meat that was being sold on the pavement near our block of flats. It was very expensive and only for Deutsche Marks, naturally. Her beloved son Saša had been left behind, yet she had made this special treat for those of us who were leaving. Incredible, but not surprising. Good deeds! I felt gratitude, admiration, guilt and fear, all at the same time. Would Ivica be able to keep his word?

We spent that night in a small room in the Community Centre, with two sofa beds that my parents slept in and a cot for me. Soon after we had arrived, Nikola came to say goodbye. I was both moved and very sad. Later that evening, by a strange coincidence, the neuropsychiatrist who had examined my mother some time earlier, came to share the room with us. I offered him the cot, feeling that it was only fair since my parents were using the only two beds. So, I slept on the floor, which did not matter much. We talked most of the night. What his Jewish connection was I did not know, did not ask and did not care.

His wife and daughter were already in Zagreb,[42] *so he would stay with the convoy until the first stop at Stup,*[43] *where all the passengers would get off the city bus and board a proper long-distance coach. He would stay behind there as he had made other arrangements to get to Zagreb.*

In the morning, several people came to give me their letters and money for their children they had sent earlier either to Zagreb or Belgrade. Our plan was to get to Pirovac and somehow get to Belgrade from there, so I turned into a 'postie' covering both new countries, Croatia and Serbia. The grapevine communication was very efficient then. How had all these people I hardly knew found out about my plans? It really did not matter. I took all the envelopes, ensuring that they put the name, address and phone number of the recipient on the front, and sealed the envelopes without telling me how much money was in them.

The morning was not only hectic but also hugely upsetting. I was both hopeful and stupefied, yet I had to function. Our 'Minja's flat cohort' came to say their goodbyes. Saša and Božo were carrying my father. The CNN journalist was there with his camera. I was repulsed, horrified by the idea of being an actor in a horror movie.

Much later, I learned that the CNN film worked for me; namely, my friend Nancy in the US saw it and recognized me. She knew I was alive. Some good came out of it.

There were masses of people around the bus, or so it seemed. Some I knew, some I did not. The atmosphere was noisy, emotional and difficult, a cacophony of blurred sounds and a multitude of frenzied faces. It was very difficult to function, but I had to. I must have been functioning on autopilot. Yet, it was very traumatic. Did I actually know I was leaving, never to return? No, I certainly did not. How soon would I realize? What would it take me to realize that?

Bane and Zora also came that morning to say goodbye. Zora put a silver bracelet on my arm, a lucky charm maybe. I was so thin that the bracelet went all the way up to my biceps. Tears. A woman approached me and told me that she knew my father; they had worked together. She asked me to look after her 9-year-old daughter, who was travelling on her own. She said the girl's name was Sara.

It wasn't. That transpired later during the journey. Why would a 9-year-old travel incognito? Unbelievable.

There was shooting, the snipers as active as ever along the route. The bus went along a 'sniper alley' and past the Faculty of Philosophy, my home from home, the place where I enjoyed my work – my students, my friends and colleagues – now sadly deserted.

Maybe it was the most appropriate final goodbye my hometown and my country could have given me. The memory of that made it easier later to accept that there would be no returning.

But, then and there, all we knew and cared about was the fact that we were alive and leaving the hell that Sarajevo had turned into. Scared but ready, we embarked on our long, winding, onerous journey.

Chapter 3

Reluctant Recognition

Journey to Pirovac

On 16 August 1992, we boarded the bus. I did not know that it would be the final farewell to my hometown and my town's farewell to me, but it was. Farewells are never easy, but absurdly this one, albeit not fully conscious, was made easier with the shooting and sniper fire, which followed us all the way to Stup, our first stop. We travelled on a rickety old city bus, full of people and baggage – there was no hold. A big coach was waiting for us at Stup along with a group of people: some Catholic priests (Stup was a predominantly Croatian area),[1] one or two representatives from the Zagreb Jewish Community, Sarajevo Jewish Community representatives, as well as Benko, my friend Lala's relative, who escorted these convoys.[2]

The passengers quickly boarded the coach, the baggage went down into the hold and we headed southwards. My family was given the long bench seat at the very back to turn into a makeshift bed for my father. We put two fur coats (belonging to my mother and me) underneath him to make it softer. My mother had her own seat nearby, while I stood by my father, making sure he did not roll over. I was leaning against the door rail. (I arrived at the destination with a solid dark bruise on my back.)

One of the first checkpoints was a Serbian one, in Blažuj.[3] All the passengers were instructed to get off the coach to have their IDs checked, while two soldiers boarded the coach. My father and I were allowed to stay on. Two paramilitaries, with guns in their hands, started looking around. They said nothing, but father and I were mortified. This went on for a while in silence until my mother came running to the coach, waving and shouting something inaudible. We learned later that, in her fear, she mistook the word for bombs (*bombe*) as the word for fur coats (*bunde*) and, since the paramilitaries had said that they were looking for bombs, she was trying to tell me to voluntarily give them the fur coats. It would have been funny had it not been under those circumstances.

The next stop was Kiseljak, a spa town near Sarajevo where my maternal grandmother's family had had their holiday home[4] before the Second World War. The spa had long been well known for the mineral water and the flat bread made with it. We had a brief break there. A colleague from the university met the coach. He told me that Nikola had asked him to wish me all the best. I was hugely touched; it was a comforting link to the happier parts of my past life amid the current frightening uncertainty. In Kiseljak, most people on the coach bought the bread. I bought some tomatoes and plums as well. I had some Deutsche Marks hidden under the lining of my shoe: the night before, while chatting with the neuropsychiatrist, he had advised me to hide some money in my shoes. That was a rather absurd idea since I had envelopes full of other people's money, as well as mine, in the bag next to my mother. However, under those circumstances it was not easy to think rationally, so following anybody's friendly advice felt reassuring.

It was at that spot that I was reminded of something one might consider a genuine Balkan irony: the reality of inheritance, or rather non-inheritance. Namely, it was next to impossible even for the next generation of descendants to inherit anything from their ancestors in any shape or form. A small, sentimental, personal example was the fact that the spa, with a holiday home once belonging to my mother's family in sight, conjured up the image of my maternal great-grandmother[5] and the tall, silver vase she had given us. It was the only memento we had of her. It had survived so many occupations and conflicts, yet this time it stayed behind. Somebody else would use it for whatever purpose they saw fit. I was repulsed and saddened by the idea: a symbol of the far greater and significant losses of many a family in that region.

When the coach started up again, some people noticed my tomatoes. They seemed popular, so I gave them to one of the passengers, who cut them into pieces and so everyone got a slice. Plums were not so popular and I gave them to my mother to keep for later. She put them on her seat, forgot about them and then sat on top of the plastic bag full of ripe plums. She was wearing her favourite silk peach-coloured suit and, needless to say, the skirt turned purple at the back. The suit was ruined, but she did not care.

A young foreign journalist was sitting on the floor, by my feet. (The space between the last row of seats and the back seat was slightly larger – it could easily accommodate him with his small bag and a recorder.) He was observing attentively. I wondered how much he could grasp, how much he could pick up, until he decided to ask me a question. He put a microphone in front of my face and asked: 'Who do you hate?' I froze and thought to myself, not that again! Hatred was the overpowering emotion present everywhere. All the radio and TV programmes talked about animosities, both exuding and provoking hatred. Hatred was the common denominator.

The young journalist obviously just followed the cliché. I was disgusted and told him the closest I came to hating was my late ex-mother-in-law, who personally hurt me[6] and I regretted that I was too polite with her instead of telling her off at the time. Now since she was dead, it was too late, so the resentment remained. I then gave him a 'speech' about the difference between hatred towards a person/s who intentionally hurt you, which could be understood, and impersonal, mass hatred, hatred of an abstract concept such as ethnicity (or race, tribe or any such group), which was rather more difficult to understand. I told him how unreasonable the latter was and what devastating consequences it had had, although both kinds of hatred were destructive in nature. Yet I almost hated him.

The atmosphere on the coach was tense. People were overwhelmed by the sense of insecurity, apprehension and confusion. Some already had children elsewhere; some did not even know where their children had ended up. Parents wanted either to join their children or bring them to wherever they planned to be. However, at that time, most parents had no clue where they would feel safe and accepted.

The little 9-year-old we knew as Sara was eventually looked after by a woman, a few seats in front of my mother, who had a child the same age. The woman realized I was busy enough with my parents so she offered to help. It was sad to see a 9-year-old trying to remember the alien name she had been told to respond to. Preparing her for the trip, the mother probably assumed the daughter would be safer with a Jewish-sounding name on a Jewish convoy and instructed the girl to say her name was Sara. (Sara was a rare name in Yugoslavia; mostly Jewish people would choose it.)

My cousins, Henika and Tanja, sat at the front of the coach. They were both distraught. Their respective children (albeit grown up) were abroad and they themselves could not decide where to head, where to try and settle. Henika was a doctor, a more transferable profession, but Tanja, an electrical engineer working in commerce, was not so sure about sticking to her profession.

That later proved to be true: their fears materialized – Henika worked in her profession, while Tanja never did.

Their aim was to stay together, bring their children to wherever they settled, and eventually bring their parents too. The parents were already in the Zagreb Jewish residential care home, temporarily.

It was terribly warm and dusty on the coach. I feared for my father – I could not forget Boris's comments made in Sarajevo about our chances. I found a piece of cardboard to use as a fan. An elderly woman sitting at the front, who told me she had worked with my father and was fond of him, gave me the real fan she was using. I was reluctant, but she insisted, so we swapped. Good versus evil again, kindness versus cruelty, affection not hatred. I also devised a kind of mask to prevent dust from getting into my father's lungs: a damp handkerchief over his face.

We did not witness further shooting. However, we did see devastated villages and towns along the way. Some houses were still smouldering, the smell quite offensive, the sight utterly depressing. With burned-out houses, villages reduced to rubble, bridges destroyed, it made a sad picture of a multi-ethnic/multi-religious country deeply immersed in ethnic/religious armed conflict. It was difficult to know which paramilitary was which. Uniforms were not necessarily recognizable. Some had insignia, some not. They all had weapons and they all looked threatening, which was definitely something they all had in common. One young man came onto the coach wearing only flip-flops, swimming trunks and a rifle slung over his bare shoulder. No insignia anywhere. Had it not been so scary, it would have been comical.

We stopped at Jablanica,[7] had a coffee break and it was here that the next part of the route was to be decided. There were two options: the Vran Mountain or the equally risky but shorter route along the Neretva River.[8] It was not clear to me what 'risky' actually meant – each route seemed frighteningly risky. Benko, who was in charge of the convoy, advised me on the options and I voted for the Neretva River since it was at least shorter. Luckily, the majority opted for that route. A great relief. Boris's survival prediction was thus more likely to be avoided: we would not be going over the dreaded Vran Mountain. So, everybody boarded the coach and the journey resumed.

Nevertheless, as we continued the journey, we were quite apprehensive. All of a sudden, after an unusual silence, I heard some loud applause. I could not figure out why. When I asked, I was told that we had just crossed the non-existent bridge over the Neretva. I had had my back turned to the front of the coach and did not see it. Two large planks had replaced the destroyed bridge and the driver had skilfully negotiated them. The notion of risk was clearer now, yet it was the only way to cross the river.

We almost got used to being checked by various, more or less scary, uniformed men – until, at one point, an emaciated man sitting next to my mother was about to be taken off the coach by soldiers inspecting the coach. Apparently, the passenger was of military age and considered a deserter. It was not clear why he was the only one picked on – he was not the only male passenger of that age – but they were adamant. My mother started arguing with a soldier. It scared me stiff; one does not argue with soldiers. Luckily

Benko, who was responsible for the safety of the passengers, had a word with the soldiers and the passenger was allowed to stay on the coach. The story – although unsubstantiated – was that human cargo at each checkpoint was worth a pack or two of cigarettes. So maybe an additional pack or even a carton was exchanged for this chap's freedom.

We went through Mostar, which was a ghost town. We only saw a few people walking about and some of the passengers started waving to them, wanting to hand them letters for their relatives in the region, to inform those relatives where they were heading – there was no other means of communication, so how else were they supposed to stay in touch? Passers-by completely ignored the passengers: distrust and fear were prevalent. Nobody wanted any contact with people on a coach that had appeared out of nowhere on streets that saw no vehicle for days. The intended relatives remained uninformed.

Sometime later, towards dusk, we arrived at a Franciscan monastery in Imotski.[9] The priests came to meet us. They carried my father in a chair. There were all sorts of food there, a real feast, something starving people had longed for, for many a month. My father was only interested in coffee: in Sarajevo, we never dared dream of coffee though my father was a bit of a coffee addict. With proper food, water, beverages and a decent lavatory (a very significant fact), we felt a bit more human. This highlighted the fact that the war had reduced us to our primary needs, our basic instincts and elementary reactions mostly, and, above all, that we had constantly felt utterly helpless, powerless and dehumanized. An overt realization, which, although kept at bay in the midst of our hell, could not have been fully ignored.

The journey from Imotski felt slightly easier. It was not warm any more. It was already dusk when we had arrived there and dark by the time we left. The next stop was Split.[10] Some people disembarked there – those planning to stay along the Croatian coast or on the islands. Yet another set of goodbyes. It was noisy around the coach in the port of Split. However, soon the rest of us were off into the night, to reach our final destination – Pirovac – not too far from Split.

The whole trip, due to the alternative route along the Neretva River rather than over the Vran Mountain, lasted a 'mere' sixteen hours.[11] We arrived in Pirovac sometime around midnight. All three of us were tired but relieved. It was a destination of sorts, albeit temporary. A promise of safety and tranquillity, a nice holiday complex located on the beach, familiar sounds and scents of the Mediterranean, reminiscent of 'the good old days' when we used to spend every summer on the Adriatic coast.

Pirovac and Onwards

When we arrived at the resort, a group of people was waiting for us, well prepared. They had a sort of reception desk outside, in the carpark, a list of all the passengers and their respective room numbers. The people in charge of running the place had allocated the rooms in advance. The frazzled passengers waited their turn. Even then, the self-centredness, the instinct of self-preservation and irritability of some people were immediately apparent. An example was the allocation of rooms. Passengers were called by surname alphabetically to be given their room keys. Yet, my family was given priority, which angered one chap, actually a distant relative of my mother's, who objected to what he saw as us jumping the queue. Although he (in early forties) and his family were much younger and fitter than my parents, he complained about our 'preferential treatment'. The fact that my father was terminally ill and frail did not matter. In adversity, strange things happen to people: when they feel disregarded, let alone threatened, the first victims seem to be empathy and humanity. However, by now, this was less of a surprise. I had learned the hard way.

A Sarajevo doctor who was already in Pirovac, a colleague and a friend of my ex-husband's, met the coach and both he and his son carried my weakened father. He then examined him and told me that, more or less, he was better than expected, but was severely dehydrated. That was not surprising because he had refrained from drinking any fluids during the trip because he could not go to the lavatory on his own – he had even refused coffee during the break in Jablanica and had only one cup of coffee in Imotski. Now the necessary fluids were prepared and he was rehydrated. Then all three of us, completely exhausted, fell fast asleep in the room I shared with my parents.

The resort was wonderfully located on the seafront. When we arrived, we did not know that we would spend quite a number of days there. My family was given two weeks to recuperate. We enjoyed lovely blue summer skies, sounds of the sea and crickets, Mediterranean vegetation and Mediterranean scents. My favourite pink oleanders were everywhere. The room was nice and spacious, with a big balcony overlooking the sea. I had been unsure what to expect. All I had known was that it was meant as some sort of respite, but nothing further than that. I could not have even imagined better.

I kept the bag with its precious contents – money, ours and other people's, and our jewellery – on the floor, by our beds, always unzipped. I was completely oblivious to the fact that the bag could have been snatched during the journey, when the bag was by my mother's feet, or here in Pirovac, where various people were coming and going. The door was never locked yet I did not think of securing the bag at all. Why such a relaxed attitude? After all, it not only contained my belongings, I had other people's money in there too. I just did not give it a thought. I had to concentrate on functioning on an hour-to-hour and day-to-day basis. Was that the beginning of the depression which would fully emerge later, in Belgrade? Or had war put things into a different perspective for me?

My family and I stayed there much longer than others. People usually stayed there for a few days and continued from there in search of a permanent safe destination. My parents just could not carry on. Our longer stay actually helped all three of us. We did recover rather well. Those two weeks were quite enjoyable. We managed to establish some sort of routine, which gave us a sense of security and normality, I suppose. We had our meals that I would bring from the kitchen, either in the room or on the balcony. My parents would have their usual siesta after lunch. In the evenings the balcony was the most pleasant place to relax, with the calming sounds of the sea and the sight of beautiful sunsets. We were even visited by a few people we knew from nearby coastal towns.

During the day, my parents stayed in the room where they received occasional visitors, among them most frequently my mother's friend Klara. She was hugely distraught. One night, at the very beginning of the war, the local militia came to her home in central Sarajevo and took her husband away. They said nothing to her. She waited for him to return because she could not think of any reason for his arrest, but he never came back. She turned to some influential people for help but to no avail. Her daughter had left for Canada with her child before the war started, so, after several months of unsuccessful searching, Klara decided to join her daughter. She suspected her husband was dead, but tried to hope for the best. Surprisingly even there, people felt the need to express distrust and spread lies and nasty gossip; all kinds of stories about her husband's financial machinations and reasons for him to hide were circulating. The vitriolic impact of life in war was still affecting frightened and lost people.

Klara's husband (who was not Jewish) was found in one of the mass graves on the outskirts of Sarajevo long after the end of the war. Their daughter travelled from Canada to Sarajevo to give him a proper burial. As in many cases, the only reason he was killed was the fact that he was a prominent man of the 'wrong' or 'enemy' ethnicity for that particular area. That was something his wife, an old communist idealist, could not even contemplate, let alone accept.

Most days I translated for various people: foreign journalists, representatives of Jewish humanitarian organizations from different parts of the world and others. All sorts of help was available for distraught, confused people.

Some needed support in choosing where to relocate to, some wanted to know procedures of immigrating to a specific country, some wanted to find out about job opportunities, what were the most welcoming countries. Most intended to go to Western Europe or to Israel. They ultimately needed support in facilitating the realization of their unplanned plans and help in finding solutions for their impossible predicament.

Those were extremely difficult decisions. What could one base the decision on? Few people knew. It was mostly about feasibility, practicality, contacts and the like. One couple, for instance, was trying to make a decision in spite of overt disagreement. The wife favoured Israel and the husband opposed it. He used the language as his biggest argument. A serious one indeed. He would bring an Israeli tin of food from the pantry with everything on it written in Hebrew and ask the wife to figure out what was inside. Genuinely impossible. Who knows why, but they eventually ended up in Israel where they did manage to make a home.

By then, most people were aware that there was no return to Sarajevo. Not I, though! My plan was to get to Belgrade and return once the war was over. (I am not sure my parents believed in returning.) In any case, our plan did differ from almost everyone else's. Except for those who remained in Split, the rest were planning on leaving the region. However, the first destination from Pirovac for most was Zagreb. From Zagreb, it was easier to organize all the necessary preparations.

Again, a foreign journalist annoyed me. The same story: the worse the story was, the better it was. A mathematician, a university professor, was returning from the beach with a plastic bag in which he had his wet swimming trunks. He wore a shirt and shorts when a journalist decided to interview him. The journalist positioned the professor in front of a grey concrete wall with no vegetation or sea in sight – and in his introduction, said that he was talking to a professor who had left home in Sarajevo with only this plastic bag in his hands. Dramatic it sounded, but not true. I was fuming, but as an interpreter, I could say nothing. Later, as we chatted in a seafront café, I complained to the journalist about his blatant lies, but he told me that shocking stories sold. He explained that this was common practice in the industry. Yet again, I realized he was only doing his job, trying to make a living – cynical yes, but understandable too.

At one point, a foreign TV reporter asked me for an interview. Without asking for whom he worked, I agreed, provided the interview was held in the garden with oleanders in the background. Was I trying to prove a point? To whom? Probably only to myself. I also insisted on shedding light on those aspects of the war that I chose. I agreed to talk only about my personal take on the detrimental effects of being compelled to leave one's home. I talked about losses, my personal losses. I had lost my home, which to me was a place of safety and security. (I still believed I was not leaving my country.) I had lost my profession, which for me was a big part of my identity. I had lost my friends or at least the immediacy of those friendships. I had lost the comfort of a familiar environment, had lost regular income to provide financial security, had lost the future; be it real or hoped for, it was still some idea of a future. A true, but a rather sad and pessimistic account. Was it ever aired? I have never found out and do not care much.

The resort turned into a busy place: journalists, aid organizations' representatives and friends and relatives from nearby towns visiting a big group of disoriented and bewildered Sarajevans. There was a large dining room on the ground floor of the resort where people met and ate their meals. I did not; I ate upstairs with my parents. That was the only way for my parents; my father could only walk a very short distance. Coffee was an important ritual for us, especially the morning coffee, which we made in the room. The kitchen staff gave me coffee and sugar while a couple in the room next door shared with us a small spiral immersion water heater they had brought from home. The two families had not known each other before, but the common lot brought us together. We enjoyed making innuendoes in front of other people about sharing a 'coil'.[12] Crude humour, but a reason to make everybody laugh and laughter has a healing power.

The couple had two children. They had sent them to Belgrade at the beginning of the war. From there, the children were then sent on to Israel. Their mother was distraught. In protest or defiance, or whatever, she wore a grey-and-white-striped sacklike dress all the time, reminiscent of Nazi concentration camps. The outfit was hugely symbolic for the people at the resort, considering that a number of their family members had perished in death camps in the Second World War. Even without those personal associations, her appearance painted a sorrowful picture.

Evenings were the best part for me. My parents would stay in the room and I would go down to the improvised café on the beachfront. We could help ourselves to all sorts of fresh fruit, alcoholic and other drinks, and the husband of the woman in the striped dress, the lead in a Sarajevo Ladino band, would sing those sad Sephardi Ladino ballads. There were also jokes, occasional black humour and laughter. Laughter again was a way of relieving tensions. It was both heart-rending and enjoyable, one of those absurd combinations of emotions. That was the time when people made a conscious effort to replace a sense of loss, sadness and anxiety with joie de vivre, togetherness and hope. Our strong need to stave off the senseless hatred we had all been exposed to for far too long brought this on. Even a suspended feeling of love started emerging. A few love affairs began. The presence of death in one's life apparently triggers the need to affirm life, to seek closeness, and that includes sexual closeness. Eros/Thanatos?

We all had free access to telephones. Everyone was frantically ringing family members, including their children, and acquaintances. Those already abroad could help them pick the most suitable place to move to. The office with the telephones was next to our room, so we often heard the desperate voices. We could hear Henika and Tanja calling their children overseas and their parents in Zagreb. Yet another sad confirmation of our distressing predicament.

I often used the phone too. I called the Lošinj family. My cousin told me he wanted to send his son to Israel. The son wanted to escape the ever-more-serious fighting he was engaged in as a member of the local national army. I talked to those arranging immigration to Israel. Most of those who wanted to migrate there were of Jewish origin, yet the nearest Jewish ancestor of my cousin's son was his great-grandfather. It was not only too distant a relation, but it was also a male connection, which did not count according to Jewish tradition. The suggestion was for the young man to join the group in Zagreb, then go to Belgrade[13] in order to convert to Judaism and from there, via Budapest, to Israel. And so he did.

I rang quite a number of people, mostly those who I assumed wondered whether we were alive. I also rang my friend Sveto's daughter in the US with the instructions he gave me back in Sarajevo when my attempt to put him on one of the Jewish Community convoys failed. He had made a list of possible contacts outside Yugoslavia who could facilitate his safe exit from Sarajevo for her to get in touch with. I also rang my friend Nancy who, far away in the US, had realized the danger much before me in the middle of it all. I wanted to let her know that we were alive and safe. I rang Stephen who had rung from the UK to warn me about the seriousness of the situation at the time that felt to me like a lifetime ago. I rang Felicity and Piotr in the UK, who had been my friends for a number of years. Felicity had been a guest lecturer at Sarajevo University. Later, she married Piotr and the three of us shared a strong bond. When I expressed my bewilderment, Felicity calmly quoted Andrić.[14] As a keen and talented observer and a 'reader' of Yugoslav life and literature, she had the benefit of seeing things from a distance, objectively, from the outside; she had a much clearer picture than those who lived it. Although I had read works of Yugoslav literature, and specifically Andrić, I was oblivious to most of the negative aspects described. Mostly denial made me convince myself that Andrić's stories, for instance 'Letter from 1920' among others, referred to a long-gone era.[15]

I could not get in touch with Saša, Mima and Božo still in Sarajevo.[16] Luckily, a new convoy from Sarajevo arrived and I found out that Saša had been granted permission to follow a convoy in his car in a month's time or so, and Mima and Božo were scheduled to leave on that convoy, too. The Community Centre president, Ivica, kept his word. What a relief! I could not find out anything about Nikola which caused me much grief.[17] Luckily, he managed to ring me and that took a burden of worry or possibly guilt off my shoulders.

I could not ring Belgrade either. There were no phone lines between Serbia and Croatia, which by then were enemy countries. Their armies were fighting on the border and stories of fierce combat and horrendous atrocities were in all the media. The only way I could contact my Belgrade family was via Goga, my second cousin living in Germany. She did her best to help and support us in her typical kind and affectionate manner. She would liaise between the two families in preparation for our Belgrade arrival.

I suddenly realized that I showered frantically several times a day, from head to toe. It must have been my need to wash out all the dirt, literal and metaphorical, rather than just the mere fact that water was again available literally on tap – something we had longed for for months. However, there was an element of vanity there too, I realized. I made sure my hair was okay. Adversity did not destroy vanity. Was it a good or a bad sign? I did not know and frankly did not care. Nevertheless, I did go to the hairdressers' in the centre of Pirovac to have my rather unruly hair done.

The holiday complex was located some distance from town. Going to the hairdressers' or post office, for that matter, was not easy; it was not within walking distance. However, I was lucky. When the resort manager drove into town, I would ask him for a lift which he gave. A trip to the post office was an important and rather urgent one. I had all those addressed envelopes with loads of money for different recipients, yet in my childlike mind money had lost its true meaning, so I did not consider the possibility of those envelopes going astray. Therefore, I took them to the post office as soon as possible and mailed them off, recorded delivery.

Sorting out the envelopes and my hair were the only 'errands' I had outside the resort. Therefore, apart from occasional interpreting, I could spend the time relaxing. Soon, the departure day for Henika and Tanja came. The anticipation was difficult enough, but the actual event was highly upsetting and emotional.

On the day, I went down to the dining room at breakfast to spend time with them. None of us could eat. It was terribly difficult to hold back the tears. The three of us went out onto a small adjoining balcony, where we had some privacy. Henika and I started crying uncontrollably, in anguish and anger. Tanja could not understand those outbursts. She was calmer. She was probably less of a pessimist and less sentimental.

After breakfast, Henika and Tanja went to say their goodbyes to their uncle and aunt. If they had hoped to meet any of us again at all, it was clear that they would never again see their terminally ill uncle. It was much harder for Henika, because her dear *onkie*,[18] as they called him, had been her only father figure[19] in her early childhood. Eventually the three cousins, all of us in tears, went to the carpark where the coach was waiting. We had always imagined that we would share our lives, that we would be together in difficult, as well as happy times, as had always been the case. That was gone forever.

Henika and Tanja were carrying large rolls of the paintings they had saved from home, holding onto the remnants of their domestic beauty.

I learned later that, ironically, they left them on the coach in Zagreb, but managed to retrieve them with the help of a Zagreb relative.

There was no time to say much, no words to describe emotions. They boarded the coach, the coach started, they kept waving and I found myself standing alone, sobbing and paralysed in the deserted carpark. And, as predicted, neither Henika nor Tanja ever saw their *onkie* again.

The next day we managed to find out that Henika and Tanja had arrived safely in Zagreb. They spent some time with their parents and decided to immigrate to the UK. The two daughters, Henika's and Tanja's, were already in London. Henika's son and his family had been in Holland for some time by then.[20]

Relatively soon, the time came for me to try to organize our trip to Belgrade. No mean feat. Luckily, representatives of various Jewish organizations[21] were there to help. I could never have expected or hoped for such support. Something that seemed completely unimaginable was not only suggested, but also organized by them. Namely, we would get a taxi to pick us up in Pirovac and take us to Split airport, where a wheelchair would be ready for my father. From there, we would fly to Zagreb, where a Hungarian driver with a van turned into an improvised ambulance would meet us at the airport. From there, we would travel to Belgrade via the only available route, Hungary.[22] The only remaining problem was the fact that my parents did not have valid passports.[23] When I mentioned this to the trip organizers, the Israeli representative gave me the names and phone numbers of people in their Budapest office whom I could contact should anything go wrong. So, everything was perfectly arranged. A dream come true, which I myself would never have been able to organize, even had I had unlimited financial resources.

We started our trip, or rather adventure, on 3 September 1992. The taxi journey was okay. The flight from Split to Zagreb had no hiccups. It was a bit tough to communicate with the Hungarian driver and his female companion,[24] both of whom spoke only Hungarian. My father, who spoke Hungarian, was in no shape to communicate. Non-verbal communication worked relatively sufficiently. However, the nightmare moment was waiting for me at the Croatian–Hungarian border. The Hungarian customs officer saw that my parents' passports had expired and said brusquely: '*Zurück nach Zagreb!*'[25] I was out of my mind and all I could remember of my childhood Hungarian were the words for 'no' and 'good'. Therefore, I said 'No good!' in Hungarian. The customs officer told the driver to park at the side of the crossing. I went to the telephone, rang the number for the Israeli officials and, within a short time, a customs officer with a pink piece of paper came over and told us to carry on. I have never seen a more beautiful piece of paper! However, I never found out what that paper was – I did not have a good look at it when they gave it to me and I had to hand it to the customs officer at the Hungarian–Yugoslav border.[26]

The journey was long and the driver decided to take a break halfway on the way to Yugoslavia. He parked on the side of the road, in the middle of nowhere, and said nothing. I was uncomfortable and apprehensive. My father was restless and my mother was scared. Due to the state I was in, and with non-verbal communication, it was difficult to figure out what was going on, but I somehow managed to conclude that it was only a 'catnap' break for the driver. Admittedly, it was the middle of the night and necessary, but none too pleasant for the already distressed family, at the mercy of all sorts of mostly anonymous people.

We continued after the break and reached the border between Hungary and Yugoslavia. My parents were allowed to stay in the vehicle and I was asked to proceed to the Yugoslav customs office to fill in forms and answer some questions. This time, my parents' passports were not a problem: they had their 'pink papers', the documents issued in Hungary. I was asked what nationality I was. I said I was Yugoslav, something I had been all my life. However, I was told that I was not. I was Bosnian, the officer said. When I objected, the officer pointed to the letters in front of the Yugoslav passport number justifying his conclusion. To my surprise, I noticed that, in my passport, it said 'BH' and that apparently denoted Bosnia and Herzegovina in front of the number. However, my parents' expired Yugoslav passports had random letters, nothing denoting any country or state.

This allocation of specific letters, depending on the Yugoslav republic of issue, apparently occurred in the period between when my parents' passports and mine were issued, unbeknown to many.

Having asked where we were heading, he asked me how much money I had. Unprepared and exhausted, I gave a childlike reply: 'Loads!' I also said I did not know how much; some money belonged to me and some to other people. He only laughed and told me to continue on my way. The reasons for his unusual and highly unexpected, but welcome, reaction remain a mystery.

Sometime around noon on 4 September, we arrived in Belgrade. On the way to the hotel, where it had been arranged we would meet the family, I noticed a great crowd of people on a street. I immediately felt uneasy: I feared groups of people on the street; they were so reminiscent of Sarajevo where shells killed so many individuals congregating in groups.[27] Then I had to remind myself that there was no civil war in Belgrade, that it was not Sarajevo. Our lives were not under threat any more.

I would learn later that the people were queuing in front of a new private bank popularly called Dafina,[28] a rather unusual establishment apparently. Namely, people would put any amount of money into their bank account, and the bank would give them 15 per cent interest on a foreign currency 30-day deposit and 280 per cent on a six-month deposit of Serbian dinars. The story goes that those who used their services did manage to make some money at the beginning, but then, a year or so later, all of a sudden, the bank, the owner and the money allegedly disappeared into thin air. So, it was a scheme or rather a scam that enabled the owner to make a lot of money.

The hotel was right across from the Jewish Community Centre and a couple of Community officials came to meet us. The family were already in the hotel when we arrived exhausted and somewhat disoriented. Having had our coffees and the use of the lavatory, we finally went to Sida's home.

A new, hard-to-cope-with chapter in our turbulent and difficult life story was about to start.

Chapter 4

Rude Awakening

Early Beginnings

Belgrade was a familiar place. My parents and I had spent a lot of time there in previous years. Apart from the family, we also had friends there and people we had known for a long time. I had even briefly been a student[1] in Belgrade. Sida's flat was also familiar. My maternal grandmother lived with Sida and each of us had spent many a day there visiting our Belgrade family. However, it was different now. Now we were not just visiting; we were compelled to move in for an indefinite period of time.

The flat was big, but not big enough to accommodate two families. Sida gave my family her bedroom and she moved into a small room by the kitchen. Sanja, Igor (my first husband's namesake) and Branko had a two of the other bedrooms. The two families shared the living room where I also slept. Not ideal for anybody. We could not help getting in each other's way. It was an inevitable, yet next-to-impossible, arrangement.

The situation our Belgrade family put themselves in must have been unbearable. Their life was completely disrupted: privacy lost, their space crammed, their flat crowded. We, the Sarajevo refugees, could not hide the fact that we needed their support, yet they themselves struggled. A recipe for disaster. We all tried to do our best, but nobody actually had any idea what the best might be. In addition, we certainly did not know how long this arrangement would have to last. What the Belgrade family did for us was astonishing: to take in for an indefinite amount of time desperate, vulnerable and ill people who had lost everything, including a secure and regular income. It was a selfless gesture of huge generosity and sacrifice not many people would be prepared to make. It must have been not only terrifying but insufferable for them.

We, now the big extended family, tried to arrange our communal life so that it caused the least disturbance for all of us. Much easier said than done. The Belgrade family tried to carry on doing whatever it was they were doing previously. For me and my family, Sarajevo and the whole traumatic experience was still very much alive in our minds. Neither my parents nor I could simply 'regroup'. The three of us were rather unsettled. Soon various rumours started circulating again. The sense of insecurity and uncertainty made us more susceptible to rumours – rumours have a strange propensity to reach willing ears easily.

Of all the rumours, the most shocking and distressing one was the story of our Sarajevo acquaintance who came to Belgrade with his wife and daughter among the first evacuees, still using air transport, with a plan to continue to Israel. His life history was very complex, yet another one of the tragic Balkan stories with the addition of a Jewish ingredient. Allegedly, as a young Jewish lad, he had fled Sarajevo in the Second World War together with his father and ended up in the Italian concentration camp on the island of Rab.[2] After Italy surrendered, they joined the partisans and he soon became a teenage soldier. At the end of the war, the family came back to their hometown, Sarajevo. They had been quite well off before the war, but they found most of their property either looted or nationalized. Quite unhappy with the new regime, they decided to immigrate to Israel. They lived there for a while. Then his father suddenly died and the young man then decided to return to Sarajevo and eventually managed to build his career and start a family. In Sarajevo, he lived a quiet life only to be, yet again in 1992, compelled to leave everything behind in order to start life all over once more at a mature age. That allegedly proved too much for him and he committed suicide in the hotel room where they were staying while waiting to leave for Israel. His wife and daughter did eventually leave for Israel, where they still live.

Yet there was no time to dwell on tragedies. I had to act. The first thing to do was to distribute all the money I had brought for various people. I rang everyone and they all came to Sida's. I gave them their envelopes and asked them again not to tell me how much money they expected or received. They all respected that. Did I feel that that was too much responsibility, or was it my refusal to face reality again, or who knows what?

We had arrived in Belgrade a bit before my birthday. It was both a happy and a sad occasion for us; happy because we were together and alive, but sad because of our predicament. We did not have a proper celebration. Somehow, it felt out of place. But Teo, Sanja's brother, and his wife[3] came and the birthday was acknowledged.

Belgrade refugee stories as well as the stories from Sarajevo were hugely distressing. However, for us, or rather for me, a difficult realization that came quite soon was that there was no going back to Sarajevo, no going back to the old life. At the beginning I had deluded myself, assuming that it was a 'temporary absence from home'. I became aware that if we were to remain in Belgrade, staying with Sida and her family was certainly not a solution. Therefore, I realized I needed to start thinking about moving out. We needed some place to call home.

Our beginnings in Belgrade were extremely difficult. Too many people sharing life and a few of them not in the best of health either. That inevitably caused a sense of discomfort, anguish, hypersensitivity and guilt too. Yet, in spite of everything, our two families managed to establish some sort of routine. Routine created a sense of security and helped us cope. Duties were divided in terms of shopping, cooking, child-minding and so on. Both families put an equal amount of money into the kitty and my mother mostly cooked. We all had meals together (until Sida fell into serious depression).[4]

I was hungry all the time. Several months of starvation did that. In addition, I had lost a lot of weight. We shared the cost of food and my mother tried to be fair. Hence, she found it embarrassing to give me bigger portions – nobody else had such a big appetite and on top of that, both Sida and Sanja were dieting. That caused the first spate of friction between my mother and me.

Luckily, later, when we moved to our rented flat, our relationship was restored.

As predicted, both my mother and I were given the clothes we needed by Sida, Sanja and others; we brought enough for my father, knowing that the majority of family were female. The household of six adults and a child functioned somehow. Even though Sida and Sanja had lived in Belgrade while we lived in Sarajevo, we had been very close. We visited frequently until the mid-1980s when my father fell ill. After that the visits became much less frequent, so we actually had not ever met Igor before. However, Sanja's husband Branko I knew: he was my ex-fling. Sanja had married him in the late 1980s. The marriage came as a surprise to me. It was actually during a short winter holiday abroad that Sanja and I had taken a few years earlier when we met him. He and I spent a few fun days together. That 'history' made our new situation somewhat awkward. Nothing was said or done about it; it was not acknowledged. It just lingered uncomfortably in the air.

Sanja's and Branko's marriage had been problematic for some time, Sanja told us. The couple had many troubles. Igor, their 3-year-old son, was fond of his father but the friction between the parents was detrimental. The saving grace was the fact that Igor had a nanny who looked after him at least half the day. She played with him and managed to distract him. That hopefully minimized the negative effect of all the unpleasantness around him, but still …

It was obvious that the family's mood had not been ideal even before we came. The adults – Sanja and her mother Sida as well as Branko – seemed to have been avoiding each other as much as they could. Neither of them spent much time at home and continued to do so (except for Sida), even more so with our arrival. The undeniable fact was that, on top of that pre-existing tense atmosphere, Sida's family had three desperate people move in with them, albeit by invitation, which made their situation far more difficult. Suddenly they had to support three needy people: one terminally ill (my father), one frail and depressed (my mother) and one 'all over the place' (me). I was looking after my increasingly dependent parents and supporting them in whichever way I could, while trying to find a way out of our hopeless situation. I was emaciated, frightened and disoriented. Of course, our presence could have exacerbated the tension between Sanja and her husband.

The Belgrade family had been trying to ignore and minimize Sanja's marriage troubles until then, but, in an overcrowded space and with three more people witnessing everything, it probably surfaced more and more. To make things worse Sida fell into a deep depression and stayed in her room day and night, unable to function. It was sad and painful to watch. The rift between Sanja and her husband intensified. It affected the entire family; we were actually a group of six tormented and needy adults (possibly not fully aware of it).

Sanja and I had always felt like sisters and she had almost been closer to my parents than to hers. We shared a lot for many a year and Sanja would turn to us whenever in trouble. Now her troubles were acute. Her marriage had been on the verge of collapse when we arrived in Belgrade. So, it was no surprise she involved my parents and me, but her request was quite surprising: she asked us to help her end the marriage. A weird request at any time, but under the circumstances even more so. My parents and I simply did not know what we could do, what kind of help was expected from us. It was an unimaginable task.

Yet, over the following days, it was all about action for me. First of all, I had to legalize our presence in Belgrade. We were required to register with local authorities. Equipped with all the necessary documents and photos, I went to the council offices on behalf of the entire family. I filled in several forms, supplied photos of each of us and was asked about our ethnicities. Since the official denied the existence of Yugoslav ethnicity (as I had claimed ours was), she declared the family and me Jewish, based on the reply in the forms where I stated we were supported by the Jewish Community. So, in my forties, I became officially Jewish for the first time in my life. Officially Jewish, yes, but how deeply did it reach? Was I aware of the emerging identity?

Having registered with local authorities, another priority was to register the family with a GP surgery. Registering with a GP was a long and complicated process for refugees. Luckily, in the culture, the fastest and most efficient way to get anything done was the 'who knows who' route, so I hoped that Sida and Sanja, both doctors, would secure access to the necessary medical support. I assumed their medical connections could be utilized. Unfortunately, it was not as straightforward as I imagined.

Then, one evening, towards the end of September, out of the blue, possibly after Sanja and her husband had had a row, he stormed into our room and started shouting at my mother and me, accusing us of 'stealing his son from him'. He hurled the obscenest insults. It was awful. Then it escalated: he threatened to shoot us; he had a pistol in his bag, he said (he had a bag in his hand). We believed him. He was very angry and convincing. I rushed into the hall and tried to call the police from the only telephone in the flat. However, he disconnected it by yanking the wires out of the wall and so I ran downstairs to the neighbours and managed to get through to the police. The police arrived and searched him. He did not have a pistol. Sanja then asked the police to make sure he left, never to come near her again. He was escorted out by the police and never came back. So suddenly Igor's father disappeared. Igor was too small to understand, but definitely not too small to pine after him.

That was a great shock to all of us. It was most surreal. Actually, when I calmed down, it all reminded me of Italian neorealist films,[5] like one of those of Vittorio De Sica's films, but in real time. Unbelievable, but true.

Soon, the time came for my father's regular medical check-up. Sida arranged for a technician from the hospital lab (where she worked until her retirement) to take his blood and get it analysed. However, when the results arrived, neither Sida nor Sanja, contrary to my expectations, could find a doctor to interpret the results. Luckily, the Sarajevo doctor friend who had examined my father in Pirovac, was in Belgrade at the time. I turned to him for help. He came, examined my father again, checked the test results and said that there was nothing alarming.

However, my father's diagnosis being what it was – advanced stage of bone cancer – he needed an oncologist who would take over his treatment. Since Sida and Sanja couldn't help, I turned for help to Sanja's paternal cousin, Sladjana, who was also a doctor. We had known her as a kind, considerate, friendly and open person. It was easy to like her and, although not directly related, the three of us had always been fond of her. She very quickly referred us to an oncologist willing to take on a refugee. We were lucky: the oncologist turned out to be a compassionate, understanding and supportive doctor. She treated my father until the end of his life. (Later, all three of us registered at the local GP surgery near the place where we moved to. They were taking in refugees.)

Those were our first steps in finding refuge in the only city we felt we could flee to. We tried to settle as much as possible after the chaos of living in a war zone. We desperately tried to emulate normality in spite of being intruders in somebody else's flat and in somebody else's life.

At the time we were living at Sida's, we assumed that very few people knew we were in Belgrade. That was why we were quite surprised to receive an unexpected visitor one evening. A tall, good-looking man with a wonderful warm baritone voice, as if just down from Mount Olympus, told Sida he'd come to see us. He introduced himself. We had never seen him before. Dejan, his name was, told us that his mother had worked with my mother and he himself had been a pupil in Sarajevo, at the school where my mother worked,[6] soon after the Second World War. He said he had come to see how he could help. He had seen our names on the list of Bosnian refugees in the Jewish Community Centre. He was Sarajevo-born, but had moved to Belgrade a long time before. He was an actor and, at the time, director of a well-known and popular Belgrade theatre. So, he suggested to me that I translate a drama[7] for the theatre. An incredible offer. He did not know me, so he could not have known whether it would be a good translation or even whether I would just take the money and run. I was delighted. Huge trust and the first chance to earn some money. So, I accepted straight away, although I had neither dictionaries nor a typewriter. (Computers were not yet in wider use.) He gave me the text and what seemed a large amount of money, in advance. I borrowed dictionaries and a typewriter and began. The risk he took was huge: as a director, he could have been accused of nepotism or any other nasty thing.[8] Dejan was a ray of positivity in the gloomy picture of overwhelming evil I carried around in spite of all my attempts to suppress it. It was hard to believe such amazing altruistic people existed and even harder that I was so lucky to be in their orbit.

I was still strongly influenced by unforgettable memories of our relatively short[9] Sarajevo nightmare. I overreacted to sounds, I disliked crowds and I felt uncomfortable and self-conscious. Many things caused irrational fear and discomfort. On the other hand, I was happily aware of the fact that the days of nettles and basil were over, although the realization that I kept noticing them in parks was somewhat upsetting. It was too much of a reminder, which hindered the recovery process. Yet I happily acknowledged that tomatoes were widely available – not in a dream any more. At a formal dinner I was invited to, a linguist with whom I was friendly, having heard about my tomato dreams, gave me all the tomatoes from his salad and explained to all why he was doing it. He thought it was funny. I could see why, but for me, it was not. Was it embarrassing? Did it hurt? Yes, it did. Was I hypersensitive? Maybe I was, maybe not. The 'tomato incident' among other things meant that I was singled out from the rest of the group, that I was not included, not *one of us* yet again! Although it made me uncomfortable, I nevertheless had to admit to myself that I was overreacting.

I felt the need to question my reactions constantly. Faced with such an unfortunate predicament, I wanted to be sure I was neither ungrateful nor unfair. For instance, I resented certain handouts, such as torn clothes or clothes size 20 (while both my mother and I were size 8 at the time). The resentment was strong but I also felt guilty about it. I realized that I had to learn to accept people's insensitivity and occasionally the logic of 'beggars can't be choosers'. All that certainly was not easy, yet on the whole, for me at least, there was a semblance of normal life; both my parents with me and our basic needs met. (A number of refugees left their elderly parents in Sarajevo, for one reason or another. I was glad I did not.) I even enjoyed some social life: I attended a few formal dinners and some lovely parties. I felt I ought to have been more appreciative. I had to admit that I was getting there! There was hope! On the other hand, the Sarajevo experience still affected me significantly. I could not stop thinking about those whom I cared about still in Sarajevo, be it by choice or necessity.

There was one piece of good news though: I heard from some people arriving from Sarajevo that my terminally ill friend, Lala, had finally left Sarajevo on a Jewish convoy. She was Jewish and about 70, so definitely eligible. She had advanced breast cancer (which she refused to treat) and was housebound. Sarajevo was certainly not the place for her to be. Lala went to Split, I was told. Unfortunately, with telephone lines cut, there was no way to get in touch with her. But knowing that she was safe was good enough.

Although my friends Zora and Bane remained in Sarajevo, their children were in Belgrade living with their relatives. It turned out that they were staying with the family of a psychiatrist who had married one of Zora's relatives. (The same amazing psychiatrist who, as a favour to Zora when I asked her a few years back, helped my dying grandmother in Belgrade.) I went to visit the children and the family. After a brief conversation, the psychiatrist told me that he thought I was much better than expected, yet nevertheless depressed. I trusted him, although I was not fully aware of the state I was in. This was my first bout of depression and I welcomed the help. He referred me to his colleague, a psychotherapist, and I started my sessions.

It was during those sessions that I realized, among other things, how much the fact that Sveto, my Sarajevo colleague and friend, was still in Sarajevo troubled me. I feared for him, for a good reason. Therefore, I took out the list[10] of his Belgrade contacts he had given me. The President of Yugoslavia[11] was one of them. The other one was the Director of the British Council in Belgrade.[12]

When I announced to my relatives that I was going to ring the presidency, they thought I was crazy. One did not do such things in Yugoslavia, especially not in the 'old days'. Yet, I did ring and, as soon as I said whom I was calling about, the president gave me an appointment the next day. I didn't expect to be given an appointment that soon so I was very pleased. It was a strange experience. From the moment I entered the building, several security officers checked me. I had experienced checkpoints, but not many civilized and polite security checks. To my surprise, I realized they did not put me off. Eventually, I was escorted to the president's office and spent quite a long time in pleasant conversation with him. I had read some of the books he'd written and liked them. I respected him, yet was not in awe of him, as those around me seemed to be. Were my senses numbed or was it something else?

The next visit was to the British Council. I knew the director from earlier times. We even shared some linguistic ideas many years prior when I was working on my PhD thesis. The conversation with him was also enjoyable.

Sveto eventually arrived in Novi Sad. I never found out who had enabled his Sarajevo departure. It was not something I felt I could ask and he never volunteered the information.

I seemingly functioned, but was actually quite exhausted. I did not sleep much at night for various reasons. The fact that I had to sleep on an uncomfortable sofa in the sitting room did not help. I also needed to be available to escort my father to the lavatory since he could not walk on his own. One night, I fractured my rib while bending down to hold him. I did not realize it immediately, but soon the pain reminded me. The same Sarajevo doctor friend who had examined my father in Pirovac and in Belgrade now examined me and told me that nothing could be done about it, except that I had to take painkillers to avoid restricted breathing. The recovery did not seem to last long. Or maybe I did not have time to think about it.

I went to the Jewish Community, mostly weekly, to draw our financial support and, on one of the visits, as I was signing the register, next to my name on the list I noticed somebody with the same surname. It was the son of my cousin from Lošinj. He had come to Belgrade to convert to Judaism and then go to Israel, as we had arranged in Pirovac. I waited to meet him. I did not know him at all. We had never met. He was a young man in his twenties, very good looking. It was nice to meet him. He had joined the Croatian army earlier, but did not want to fight any longer, hence his plan to flee to Israel. He did not look us up because he was far too scared, he said; actually, he was terrified about being in Serbia where he was considered an enemy combatant since he had fought in Croatian national army. He expected to be taken to Budapest to sort out all the necessary requirements for going to Israel. When I thought about it, I suddenly realized the absurd reality of a hypothetical situation in which the sons of my three relatives[13] from three different regions could have found themselves: they could have joined their respective national armies and could have ended up inadvertently killing each other. Members of the same family, albeit extended, not even realizing it. How outrageous was that?

In September/October 1992 a significant number of Sarajevo refugees came to Belgrade. (By then, along with Jewish convoys, all sorts of ways of fleeing Sarajevo were actively in operation: Red Cross, UNHCR,[14] a secret tunnel under Sarajevo airport, and so on.) A few of them were Jewish and came to the Jewish Community Centre. Immigrating to other countries was easier with the support of the Community. Again, some wanted to go to Israel, while most preferred Western Europe. For those who were planning on Israel, it was preferable to prove their Jewish origin. That was why, either at the request of the individuals themselves or their relatives, my mother and I agreed to vouch for some that they were Jewish. We vouched for quite a few. We personally knew several and knew they were Jewish. However, we also knew that some of them were not, but that did not matter much.[15] What did matter was any sort of help we could provide. Good versus evil again? Possibly.

There were still no channels of communication between Sarajevo and Belgrade. The Jewish Community Centre organized an amateur ham radio, used not only to replace telephone communication, but also for emergency money exchange – money would literally change hands – namely, somebody in Sarajevo would hand a certain amount of Deutsche Marks to a designated person in need there, while a relative of that person in Belgrade would hand the equivalent amount to a Belgrade person in need, usually a Sarajevo refugee. At the same time, I heard that the church charity ADRA[16] had started delivering letters and parcels between Belgrade and Sarajevo. By then, I had enough clothes, but shoes were a problem. I decided to send a letter to Zora via ADRA to ask her to go to my flat and get a few pairs of shoes from those I had left behind. The new occupants (not the one I had left the flat to) would not let Zora in and refused to give her any of my items. I was surprised in spite of everything: few people could wear my small, narrow shoes, so why not give them back to the owner? Then I remembered the binary way of thinking there: friend/foe, love/hate, us/them etc. That explained most things.

Our living arrangement in Belgrade became more and more difficult. I started looking for flats to rent. Not an easy task. Great demand and meagre offerings. Very high rents, always in Deutsche Marks, made matters worse. I visited various flats on offer. None was acceptable mostly because they did not meet my father's requirements (reduced mobility). Either there was no lift to get him to whichever floor the flat was on, or the bathroom layout was such that he could not be escorted there. In one case, there was no hot water in the bathroom: one filled the bathtub with water heated in the washing machine[17] next to it, which was a weird and scary solution. There were many such unforeseeable obstacles.

Sometime around the beginning of October somebody at the Jewish Community Centre told me that a woman was preparing to move to Israel temporarily, so she would be renting out her flat. A perfect flat; everything I needed. This one being one of the rare acceptable flats, I gave the woman six months' worth of rent in advance, as requested, naturally in Deutsche Marks. I did not think much about it. The flat would be available in a month, she had promised. That meant we would have a place of our own some time in November; not bad at all. I naïvely believed her. It never occurred to me that she might not have meant it.

Along with looking for a flat to rent, I was looking for a job. I urgently needed regular income. Finding any kind of acceptable job was not easy, considering that many refugees were looking for work. In terms of money, we were lucky because we received financial help from the Belgrade Jewish Community Centre – they later distributed donated food and clothes too. That helped a lot. However, we needed the money not only to live on, but also to pay extortionate Belgrade rents. That created an unbearable pressure on me.

Suddenly, my father developed a high temperature. We needed medical help. In his case, any minor ailment could easily become fatal. Therefore, I asked Sanja to find a doctor urgently. Sanja could not think of any of her colleagues who would make house calls. The only thing I could do was to ring the emergency services and hope they would accept a refugee patient. We were lucky. An exceptionally kind-hearted doctor came and did all he could to save my father. It was pneumonia. He would visit daily and he prescribed all he could. At the same time, he did express his doubts about my father's recovery. This was a huge blow to my mother and me. Yet my father did recover. The worst was over.

One day, all of a sudden, my American friend Nancy rang up. I was hugely surprised. She had seen us on TV, leaving Sarajevo, she said. How on earth had she managed to find Sida's phone number? Nancy wanted to bring my family and me to the US. She tried everything, but failed. The family did not fit the American criteria[18] for accepting Bosnian refugees. I was relieved; I did not want to go and, even had I wanted to, it would have been impossible with my parents. Leaving them behind was out of the question.

In addition, I still cherished the illusion that I would not leave my country of origin and had hopes for the future, admittedly not fully articulated hopes. I could not imagine living in a foreign country, with a foreign language, albeit one I was fluent in. The question that loomed large in my mind, ever since my student days in the US, was 'How could one love in a foreign language?' A dubious argument – although I never gave up hope of finding love! – but happily I found confirmation for that argument in Eva Hoffman's book[19] and kept quoting it. That made my reasoning more convincing. I did not realize then that it was fear of the unknown that made me hold onto a flimsy defence.

Little did I know that I would later not only love deeply, but also grieve profoundly, both in a 'foreign language'.

I thought a lot about Nikola, who was still in Sarajevo. That worried me. He rang to see how I was and I was somewhat relieved. He sounded alright. Nevertheless, I stubbornly wanted to save him and wondered whether anything could be done to facilitate his escape from Sarajevo. Some people who knew him suggested that they would help with it. However, he did not want to or could not leave Sarajevo. He was a member of the new Bosnian government and his son had been drafted which also complicated matters.

To my relief, he left Sarajevo relatively soon after as an accredited diplomat. He was able to take his family with him.

Belgrade friends and acquaintances were trying to help any way they could. Mira was one of them. I had met her through my Sarajevo friend, Lala; she was Lala's relative and only an acquaintance of mine until my arrival to Belgrade. I had always liked Mira, but once I came to Belgrade, she was one of those unexpected and very pleasant surprises. She showed enormous empathy, something not too many people possess. She did all she could to make my unhappy predicament easier. She immediately became much more than just an acquaintance. She came to visit soon after our arrival to see how she could help. She brought me some very elegant garments. (Luckily, we were the same size and had similar tastes.) Then she invited me for a meal at her home. Joca, her husband whom I hardly knew, was truly welcoming and supportive. I took to his quirkiness straightaway. I felt very relaxed with them, which did not often happen those days. After a pleasant evening, Mira brought me back in her car and, a few minutes later, rang me up to tell me that the car was parked on the pavement across from the house and that the car keys were on the table in the sitting room. The car was mine, she told me. She would not take no for an answer. She obviously had arranged it all with her husband earlier on. He had come and picked her up. She said they had two cars and that I needed a car, if for nothing else, to take my father for his medical check-ups.

Mira also took me to a party organized by her friends, husband and wife, Beba and Jadran. She wanted to help me integrate. To everybody's surprise, it turned out I already knew some people there. A small world! One of my close Sarajevo primary-school friends was there and some others. The evening was extremely pleasant. I felt I was accepted; there was a rapport among us. We were people of similar age and background, similar values, similar outlooks and similar sensibilities. The sense of togetherness was strong, something I craved. The external hostility, which became the way of living in Sarajevo, made me eager to look for friendliness and acceptance, I believe, more so than before. One develops special radars. I guess people, especially vulnerable ones, seek out like-minded people, those they can trust and with whom they have some commonality, basically those who make them feel safe. Both couples, Mira and Joca and Beba and Jadran, were such people. They exuded empathy and I felt I could relate to them. They had an exceptional skill in providing unobtrusive support. With time, we established a close bond and we have remained firm friends ever since.

My search for a job became frenetic. The pressure was incredible, not least because my parents, like many other elderly people, could never access their well-earned pensions; our financial resources depended on me mostly. Admittedly, the Belgrade Jewish Community Centre arranged special financial help for the refugees. It was the only regular income we had at the time. Yet it was not sufficient, hence the urgency to find a job.

After a while, it was only the elderly who received money; other refugees were given food and clothes

I had a job interview at a nursery.[20] The job was teaching toddlers English. I panicked. What did I know about teaching toddlers? My linguist friend, a professor at the Belgrade English Department, asked his friend Eva to help me. She was an expert in teaching children. She gave me the relevant literature and, after a long conversation, we both decided we liked each other. Eventually we became close friends. Eva gave my family some home necessities before she herself moved to Israel. She was an exceptional person: generous, friendly, eccentric and intelligent. We remained friends for good. However, I did not get the job.

I then had an interview at an English language school for adults. I had confidence there; I had some experience in that. I had taught at a language school for adults in the final year of my studies and also in late 1980s, to supplement my income,[21] not to mention the fact that I had been a lecturer in English language and linguistics at Sarajevo University. So I was not too anxious about getting a job there. They did not hire me because I was not a native speaker, the argument went. However, neither were most of the other teachers employed there. Disappointing and unfair. But life is not fair, is it?

Although I thought I functioned well, I realized I was not as well prepared for my predicament as I thought I was. I did not always know how to react; the concept of giving and receiving seemed to have acquired a different dimension and I was quite clumsy with it. I knew I was the one in need yet I resented it hugely. For instance, the former American lector at Sarajevo University and his wife, with whom I had become quite friendly, managed to find me in Belgrade, rang me and offered to send me $1,000 as a gift. It shocked me and I turned it down. I bluntly refused. I realized I disliked handouts; I was none too comfortable collecting the money at the Jewish Community Centre either. Was I too proud and arrogant to take gifts and charity? Was I trying to deny my actual position, the position of one needing a lot of support, the one who could not be self-sufficient? I convinced myself that I could manage somehow, that it was too generous a gift. My argument to myself was that I was not in such a dire need. In my mind one should accept support, in any shape or form, only in cases of dire circumstances. As a consequence, unfortunately, I never heard from those friends again. I lost a nice friendship due to an unreasonable reaction, which even I found difficult to justify.

My friend Sveto later pointed out to me that it was equally important to know how to receive as it was to give. He was right again. I had never thought much about the art of giving and receiving, a rather delicate balance. How could one decide when and why either giving or receiving might turn out to be demeaning rather than generous? When a gift feels like charity (in my mind humiliating), rather than an act of kindness? That became a new dilemma. I had not encountered anything like it in my peacetime life experience which now seemed so far away.

Attempt at Settling Down

It was true that the kind of life I lived previously, in peacetime, seemed far away, but it was alive, lurking in the background. It still had the power to comfort. One of the extremely important elements of that life was my friendships. Among the prominent ones was the bond with my childhood friend, Goran. We had been friends since early childhood and had been very close. Having no siblings, I felt he was a perfect sibling replacement for me. I used to turn to him every time I needed support, especially emotional support, either with my early love troubles or the more serious ones later. He was a man with a big, warm heart. However, lucky for him and his family, during the war they were not in Sarajevo. The family had gone to Israel in 1988 for a specific period of time so that he could specialize in a particular field. However, the Bosnian war broke out in the interim and they had been compelled to stay there.

In my distraught state I needed to feel cared for more than ever. Goran made sure I was. Every time anybody travelled from Israel to Belgrade, he would send us gifts such as huge tins of Nescafé, powdered chicken soup[22] and the like, for us at that time, luxury items. I cherished those kinds of gifts. He also sent me money from time to time. I accepted that too and even appreciated it and this time I managed not to destroy a precious friendship! Had I learned my lesson or was it something else? In the case of Goran, pride or oversensitivity did not intrude. Or maybe pride never entered our relationship as we knew each other so well that we could easily second-guess our respective intentions. Or else was it because these gestures confirmed the depth of our friendship and symbolized his concern for me? One thing was certain: I did not perceive his gifts as charity.

Being in touch with old friends was invaluable. It was proof that I had not lost their friendship while displaced. They managed to reach me! One evening, my UK friend, Felicity, rang me. That was not too much of a surprise because she knew where I was. I had told her about my plans when I called from Pirovac. What was a surprise was the fact that they – she and her husband, Piotr – were hosting Tanja's daughter. Such a coincidence made one wonder how small the world was. Ivana had started university, supported by one of a number of Bosnian aid organizations. Felicity and Piotr were involved with one of them and Ivana had ended up at their home one day. Talking about Sarajevo with Ivana, the hosts mentioned me as their friend and Ivana said that I was her relative. So, the connection was immediately acknowledged.

It was actually with the help by Felicity and Piotr that, shortly after that, I was offered a job. Their recommendation opened the door to the English Department of Novi Sad University. So, I ended up working with two Sarajevo colleagues also working there and we worked together until I left.[23]

In October 1992, I started commuting from Belgrade to Novi Sad which was a distance of about 110 kilometres (70 miles). Initially, a university-run coach took all the Belgrade staff (which were many) to the university. The coach trips were quite pleasant because I met a lot of people. It was also convenient for me because we were still living in Sida's flat which was near the bus stop.

The beginning of the academic year coincided with the beginning of cold weather. Unfortunately, I did not have a coat. I asked Sanja if she had one she could give me, a spare one. She pulled out an old coat she had put away, tried it on and, saying that there was more wear in it, decided to keep it. Painful though it was, I tried to understand.

Eventually I turned to Vesna, a Jewish Community Centre volunteer.[24] She was a person hugely dedicated to helping refugees and had joined the Centre with that aim in mind. Yet another exceptional person, the type one rarely meets. Yet again, we were lucky to have come across such a person. She helped us and many others in all sorts of ways. She immediately found me a coat that had been donated. It was lovely, warm, fur lined, but a bit too small. It cut under my arms. Still, I wore it happily. In addition, she gave me a hat. It was very windy in Novi Sad.

Overall, I considered myself lucky. In the end, I had to admit I had not waited too long to get a job. It felt long due to all the pressures, but actually, all things considered, it was a relatively short period. I had the kind of job I had always loved and a salary! My old friendships were confirmed and I met a lot of exceptional people. I felt much better. I did not even need further therapy. We, as a family, became hopeful; things started falling into place.

I did not work every day, so I could spend time looking for additional work. As the breadwinner I needed an extra income. Although money was important, I believed other things mattered more. Our sanity above all. So, I tried to keep my anxiety under control. How much I succeeded, I cannot say. There were so many things going round in circles in my head. Among other things, I missed my Sarajevo 'cellar friends' and worried about them. I kept hoping they would join me soon. They did: less than two months after us. Mima, Božo and Bennie (the dog) arrived in Belgrade. They brought with them the son of Mima's middle sister. The sister was a widow with a teenage son and a daughter in her twenties.

The flat where the three of them lived was demolished at the beginning of the war and they had moved to our neighbourhood, to the flat with the elderly parents of Mima and her sister. When Mima and Božo decided to leave for Belgrade they took the sister's son with them, while the daughter stayed in Sarajevo to nurse the mother whose breast cancer had returned. The ill sister and her daughter eventually arrived in Belgrade after Mima and the rest of them had left.

Almost at the same time, my 'husband' Saša arrived, with his girlfriend Cica.[25] Their journey was dramatic, but successful. Hence, the entire Sarajevo 'shelter group' – except for Minja, Saša's mother – was now in Belgrade. It was a great feeling – together again. People who shared such appalling experiences.

The bond[26] was hard to describe or define; we could fully understand each other, fully empathize and tune into each other.

Hence, in Belgrade too, we kept close as much as we could. Often various acquaintances would invite us to parties and I would introduce Saša as my husband and Cica as his mistress. People would be shocked, while the group found it hilarious. The fact was it was neither shocking nor hilarious. It was our grim reality: it was about staying alive. I was officially married to Saša, yet he lived with his girlfriend. None of us would have chosen to live our lives that way.

Soon, Mima and Božo and Saša and Cica decided to go to Denmark. They wanted to escape insecurity, tensions and emerging animosities. They wanted to start afresh, which they realized was impossible in Belgrade. Therefore, my 'husband' decided to get married. I was invited to be a witness at the wedding and, as was customary, my task was to buy a bridal bouquet. Not an easy task under the circumstances. I could not afford what I liked and did not like what I could afford. Not the only absurd situation by any means. I eventually found one, the most suitable one. The florist appeared stunned by my 'wedding story'.

After the florist, I went to the registry office with the second witness to book the wedding; two were needed, the other one was Cica's friend. As requested, I claimed that there were no impediments to Saša's marriage, knowing full well that I was still his legitimate wife. However, I also knew that the divorce proceedings were scheduled for the next day, a few days prior to the wedding. We found this both sad and amusing.

The divorce proceedings went well. A solicitor, a friend of a friend, prepared the arguments. He argued that the couple, with a great difference in age,[27] had met under unusual circumstances, a war, and spent a lot of time in the shelter during the shelling. Once they started life together, in peacetime, under normal circumstances, they realized how incompatible they were, the solicitor argued. (Our private joke was that, when Saša saw me in broad daylight, he decided to divorce me!) Whether the jury believed us or not, the argument was accepted and we got divorced. Straight from the courthouse we – Saša, Cica, his future wife and I, his ex-wife – went to celebrate in a café.

The wedding was bittersweet. We all genuinely rejoiced in the fact that the two had not only survived the Sarajevo hell, but had also managed to get married and had plans for the future. At the same time, splitting the group did not sit comfortably with any of us. Their trip to Denmark was soon booked. We did not fancy the idea of yet another bond being challenged. However, needs must and Mima, Božo and the children,[28] and Saša and Cica left for Denmark. Bennie, the dog, followed later.

I never saw Saša or Cica again. I never met their children. However, the bond remained. As for his mother, he and the family managed to visit Minja soon after the end of the war. She died shortly after that, of leukaemia.

The bond and solidarity between Mima and me became even firmer and never stopped. Soon after their arrival in Copenhagen, while they were still living on the awful floating 'hotel', Mima managed to send me a gift, a lovely second-hand Burberry mac. In spite of coping with her family's terrible living conditions and humiliation, she found it in her to think of the needs of others. Having learned that somebody was due to travel to Belgrade, she went to a Red Cross depot of donated clothes and found it there for me so it soon arrived with some other stuff she had found. Needless to say, I was both surprised and hugely moved. Luckily, struggle for survival does not necessarily kill altruism.

I was sad to see them go. But I could not dwell on that too much; I had serious matters to sort out. I was getting impatient and nervous about the furnished flat I had paid for in advance. We were three weeks past our moving-in date and the landlady was stalling. She kept ringing up with strange stories. First, she said she could not leave the beds so we would have to provide these ourselves, and then, the following week, she said that the fridge had broken down and eventually she said she had had a bad dream about her new tenants being killed in the flat. Each time, she asked whether I was sure I wanted the flat, and each time I said I was. Eventually, well over a month later, the woman informed me that the flat was not available any more. I panicked. I had no receipt for the money I had paid her. Stupid, but too late for regrets. I was hoping to engage a solicitor to help me with that, and I asked Sida's family if they knew of any lawyers. They did not. Therefore, I rang up the woman and demanded my money back. She agreed immediately, which surprised me.

Without a solicitor, I felt I needed some authority added to my rather unremarkable, small, miserable self. The only thing that came to mind were physically strong men to accompany me. Not that I knew any men who would use their physical power, but their appearance might do the job, I hoped. Hence, I asked Dejan, my new friend and saviour, the theatre director and a Sarajevo refugee friend, an avid theatregoer (hence they knew each other) who were both hunky men: two unsuspecting people suddenly turned law enforcers! However, there was no need. The woman returned the money straightaway. We saw her take it from the table by the front door where we could see many other similar envelopes. All three of us were both repulsed and relieved.

FAMILY AND FRIENDS

Above: Summer holiday in Dubrovnik with my parents, 1950s. (Author's collection)

Below: First wedding – Sarajevo 1970s: Tatjana (my witness) and both my husband's and my families. (Author's collection)

Sarajevo University colleagues and students, late 1970s or early 1980s. (Author's collection)

Onset 1992 – with my parents: staying or leaving? (Author's collection)

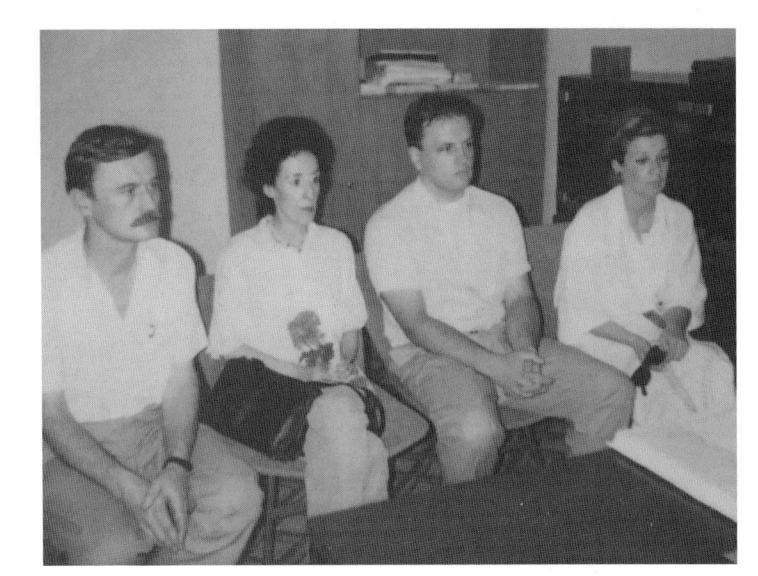

My bogus wedding, Sarajevo, 1992, with witnesses Mima and Božo. (Author's collection)

Above: Belgrade – with friends Jadran, Beba, Joca and Mira. (Author's collection)

Right: The wedding of my bogus husband Saša to Cica, Belgrade, 1992 (with me as Saša's witness, far right). (Author's collection)

Above left: Family reunion in London, 1995. From left: Ivana, Tanja, my mother, Ella, Moni, me and Henika (with her back turned). (Author's collection)

Above right: With my mother in London. (Author's collection)

With Duško and Celia (far right) with our SSEES students at Celia's. (Author's collection)

With Ned, HOME, Cambridge. (Author's collection)

Getting ready for New Year's Eve celebration, 2000. (Author's collection)

Above: With Melanie (above, comparing profiles) and Ned and Richard (below). (Author's collection)

Below: Ned and my mother in Cambridge. (Author's collection)

With Milica in London. From right: Milica's father and mother, with my mother between them, Ned, Milica's grandfather and Milica. (Author's collection)

Right: Sida and Sanja visiting the UK (on different occasions). (Author's collection)

Below: With Igor, Linton Zoo, 2001. (Author's collection)

Henika and Tamara in Cambridge. (Author's collection)

Goca, Jasna and Goca's son at a party – after Ned's death. (Author's collection)

With Nina and Goran in Germany (as a UK citizen). (Author's collection)

PEACETIME SARAJEVO

Former Yugoslavia. (Wikimedia Commons)

Sarajevo panorama. (Wikimedia Commons)

Left: The street in *Centar* municipality with the JAT 'skyscraper' in the background. (Wikimedia Commons)

Below: The Parliament Building with the Faculty of Philosophy next to it and the National Museum. (Wikimedia Commons)

Above: The bridge by the 'Museum of Young Bosnia', a revolutionary movement pre-World War I (now renamed). (Wikimedia Commons)

Right: Bridges over the Miljacka River. (Wikimedia Commons)

Sebilj fountain – Baščaršija. (Wikimedia Commons)

The 'new' railway station built in the 1950s. (Wikimedia Commons)

Above: The *Novo Sarajevo* municipality with 'dormitory' cities further down. (Wikimedia Commons)

Below: Early gravestones at the Old Jewish Cemetery, covered in snow. (Wikimedia Commons)

Left: The Catholic Cathedral. (Wikimedia Commons)

Below: Gazi Husrev Beg mosque with clock tower. (Wikimedia Commons)

Right: The Serbian Orthodox *Saborna* church. (Wikimedia Commons)

Below: The only functioning synagogue, at the Community Centre. (Wikimedia Commons)

Above: The main street in *Centar*. (Wikimedia Commons)

Below: Snow in Sarajevo. (Wikimedia Commons)

WARTIME SARAJEVO

Above: Total destruction – nothing left. (Wikimedia Commons)

Right: The Parliament Building burning. (Wikimedia Commons)

Above: *Momo* and *Uzeir* (Twin Trade Buildings), singed and damaged. (Wikimedia Commons)

Below: Erstwhile Hotel *Evropa* (Europe). (Wikimedia Commons)

Dobrinja, one of the newly built parts of town, with smaller houses, ruined. (Wikimedia Commons)

'Dormitory' city under fire. (Wikimedia Commons)

Above: No more residents here; only graffiti. (Wikimedia Commons)

Below: *Grbavica*, the first 'dormitory' city, heavily bombed. (Wikimedia Commons)

Above: Only the shell remained. (Wikimedia Commons)

Below: Media Centre gone – no more news bulletins from here. (Wikimedia Commons)

Above: Once an office building, and now?
(© Murat Tellioglu | Dreamstime.com, Photo 136822703)

Below: Firefighting with a bucket of water – the only way available.
(© Mark Milstein | Dreamstime.com, Photo 42465239)

Above: Precious water. (© Mark Milstein | Dreamstime.com, Photo 42464762)

Below: No going back to these buildings. (Wikimedia Commons)

Above: City centre standstill – hanging wires, rubble, burnt-out cars and trams, fear. (© Mark Milstein | Dreamstime.com, Photo 42465052)

Left: An old man, desolate. (© Mark Milstein | Dreamstime.com, Photo 42465377)

I learned later that the woman never intended to rent her flat. It was a clever swindle to earn some money. She took deposits from several naïve people, put the money in the Dafina bank and made a nice profit. The original amounts she calmly returned to the victims. Some people are unscrupulous in taking advantage of vulnerable people.

I certainly was one of those vulnerable ones in dire circumstances and quite desperate. I had the money, but no flat in sight now. As luck would have it, my primary-school friend, with whom I had rekindled our friendship at Beba's and Jadran's party, rang me, just after the incident with the landlady, and told me that somebody she knew intended to rent their furnished flat. It was a small flat – one bedroom – but quite suitable for our needs. I would again sleep in the sitting room, but that was the least of my worries. I gladly agreed to take it, the arrangement being that we would move in as soon as the flat was ready. Luckily, it did not take long. Sometime in December 1992 we were able to move in. The remaining problem was to organize my father's transport down the three storeys from Sida's flat. It was eventually solved: Teo and Pepe,[29] Sladjana's husband, carried him down. In the apartment building we were moving to, thankfully, there was a lift.

The curious thing about the sense of time both in Sarajevo and during our Belgrade beginnings was that the days were compact, full of events. Hugely significant things happened one after the other in quick succession – a brief period of time jampacked with action, literally, not in relative, but in real terms. Fleeing home, relocation, living in temporary accommodation, setting up a new home, adjusting to the 'new country', a new workplace, finding new doctors, acquiring new friends and renewing friendships – the lot, even finding a new identity. (At least the language was the same, or so we believed.)[30] Hence, our perception of time was considerably disturbed. It was difficult to fathom that it had only been about four months since we had left Sarajevo and moved into our new home.

The story of our new rented flat was a rather interesting one, illustrating the absurdities of the times. Namely, in Serbia sooner than in Bosnia, the post-socialist transition period provided a chance for people to buy the flats they lived in from the owners, for a reasonable amount. The owners could have been the state, a firm, an institution or any other organization as there were very few private property owners.[31] Most often it would be one's employer that had allocated a flat to a particular employee during the previous regime.

It turned out that our new landlord was one of those who had recently become the owner of the flat. It was the same with Sida's flat – when we first moved in, she still did not own her flat, she only had a document proving that the flat had been allocated to her late husband to live in together with his family. Soon Sanja and Teo, with the help of their solicitor, bought the flat on behalf of their mother. Absurdly enough, the total amount they paid for the large flat was the same amount we initially paid[32] for about two months' rent for a one-bedroom flat.

We knew the owner of our rented flat was a former Bosnian representative, an apparatchik,[33] who worked for the Federal Socialist government, and had actually lived permanently in Sarajevo, but had been granted the use of a furnished flat while in Belgrade. He bought the Belgrade flat from the government as soon as it was possible and, by the time we moved in, he had left the country and was living abroad.[34] We were genuinely surprised to see that the furniture still had little metal plates indicating state ownership (my parents recognized this socialist practice). In other words, it was paid for out of government funds. The furniture in many VIPs' flats was of the same provenance. It was a typical remnant of the way socialist governments treated their VIPs and apparatchiks.

The story of the flat was not a grand revelation, yet it made us somewhat uncomfortable, but we decided to take no notice of it. Having settled in, we tried to ignore every negativity around us as much as we could. We even made an effort to arrange occasional pleasurable moments for ourselves; we desperately needed soothing. A special treat was a visit to a cottage on a nearby hill, owned by the family of my newly acquired friend Božidar[35] who invited us there. Occasionally we would go to an open-air café we used to frequent in years past or visit friends whose flats were accessible by lift. Sometimes, we would simply enjoy a modest coffee and pancakes of an afternoon when I was at home. Our harmonious, loving relationship was restored. Again, our small family lived a life of sharing – good, bad and indifferent – a life of closeness and togetherness.

Relatively soon after Mima had left for Denmark, Mima's ill sister, escorted by her daughter Taša, arrived in Belgrade on a UNHCR convoy. They arrived at the end of December 1992 and were supported by some relatives. Mima's sister had breast cancer, final stage. I had adapted to living in Belgrade by then, so I felt I could be of some help. We stayed in touch. Taša devotedly nursed her mother at home. Her mother was in very bad shape. Soon she needed a blood transfusion. Where could a newly arrived refugee get one? I turned to an old Sarajevo friend, who had lived in Belgrade for ages. She was extremely well connected, with plenty of *vezas*. She could do it, I thought. And she did. Taša's mother had her blood transfusion. It postponed the inevitable.

Due to the international sanctions imposed on Yugoslavia[36] at the time, importing goods, including medicines, was hugely hindered, if not impossible.

Consequently, there were shortages, which gave rise to an ever-present, thriving and out-in-the-open black-market economy. Whether it was with official approval or not, it was the way to get what you needed. Among many items, those most in demand were petrol and medicines. Luckily for us, the Belgrade Jewish Community had a pharmacy and it had a good supply of medication, so we did not need to depend on the black market. The pharmacist could even order particular medication for specific individuals.[37] At the beginning, my mother would go there to get all we needed, but later it became my duty.

As for petrol, Pepe mostly took care of that. He was a big softie, with a huge heart. He exuded affection. No wonder my parents and I accepted him wholeheartedly when he and Sladjana got married, even when some other family members disapproved of him. He worked for an embassy and brought my father cigarettes and filled my car up with petrol on several occasions. He claimed the petrol was free for him. (At the time, petrol could only be found on the street corners, in big Coca-Cola bottles – a rather dangerous enterprise, but nobody paid any attention to that.) I knew that his story of free petrol was not true, but could do nothing and did nothing. I just appreciated it. Not only that, he was skilled in giving discreetly and with kindness, but also, by then, I had probably mastered the skill of receiving as well.

Although we were not religious, as members of the Jewish Community, we were included in the tradition of receiving gifts on Jewish holidays. On the first Passover in 'our' flat, we received, not only a food parcel, but also a bunch of flowers. (An Israeli donor, domiciled in Belgrade, financed these gifts for refugees and included flowers.) Yes, we appreciated the food; we desperately needed it. However, the flowers meant something else. Flowers had a deep symbolic value. They were outside of our basic needs: they represented beauty, another human need but less acknowledged. The flowers confirmed to us that we were seen as human beings not reduced to satisfying basic needs only. It proved that there were those who perceived us as 'normal' people who happened to have been caught up in unhappy circumstances, rather than just scroungers and a burden, which, unfortunately, was becoming a widespread view.

Much later, in London, I received a plant as a gift from one of my newly acquired synagogue friends. Again, I assigned huge symbolic value to it; again, I felt I was perceived as a 'normal' human being, which was something I craved.

Receiving a regular income, a monthly salary, was significant, not only in terms of financial security. I felt less like a second-class citizen, the way refugees were made to feel. Unable to fend for themselves and with lost autonomy and independence, the feeling of being less worthy was inevitable.

Once I received my first Novi Sad salary, I gained some of much needed confidence. It also enabled me to think about my starving colleagues in Sarajevo in practical terms. Hunger was still fresh in my mind, so I could easily imagine how they felt. By then, ADRA had also started delivering parcels from Novi Sad to Sarajevo, so I bought mostly potatoes and other lasting fresh produce in Novi Sad and packed it all into a sack. I sent the parcel to colleagues at my department in Sarajevo, to one of my favourite former lecturers who had previously saved me from the political minders, as well as to my friends Omer and Zvonko and their families.

It was a good feeling to be able to help rather than depend on handouts and charity (which I did appreciate, but still resented). However, reality soon kicked in. The Novi Sad salary was important, but not enough. I then intensified my search for additional jobs. First, I was offered a job (paid in Deutsche Marks) at the Jewish Community Centre. Once a week I would, as a cultural officer, organize various cultural events. I cannot say that I felt very competent at it, but I knew I could make an effort to find the best way of doing it. The drawback, though, was the fact that the refugee stigma which, among other things, meant being seen as inferior, weighed heavily on my mind and, to add insult to injury, some at the Jewish Community Centre reinforced it. For instance, a tabloid journalist was surprised at the fact that I 'was literate', as he told me. A Board member who was supposed to induct me decided to make sure I knew 'my place'; she often undermined and bullied me. But that did not last long. I managed to prove that I was up to the job, especially since the job also included writing for the Jewish Community magazine and translating summary of texts published in each issue, the part I was confident about from the start.[38]

Although my terminally ill friend Lala was safe having left Sarajevo, she was still much in my thoughts. One day, in January 1993, I received phone calls from two people, Beba my new Belgrade friend and somebody I did not know, from Prague: Lala had died in Split and would be buried there.

Another case of ironic coincidence, Lala's mother had been buried in Split during the Second World War. She had been a refugee there, while Lala worked as an English language interpreter in a hospital on the Adriatic island of Vis, where the British and the Partisans were collaborating. Now, in 1993, some fifty years later, Lala, also a refugee, was buried in the same cemetery as her mother.

When I heard about Lala's death, I contacted Mira as soon as she returned from her winter holiday. We got together, trying to decide how to commemorate Lala's passing. New circumstances called for new customs, ones made up on the spot. The only idea we could come up with was to pay for a prayer for the dead at the local synagogue and be there at the service. A strange addition to the myriad absurdities. The four of us: Mira, her husband Joca, her father and I attended. (None, including the deceased Lala, was religious.) None of us had a clue about any customs, unsure whether women were expected to cover their heads or not, for instance. Both Mira and I had a scarf in our pockets, just in case. Joca (who was not Jewish at that) and Mira's father helped themselves to paper kippahs provided for the purpose. Since it was the middle of winter, the service was held in a 'winter synagogue', a euphemism for the small room above the actual synagogue – the economic crisis made it too expensive to heat the high-ceilinged synagogue. There was an atmosphere of gloom. The room was crammed with Sarajevo refugees looking grey and miserable, most wearing donated dark clothes that did not fit – a bunch of shrivelled people, a depressing sight. We felt awkward and saddened. Later we found out that a group of Lala's friends from her student days[39] had had a get-together at a nice café where they had a stiff drink in her memory. A much better and more appropriate solution.

Desperate situations affect innumerable areas of life, which was the case in our lives too. One aspect frequently affected was human relationships. They were constantly tested and challenged. Unfortunately, even within seemingly cohesive families, cracks appeared. Dormant disagreements and tiffs surfaced. Potential new misunderstandings often appeared and tolerance became an aspiration, rather than reality, self-restraint more difficult. This all seemed to have insidiously happened to our extended family. Although our rented flat made us feel more at ease and relaxed, we actually missed Sanja and Igor. They did not visit often. There had to have been a reason for it. It was true I was not always pleased with Sanja's conduct and I showed it, in spite of efforts to the contrary. In addition, Sida, whose fit of depression was over, would visit, but only when I was not at home. I wondered why and was unhappy about it. There was no obvious reason for that kind of behaviour so both my father and I asked my mother to have a word with her sister. My mother refused, arguing that very little could be done about it without creating an overt rift. Admittedly nobody wanted that. So, the reason remained a mystery.

Sometime in spring or summer 1993, having seen my CV, the Jewish Community Centre officials, realized that I probably knew and might have even been friendly with some of the leaders of the Republic of Srpska government[40] and turned to me for help. They were right. I had been friendly, especially with one or two high-ranking officials. I was only happy to be able to help.

The problem for the Jewish Community officials was the fact that, unlike in central Sarajevo, the part of Sarajevo under the jurisdiction of the Republic of Srpska, known as Grbavica,[41] was not receiving any support from the

Jewish Community Centre: no pharmacy, no soup kitchen, no food parcels. The Jewish Community Centre in central Sarajevo served the boroughs of Centar, Stari Grad and Novo Sarajevo – the Centre, the Old Town and New Sarajevo – but was completely cut off from some other parts including the borough of Novi Grad (New City). Therefore, a group of Jewish aid organization officials were keen on starting a Jewish Community branch there. They needed contacts and permission from the authorities in the Republic of Srpska in order to access Grbavica.

I was asked to put them in touch with some of my former colleagues in Pale, which I easily could, since the wife of Sveto's brother, who was a high-ranking Republic of Srpska official, lived in Belgrade. I got in touch with her and she was very pleased to help. The group (consisting of several aid organizations, both Jewish and non-Jewish) went to Pale where they were warmly received and even offered whisky by Sveto's brother, I was told. They were given all the necessary permissions, as well as a military escort into that part of Sarajevo; and so, the branch of the Sarajevo Jewish Community began operations in Grbavica serving the wider area under the jurisdiction of the Republic of Srpska.

I was quite busy by then, looking after my parents as well as working. Nevertheless, I still needed more work to increase my income. I was lucky again. Several people asked me to give them English lessons and they paid in Deutsche Marks. I tutored a young Sarajevo woman intending to move to Canada, her brother, Pepe and one of his colleagues from the embassy.

I still, to this very day, wonder whether Pepe genuinely wanted to learn English or whether he was finding a way to help me financially without offending me.

With time, I noticed that I had slowly started recovering; my old interests and ambitions reappeared. No amount of hardship and adversity could kill the sociolinguist in me. My time in Sarajevo, and my exposure to both the media and public narratives of 1992 Sarajevo, was almost a field study. I realized I had stored the data somewhere in my brain. It was simmering in my mind and I soon produced a paper entitled 'Language War – War Language',[42] which I presented at the Belgrade British Council.[43] It was well received, a boost for my shaken confidence.

I was regularly in touch with Taša. Her mother was struggling more and more with her illness and eventually died towards the end of 1993. It was very traumatic for Taša. After the funeral, I did not hear from her for a while. I stupidly assumed that Taša needed some space. Eventually I rang her. The gist of the conversation was that Taša was exploring the position of the flat, wondering whether she would be so unlucky to survive by landing in the bushes below when she threw herself out of the window, on the eighth floor. I was horrified. I somehow managed to convince her to come and visit, knowing that talking to people who 'understood' helped one hugely. I also realized how much a meaningful job meant to me, so I assumed the same 'medicine' could help her. Taša came to visit, we talked a lot and she, a law graduate, agreed she needed a job.

I was unsure where to turn. But then, I remembered that Božidar, the Director of the Institute for Philosophy and Social Theory, was one of those rare people one meets for the first time and feels comfortable talking to. I had been pleasantly surprised to see that he understood my position and did not pity or judge me. He had been a Sarajevo university lecturer in the 1970s so he understood the Sarajevo mentality. I regularly had long talks with him; his wisdom was inspiring. He had enormous empathy, a big heart and could understand our situation, sometimes even better than we Sarajevans could ourselves. Talking to him was healing. There was nothing phoney about him, no fake sentimentality, just overt readiness to help. He was a tough softie! He tried to help me in whichever way he could. Among other things he invited me to attend a conference organized by the institute, which enabled me to resume my place in the academic environment. (Admittedly, I refused to prepare a talk for the first conference because I did not feel up to it, but I did attend.) Hence, I hoped Božidar might help Taša with finding a job. It was not only Božidar whose company I enjoyed though; the institute became a pleasant and safe place to visit and I went there quite often. I used one of those visits to talk about Taša, her circumstances and her need for work. Taša needed to feel useful again, to feel alive again, I said. I was sure Božidar would and could help. He offered to interview Taša. After the interview, Taša was offered a job. She accepted and took on the role of organizing their international conferences. She was very well received. She felt fully accepted and was hugely moved when they celebrated her birthday by giving her twenty-eight bars of chocolate, one for each year of her life. She could not stop talking about it. Yet, once she had somewhat recovered, she realized that living alone in Belgrade was not an option, that she missed her younger brother, her aunt and the family in Denmark. She was compelled to go there, above all to be with her brother. She arranged everything for the trip. She also organized a proxy marriage[44] (two options 'just in case') to her boyfriend whom she had to leave behind in Sarajevo and whom she intended to bring to Denmark to start a new family life with. I was sorry to see her go, but at the same time, I knew she needed to join the family, to regain that sense of belonging.

The proxy marriage was successful, but little did she know that there was a huge disappointment in store for her! When the boyfriend eventually came to Denmark as her legitimate husband, he brought along his girlfriend, the one with whom he had spent the war in Sarajevo. Taša started divorce proceedings immediately. How that made Taša feel, only she knew. Yet the other side of a coin was that, ultimately, she had saved two lives, albeit not by design.

With time, commuting to Novi Sad became more and more difficult. The economic situation compelled the university to abandon the coach. We firstly had to take public buses and then, later, the train. Both were difficult and expensive – we had to finance the trip ourselves. However, for me, it was the work I enjoyed and nothing could put me off.

When I began taking the train, which was the most difficult option, I had to get up at about 4 a.m., not my favourite time – I like sleeping late. However, that was not the worst of it. Trains were dirty and overcrowded, the people impatient and aggressive. I would usually have to take the notorious 'smugglers' train' going from Montenegro to Budapest and back. Due to shortages, goods were smuggled from Hungary and sold at various, numerous, open-air markets in Belgrade, as well as from stalls along central Belgrade boulevards. One could buy everything and anything from cigarettes to clothes, household items and food. All those smuggled goods filled half the available space in the carriage. I never even thought of finding a seat. I was happy being able to stand in the corridor, provided I was not squeezed between bodies, which often happened. On one occasion, I was squeezed between people with my back next to the carriage door when suddenly I found myself on the platform (the train was stationary). I was in the way of a fellow passenger who wanted to get off the train because he realized he had boarded the wrong one. He simply had no patience. Being a female and rather small, I was an easy target. He did not let me turn around so that I could step down onto the platform – he just pushed me out. I found myself sitting on the platform. I noticed several hands signalling me, which I grabbed hold of and they pulled me back up on. It all happened so quickly that I had no time to get frightened. The bruises though reminded me of the incident and in hindsight the incident seemed even worse.

In the spring of 1994, the Institute for Philosophy and Social Theory organized another international conference and I was again invited. The conference was entitled 'Interculturality' and this time I decided to prepare a talk,[45] probably due to my pride and stubbornness – I was not going to let circumstances destroy my integrity and identity. I lacked new ideas so in order to prepare a paper, I decided to have a look at my doctoral dissertation to see if I could use some of the material from it. Since I had failed to bring my own copy to Belgrade, I went to the university library to get a copy. I filled in all the necessary forms and was given a copy. Ironically, I had to sign a document vouching that I would not abuse or make unauthorized use of the dissertation. I did it and said nothing. However, when the librarian saw the name on the form and then the name of the author on the copy of the dissertation, she realized that it was the same name. She asked whether I was the author. Tears ran down my cheeks. Suppressed frustration or something else maybe came out uninvited.

The next conference, 'Towards a Language of Peace' in 1995,[46] organized by the same institute, where I gave a talk turned out to be less traumatic.

I was offered yet another job in the autumn of the 1994 academic year. My earnings were still insufficient under the circumstances, so I started teaching English at the Faculty of Electrical Engineering. Pavle, who was then just an acquaintance from Sarajevo[47] and a refugee himself, suggested that management employ me. (He was teaching there at the time.) I worked a lot, but at least I had enough money for a few 'luxuries' for us from time to time and finally I could buy an odd present. For instance, I bought a set of bed linen or occasional petit fours[48] which were our favourite. And later, for my parents' fiftieth wedding anniversary, I bought a set of coffee cups, nice red cups (sold at an open-air market for a very reasonable price). They did like them.

Overworking, travelling, stress, too much responsibility for too many things, all took a toll on my health. Actually, not much was wrong with my physical health, but I was worn out and exhausted. On top of everything, I tried very hard to put on a brave face on, not only for my parents but also for everyone else, including myself. I realized that, above all, I resented other people's pity or my own sense of helplessness. Was it pride or something else? I did not have time to think about it. What I could not ignore was feeling faint, a kind of blackout I had from time to time. It was alright when it happened at home; I could cope with it. I would lie down briefly and it would pass. My mother panicked a bit, but I managed to calm her down. My father was more practical. He would tell me to lift my legs above head level. The problem was, however, when it happened in public. There were two such quite drastic occasions. One was on my way home from a visit, where I already felt unwell and left early in order to avoid being fussed over. However, as I got off the tram, I found I could not walk and felt faint. I managed to lie down on the pavement. I did not lose consciousness, so I was embarrassed, yet could do nothing. A woman, living on the ground floor of an apartment building overlooking the pavement, saw me and came out, gave me some water and a spoonful of sugar. She then hailed a taxi and the taxi driver took me home. He refused to take my money.

I could never figure out where this kindness and empathy came from. Why did they not think the worst of me?

The second time, I fainted on a train. The train was as overcrowded as ever and I had to stand in the corridor. Luckily, I was not crushed this time; there was enough space to move my arms. I was returning home from Novi Sad, on a Saturday, having spent all day examining students. The canteen was closed, which I did not know beforehand, so I had had no food all day. When I came round, I was sitting in a compartment with people gathered around me. They were quite upset. A woman told me I had scared her because I 'looked more dead than a corpse'. Not exactly encouraging! An elderly man handed me a bottle of plum brandy[49] and told me to have a sip. I was moved; they genuinely seemed to care.

Yet again, I could not stop being amazed at the kindness and generosity of not only family, but various individuals – strangers, acquaintances and friends alike. I wondered how come there was so much compassion and caring. Where did it come from? In spite of the deteriorating economic situation, most people managed to retain their integrity, I felt, especially during the first few months after our arrival. The explanation could be that there was no shooting and shelling in Belgrade, no literal struggle for survival, no overt presence of death. In spite of difficult living conditions, people there were not reduced to only satisfying their primary needs. Their lives still had some depth. They had space for various feelings and reactions; they had time to think and feel, to love as well as hate, and most importantly to reflect on both.[50]

I kept in touch with Zora's and Bane's teenage children. As time passed, they started complaining about their parents not leaving Sarajevo. They took it personally. Parents of their Sarajevo friends came to Belgrade, while, for their parents, 'not losing the flat was paramount', they complained. Neither the children nor the parents ever told the truth in their ADRA letters, so all sorts of assumptions were in operation. The parents sent the grandfather to Belgrade (to die) yet they were 'almost having fun', was the teenagers' argument. When the family from Belgrade sent lentils mixed with unroasted coffee beans (ADRA would not accept coffee) to the parents in Sarajevo, the parents wrote back saying what fun it was to try to separate the two. On evenings without electricity, with candlelight only, that kept them busy, they claimed.

It was stories like that that caused confusion. Sparing the children from ugly reality. At the same time, the children never told the parents the truth about their feelings. The teenagers missed their parents so much that they were incapable of reading between the lines, unable to anticipate the parents' desperation. And the parents? Did their desire to protect their children from uncomfortable truth achieve any goal? Hardly!

Both parents eventually, quite late into the war, arrived in Belgrade; first Zora, in a rather bad shape, and Bane even later.

These rather uncharacteristic reactions of the two teenagers, however, made me think about my own reactions. I worried about the mental damage Sarajevo could have caused. I was aware of my Sarajevo attempts to neutralize evil by doing good, but I wondered how much of the widespread Sarajevo evil had rubbed off on me. Did I have some nasty reactions stored away that I was not aware of? My need to question my own reactions increased when I overheard Sanja telling her sister-in-law that they should hide the fancy winter jackets they had bought because seeing the jackets would make me envious. That was upsetting to hear, but also made me wonder. Was I prone to envy? I did not think I was an envious person, but conditions in my life had significantly changed, so I might have turned into one. Therefore, I started monitoring my reactions. Walking down the street in the evening, I would register windows with warm, pleasant glows coming from inside and imagine happy families enjoying their cosy evenings – something we, as a family, had had but could not easily conjure up under the circumstances. Did I envy them? The answer was no; it just made me long for the good old days gone forever. Occasionally, I would also notice people coming out of a pastry shop with little bags full of desserts we could not afford (I had always had a sweet tooth). Did that make me envy them? No, I would just ask my mother to make improvised jam tarts with the jam and flour we received as gifts. That reassured me. It was not a great achievement, but it was a big comfort to me.

Although my Belgrade experience, overall, was good, Novi Sad did not match it. The English Department at Novi Sad University was not a welcoming environment from the start, possibly understandably. The town itself was brimming with refugees (more than Belgrade) and the view that refugees were taking jobs from the locals was widespread. Maybe that was the reason. Maybe the Sarajevans were not forthcoming and friendly enough, or maybe the Novi Sad people resented us for whatever reasons. In any case, somehow, we, the three Sarajevo lecturers, ended up relying on each other. I missed the kind of departmental camaraderie we had had in Sarajevo before the war.[51] Whatever our camaraderie had been about, it was a gesture of inclusion and gave us all a sense of belonging. That was what I yearned for. Among the few people at Novi Sad University who showed empathy and made me feel included was a distinguished linguist who also commuted from Belgrade. She knew how to help and was willing to help. She made me feel accepted and appreciated.

The students, on the other hand, were students, more or less the same. I felt very comfortable and fulfilled with them, albeit rather sad. They reflected the unfortunate predicament they were caught in. Their faces were strained, their expressions hinted at hopelessness, their clothes were dark and drab. The general atmosphere was grey. Quite a number of them were refugees from Bosnia. I felt both empathy and the need for offering extra support and pastoral care. Students had always been a group of people eager to learn and quite receptive, but now caught in an unfortunate set of circumstances, even more so, especially the refugee students. They were in a hurry to graduate and start their lives afresh somewhere, somehow. I was there to facilitate that and that certainly gave me both pleasure and satisfaction.

In a way, with the students I was back to my normal 'mission', parts of my identity reclaimed, especially the professional parts. That gave me an impetus to start creating some sort of existence almost to my liking. I had old friends, new friends and my old profession back. I was especially happy and proud to have acquired such a wide circle of friends, either those who had chosen to befriend me or those I had met through mutual acquaintances; from Beba and Jadran whom I met through Mira, to Brana, a kind soul I met at the Jewish Community Centre and immediately took to.[52]

Emerging Doubts

The attempt to create a new life almost to my liking was the 'tool' that helped me ignore every argument in support of emigrating – both those of the 'shelter group' earlier and everybody else's during this refugee period. Maybe it was alright for them, but, in reality, the reasons overall were not convincing, I told myself. After all, I had such a great social network, with exceptional people around me. My profession was restored, my life was alright. All convincing arguments. Yet, that was only partly true. My life, in many respects, was actually quite unacceptable. I was in denial again. The denial was reinforced by the circumstances. I could not ignore the state my parents were in, especially my father, and his need for serious medical care. To leave them behind was unthinkable, yet for the three of us to go anywhere was impossible. So, what option did I have but to bury my head in the sand? I was fully responsible for my family's life. My father was too ill to be active in any shape or form while my mother just about managed to do the cooking with the food I bought.

Our family almost entirely depended on me. Most of the money we had at our disposal I earned and some of it in Deutsche Marks.[53] Only a selected number of things could be paid for in dinars, for instance utility bills, transport fares, or in various shops and supermarkets where hardly anybody shopped. Most items were bought from smugglers at more reasonable prices, albeit often in Deutsche Marks. The Deutsche Mark was the currency most widely used, for instance to pay the rent (landlords would only accept Deutsche Marks) or for purchasing any of the smuggled goods sold on the street. Although dinars were not much used, still my early dinar earnings were not sufficient to cover all our dinar expenses. So, in our early days in Belgrade I would exchange my hard-earned Deutsche Marks for dinars on the street to supplement the income and pay the rent with the remaining Deutsche Marks. Many people earned their living changing money illegally. There were many street-corner foreign exchange 'offices'. Police turned a blind eye. I struggled with the arithmetic, as ever, but those 'exchange clerks' were fair, and always gave me the right amount. Most of them were Bosnian refugees and they empathized.

However, soon international sanctions and the half-dead economy caused inflation to grow exponentially. The dinar would devalue every few hours, so my dinar salary would be worth next to nothing within a short time. The foreign currency market was again the solution; this time the exchange went in the opposite direction. In order to preserve some value, one exchanged all the dinars for Deutsche Marks as soon as one could.[54] I would usually do it somewhere near the railway station in Novi Sad, at one of many locations. One saw mostly young men slowly walking about, producing a strange sound, which one perceived as a barely audible buzzing sound: '*z,z,z*'. They were actually advertising their 'merchandise', repeating, in low voice, the word for foreign currency '*devize*', but the only audible sound was the 'z' sound.

I worked on Fridays in Novi Sad (the day few people wanted to work on). We would pick up our salaries, in brown envelopes, in person (also possible by proxy) from a faculty cashier, once a month, on Fridays. Therefore, I again became a 'postie', bringing salaries to all the colleagues living in Belgrade. I had big envelopes for each department, with smaller ones for each member of staff inside. I would ring the person named on the big envelope (a sort of representative) to let them know that I had arrived and they would come to my house, take their big envelope and distribute the smaller ones to respective colleagues. They would then immediately buy foreign currency, mostly Deutsche Marks, at the nearest black market. I had a financial advantage: I bought the Deutsche Marks in Novi Sad straight away and achieved a better exchange rate, i.e. the dinar was a fraction less devalued an hour or two earlier.

On the days when I did not or could not get Deutsche Marks in Novi Sad, I would take a tram from the Belgrade railway station, get off near a popular supermarket and buy, for dinars, everything the family needed (either immediately or longer term). I would organize the items at the till so that the perishables were first, then the necessary ones, then those less needed. I would tell the cashier to stop once they had reached one million, or billion or trillion (depending on a month).[55] Then I would leave behind the items at the back of the 'queue' because I could not afford them.

I could say that, more or less, I succeeded in organizing our life as best I could. All three of us managed to do with what we could afford. We tried never to pay attention to the fact that what we could afford was actually minimal. We managed to convince ourselves that we had everything we needed. Yet, something that we had to admit we missed were the mementos people commonly have. No old love letters, no school reports, no favourite books, not even my parents' medals and decorations, for instance. (Luckily, soon after we moved into our rented flat a friend of mine from my Belgrade student days visited Sarajevo as a member of an international group.[56] He brought us the family photos from my friend Tatjana's parents' home. Some got lost during the journey, but that did not matter. At least part of our documented past arrived.)[57]

I often thought we could be defined as 'people with a lost past'. I believed many a refugee shared the feeling. We were not alone; there were many refugees in Belgrade. Our already miserable life began deteriorating. The economic situation made the refugees' predicament even more challenging. Hence, local authorities started distributing to refugees donations from various international humanitarian agencies. It was a great help; there was food and some hygiene products. One less thing to worry about. We were also told there would be some flour for us. I regularly went to pick things up. I also went to pick up the flour, not knowing how heavy it would be. It was a sack of fifty kilos. None of the refugees around me offered to help. Not surprising; all buried in their own misery. The sack weighed more than me,[58] but I managed somehow. Admittedly, my fingers were bleeding under the nails, but not too badly. Food meant survival!

My mother had several relatives living in Belgrade. We did not see much of them, an odd visit from time to time, or a phone call. Everybody was busy with their own struggles. There was one family, though, who had to face the ultimate loss; the mother and twin sister of Goga, my second cousin who lived in Germany and who had liaised between Sida's family and mine while we were in Pirovac. When we spoke to her from Pirovac, in 1992, she was well. But soon she fell ill, passed away and was buried in Belgrade in 1994. Unfortunately, this sad occasion brought us all together again. Emotions ran high. It was yet another blow.

The best way to alleviate our frequent sense of gloom were visits by sympathetic people. Actually, various truly affectionate and devoted friends often came to visit my parents. Among them were their good friends,[59] with whom they had been friends since the 1940s. There was an obvious emotional bond between the two couples; they were my parents' 'war friends', the Jewish friends who had shared their terrible lot of the Second World War. Another special person was Sladjana's mother[60] who was an exceptionally warm-hearted, understanding, quietly selfless and supportive person. Their presence and backing meant a lot to me, too. I knew I could rely on them to provide an emotional lifeline for the family. There were quite a few others, too. My parents enjoyed their visits. However, my father was getting weaker and weaker, although he was still fighting.

I was sometimes away from home for longer periods; from morning to evening some days. When I was away my parents needed somebody to stay with them. There were two men who frequently visited and stayed with them while I was not there. I felt my parents were in safe hands. They were both generous, affectionate and kind-hearted people. One was Djordje, who lived in Belgrade with his family. He was orphaned in the Second World War and had lived in a children's home in a village in Croatia where my mother was a teacher. So he ended up being my mother's pupil during the war, some fifty years before. This second war brought them close together again. As a child Djordje became attached to my mother and forever stayed attached to her. He selflessly supported us. He never wearied of giving my mother a helping hand in whichever way it was needed.

The other one was Cveja, who would even move in for several days when I travelled. He was Henika's partner from Sarajevo, of whom the entire family immediately grew fond. He exuded unadulterated humanity and kindness. He did not have a selfish bone in his body. In early April 1992, he and his daughters left Sarajevo for Belgrade but he could not return to Sarajevo since the siege had started – nobody could enter or leave Sarajevo any more. He missed Henika and, so coming to the family, in a way, meant both for him and for us a connection with Henika, who was in London by then.

She missed him too. Unfortunately, he died before the two of them could ever be reunited.

It was the help of these two generous men that enabled me to accept a few invitations to give lectures abroad. It was not often, but I was invited to several lecture tours and conferences and that meant a lot for both my confidence and my career. I gave talks in Bratislava, Warsaw, at several universities in the UK and in Rome. The invitations came thanks to Piotr and the European Erasmus Tempus Programme.

Travelling abroad also meant that I needed a passport; my previous one had expired. However, a passport was not the only problem. Due to international sanctions and the UN arms embargo, flying in and out of the country was not possible, no flights allowed. There were vans that would take one to Budapest airport and back – certainly not the most convenient way of travelling, but not a reason to refuse such an attractive proposition. Getting a new passport took some persuading of the officials. It became yet another politically paradoxical situation to get one's head around. The country where we now lived retained the name Yugoslavia (yet it was a different entity), it kept some of the federal institutions, but with different remits. I applied for passports both for myself and for my parents ('just in case') and I managed to get them, the Yugoslav ones, admittedly with a bit of *veza* at work. The old red passports books were still in use, so our new passports actually did not differ from the old ones. With my new passport and a good plan for my parents – leaving Cveja to look after them – I could happily attend the conferences and give lectures.

One also needed foreign currency for travelling abroad. Therefore, I wanted to withdraw some money from my foreign currency account, for which I had all the necessary documentation. However, I was refused. The argument was that I was a Sarajevo client, even though the branch in Belgrade was the head office of that particular bank.[61] I even had a strong *veza* but all I achieved was to draw the latest statement for my account.

I never managed to get any of that money out; not even for my father's funeral, although regulations then stated that the money could be withdrawn for 'exceptional needs'. Death and funerals, after all, probably did not constitute 'an exceptional need' under the circumstances. And even years later, to this very day, various regulations and arguments have made it impossible to get hold of one's money.

Several of these trips abroad meant getting together with my Sarajevo friends or family. When, in 1993, I attended a translators' conference in Bratislava, Marina, my writer friend, joined me there. It was a lovely reunion. She lived in Warsaw then; she was a lector at Warsaw University. So, when I was invited to Warsaw University the same year, I stayed with her. During my lecture tour in the UK, in 1994, I stayed with Henika and Tanja in London while giving a lecture at SSEES.[62] I stayed with Felicity and Piotr in Leicester while I gave a lecture at both Leicester University and Warwick University. On my way to London, on a stopover at Schipol-Amsterdam airport, Henika's son came to see me with his wife and daughter.[63] In Rome both Felicity and I gave a talk at the same university, the same day. Hence, those trips meant for me, not only professional affirmation, but also affirmation of my friend and family ties.

All in all, I persuaded myself that I managed to establish myself: I had my work, I had my friends, I took part in various conferences and received invitations for foreign lecture tours. My parents were delighted, especially my dying father who felt that I had managed to prove myself that I had 'arrived'. No more fear for my existence. The 'investment' in my 'head' was working; I had secured a place for myself in the new setting.

The concept of the 'head investment' was yet another reflection of the Jewish tradition alive in my family's psyche, although we were mostly oblivious to quite a few aspects of that tradition, or denied it altogether. The new Yugoslav ideology, the new identity overshadowed family roots. Yet, it seemed that some things could not be easily uprooted. The threat of being forced to leave one's home, to flee one's country, seems to have never been far from Jewish consciousness and my family was no different in that respect.[64] Mazower in his book about his Russian Jewish émigré family quotes his grandmother's family motto: 'A suitcase in the head, a suitcase in the hallway',[65] which clearly reflects that attitude. Probably, for many a Jewish family the message has been stored somewhere in their (our) unconscious. As a part of their (our) DNA and imprinted on their (our) collective memory, it often becomes their (our) life 'philosophy'. In any case, for whatever reason, many Jewish families believe, among other things, that the most important asset for survival is good education i.e. 'a suitcase in the head'. The wealth one acquires cannot usually be carried around, or transferred to a different country, while education, safe 'in one's head', can. If the head is still on one's shoulders, it goes with one anywhere and everywhere. It cannot be stolen or requisitioned or be taken away in any other way. It seems that among Jews it is generally considered the best kind of safety net and a way to establish oneself in the new environment.

Pointing to my 'successful' life, as I defined it – job, lecture tours, parties and so on – as well as some other strategies, helped me keep my parents unaware of the tense antagonistic atmosphere developing rapidly into the mid-1990s in Belgrade, especially targeting refugees. Besides, my parents only had contacts with friends and family, with likeminded people. They had almost nothing to do with the outside world. Those around us were all a special kind of people. As for friends, it is not for nothing that it is said that one chooses one's friends. It seemed they were the kind who cherished kindness over nastiness, good over evil and believed in generosity not selfishness, regardless of the difficult conditions they also lived in.

Actually, as far as I was concerned, I also felt I had managed to consolidate my life to a certain degree. I believed I had managed to create a sense of belonging, albeit to a small group. However, there were not many places where I was not made aware of my refugee status. (My parents did not need to know that.) Refugees were becoming more and more resented. People tried to be kind to us, but they did not always succeed. The difficult living conditions, the incredible rate of inflation and the sense of insecurity caused a change in many people. They probably needed a scapegoat to blame for their misery. Refugees became a safe option.

By then, 'refugee' gradually became more and more of a dirty word. It was especially difficult to be a refugee in your own country[66] – as I considered the country I had arrived in, in spite of the fact that actually it was the new, shrunken Yugoslavia, the fact I tried not to see. Everything seemed the same, but it was not. I held onto the illusion of continuity, I held onto the false sense of belonging. The reality, though, was that I was a refugee, the worst kind of a foreigner, that the country was not the same and my life had very little in common with my previous life. So, actually, it was a delusion that was getting harder and harder to sustain. What it meant was holding onto something that did not exist and thus preventing a fresh start. Exactly as Towles, talking about exile, put it: 'But when you exile a man into his *own country*, there is no beginning anew.'[67] That was probably why I tried to convince myself that I was just continuing my life as it had been, only in a somewhat altered environment. However, the fantasy did not work so efficiently any more. I had to admit to myself that life in a foreign country, which inevitably calls for beginning anew, might be the only solution.

In the meantime, in Belgrade, the worsened economic situation also called for new behaviour. It was not about a new beginning, but about 'revised' rules for everyone, the 'new normal', for locals and refugees alike. It was not only about accepting and using the black market, previously unthinkable, but also about behaving in an unorthodox and borderline illegal manner. I found it difficult to break rules, to get anywhere near borderline illegality, although I was aware that that had become a standard. People were nudging me into doing these things. One of the most common was issuing cheques knowing that you had no money in your account. People issued cheques knowing that they would bounce, but I was reluctant. However, even if you had money in your account, banks themselves often had no money to give to customers. It may sound absurd but simply, at times, there was no money in circulation.

I resisted issuing cheques that would bounce until the end of December 1994. A friendly bank clerk advised me to do just that. I had no money in my account (quite a usual occurrence) when the bank clerk suggested I write cheques for anything I needed to purchase. Therefore, for the coming 1995 New Year's Eve[68] celebration (which was a big event in the family), I bought a roast for dinner and minced meat for the stuffed cabbage leaves for 1 January, as was the custom. I wrote a cheque (knowing I had no money) at the butcher for an incredible amount, trillions of dinars. At the time, it was worth the equivalent of some 300 Deutsche Marks. A lot of money to pay at the butcher by anybody's standards. However, when the cheque was cleared, at the beginning of January, it was worth only 4 Deutsche Marks (which I did have). An astonishing rate of inflation.

So, eventually I was doing what everyone did. Maybe that was the sign that I did belong? I wanted to believe it, I tried to ignore the refugee stigma. Yet, it was all too painful. One of the rare occasions where I could successfully ignore it was a 1995 premiere of the drama I had translated when we first arrived – thanks mostly to Dejan, the director of the theatre, who invited me. I was a guest of honour and I genuinely felt honoured. That evening, there was an announcement on TV news mentioning my name as a translator of the drama premiered at a well-known theatre. My parents were very proud.

But back to our 1995 New Year's celebration. We went through the motions, but my father's health was seriously deteriorating. He just wanted to die, he said; he had had enough. I found it hard to accept. I pleaded with him and even asked Henika to talk to him. I could not face losing him; the bond between us was exceptionally strong. In vain: he soon contracted pneumonia again and refused treatment. My mother and I tried to persuade him but to no avail. One day, in mid-March, I came home from work and my father was in a coma. The family were there, as well as Sladjana and her mother (both doctors). They assured me that he was not in pain. I believed them, yet I called my psychiatrist friend and asked him for advice. He told me just to hug my father, moisten his lips and that it would not last long. My mother and I sat by his side and, in the early hours of the morning of 14 March 1995, he passed away peacefully. I was both devastated and relieved. My father's suffering was over. I rang up the London family (his sister and her family) to tell them the sad news. It was too early in the morning, but I could not wait. I needed to share my grief with them.

The regular commotion began. Things were done quickly and efficiently. Friends and family helped. Božidar, who had been my confidant almost since I first met him in Belgrade, came early to offer me emergency money. I told him off. I needed no money, I needed his friendship, I said. Rude, but true. He understood, as ever, and did not take offence. The funeral was arranged. Both my mother and I were in a state of shock. Even though it had not come suddenly, it was still painful and hard to accept. The three of us were no more.

I found it difficult to accept the idea that our Sarajevo part of the family would not be with us, that they would not be able to share the grief with us, to help us lay out my father's remains, to say farewell to him. My need to be with them, especially Henika, was so strong that 'out of nowhere' – or was it out of nowhere? – I came up with a plan. I rang Henika and asked her to take the family to a synagogue in London – they were all in London by then – at the same time as my mother and I were to attend a service in the Belgrade synagogue. I said we would then at least share the firmament. Whatever I meant by that. We all did as agreed. My mother and I went to the synagogue, now the proper one – it was March, so not the 'winter synagogue' in operation. Yet again, I did not know whether our heads needed to be covered or not, what was expected of us, but I asked the rabbi and did as I was told. Did I not realize then how profoundly Jewish I actually must have felt?

The ever-helpful Vesna from the Jewish Community organized transport to the cemetery for my mother and me. Cveja, Henika's partner, was her proxy at the funeral. I held onto him. It caused some friction in the family, a rather unpleasant attempt at 'regrouping' during the funeral. Difficult to comprehend, but soon forgotten. We buried my father in the Jewish cemetery with a rabbi and Jewish rituals although he was a confirmed atheist (as was my mother)[69]. Djordje claimed it was my father's wish. I doubted that, but had no will or energy to dwell on it further. Both my mother and I went along with it.

It was only much later, in Belgrade, that I learned from Djordje's daughter, that it had been a lie Djordje used, in cahoots with my mother, in order to convince me to accept such funeral arrangements. Actually, I realised only then that it had been a good rational decision since the alternative would have been a typical, undignified burial of a refugee, of an 'irrelevant' displaced person.

Then people started coming to our flat to pay respects. Many of them, for days. It was the custom and it did actually help both my mother and me. It distracted and tired us enough so we could get some sleep. When we eventually ventured out, we came across some surprisingly kind people. For instance, the tellers at the bank where we had had our accounts since our unhappy arrival, greeted us with kindness and expressed their condolences. It moved us and comforted us. For us it was a sign that we were not perceived as faceless individuals, one of 'too many refugees around'. We craved for gestures like that in our sad and depressing predicament.

My father's death was a great loss for both my mother and for me. The three of us had gone through hell; we had shared so much, not only in the past few years. I had lived with my parents, except for a short period in my first marriage, so our lives were intertwined to a great degree. There was very little we did not share. Now my mother was quite lost, after fifty years of a happy marriage, and I felt it was my duty to support her. I tried to replace my father as much as I could, although it was an impossible task. Ultimately, I also needed help and support. I missed the closeness and understanding my father and I shared. I always felt he was not only my father, but my true friend as well.

It was only then that I realized that my mother had become agoraphobic. All the time in our rented flat of almost three years, she did not go out much. Not on her own anyway. Therefore, I had to start taking her out, little by little. First, to the nearest street corner, then to the next, to a nearby shop, then to the bank and so on. It didn't take her too long to get back to her old self, albeit grieving and somewhat frightened. She even went to visit a friend or two on her own.

At about the same time, cracks between the two families, Sida's and ours, became overt. Various adversities and hardships had taken their toll on both families. In Sida's case, there was constant anticipation of the recurrence of her depression. In addition, Sanja, albeit keen on ending her unhappy marriage, had to readjust; ending a marriage is a traumatic event in the best of times. To make things more difficult, by then the economic situation in the country was dire, so the quality of life inevitably deteriorated for everybody. Organizing simple daily life in Belgrade became a strain. Making regular income stretch far enough was extremely difficult and complicated. One had to resort to various ways and means.

It seemed to me, though, that the difficult situation in the country affected our family more. Possibly it was unfair, but that was how I felt. We had no money 'under the mattress'. Neither did we have any of those forgotten-about home supplies, which could help and replace that which was not available or accessible any more. We had no old clothes, no old household items, no forgotten tins of food nor anything else to fall back on. We could not even draw our own money from the 'old savings account'. All three of us, including my terminally ill father, had been desperately trying to establish some sort of normality while struggling with making ends meet. My resilience had started to fray around the edges. My father's death was the final blow.

I became increasingly oversensitive. Or was I? Was I overcritical of others while not self-aware and self-critical enough? It was hard to tell. Probably, but I wished I were not. I tried quite hard. However, I certainly became aware of the amount of unpleasant behaviour that I seemed to have been exposed to. It was not only Sida who showed inexplicable resentment towards me, but also Sanja's overall behaviour started making me feel uncomfortable. I kept remembering things. I could not hold back any more. Impatience and indignation surfaced, especially after my father's funeral. Funerals and weddings are notoriously the cause of rifts in families. Who knows why? Raw emotions maybe.

Anyway, I wanted to believe the gap was not unbridgeable. We surely all wanted to overcome it; we all wanted to go back to being a loving family. Therefore, with my typical undiplomatic (and often detrimental) candour, I wanted to clear the air. I wanted the truth; I wanted it all out in the open.

My Belgrade friend, Brana, once said that if she wanted to hear the naked truth, she would turn to me; if she needed comfort in place of truth, she had plenty of others to turn to.

After a rather nasty row with Sanja, I wrote her a letter. In it, I tried to appeal to her by reminding her of the harsh conditions we had all lived in. I hoped she would look at our mutual predicament from the time our lives became entangled and fathom all the intricacies. My aim was to reclaim our loving relationship. Surely, things could be rectified. An apology and a big hug would do! That was what I hoped for. Childish and simplistic, most likely. Wishful thinking too.

Was there any point in doing that? I had to try. I knew that under adverse and painful circumstances people rarely manage to get a clear and objective picture, and even more rarely do they achieve a level of self-awareness, but I hoped against hope. I somehow thought we both might make an effort. Too naïve and optimistic probably. Or else denial again? Things had gone too far by then and it was too late, maybe?

It was my typical inner conflict, the one between forgiving and forgetting on the one hand and, on the other, giving up, nursing my wounds and ultimately accepting the loss. I always feared losing relationships, held onto them stubbornly, often deluding myself, until eventually I had no choice but to admit the reality and let go. That had been a struggle for me for years and in various instances. I had been doing it before and probably would continue doing it. Hence, it was not surprising that I struggled with it again.

That covert/overt conflict between the families did not make life any easier. However, it certainly was not the only uncomfortable situation for me. As time went by, I felt more and more uneasy in both Belgrade and Novi Sad – apart from the life I shared with my friends. There was again a significant, and difficult-to-cope-with discrepancy between my private life, which friends made easier, and my public life, hugely influenced by palpable antagonism towards refugees that was widespread throughout the country.

That made me hold on to my Belgrade friends more firmly, but I also kept in touch with some refugee colleagues from Sarajevo University. That also helped. I could talk about anything and everything with them. We had quite a lot in common and we offered each other emotional support. I could openly explore with them my feelings of being an outsider; we shared the misery caused by resettlement. However, many of them did not seem to have such strong feelings of not belonging. In my case, the feeling of being the intruder or outsider seemed much stronger.

My feelings could have been intensified by my not fully recognized and acknowledged, yet emerging, sense of Jewishness together with the identity confusion the disappearance of Yugoslavia caused – most of my refugee colleagues saw themselves as Serbs, not Yugoslavs. Or maybe it was my inherent hypersensitivity or something else. Yet, I had to admit to myself, although I believed I was in the country I considered my own, that the country did not accept me as one of its own. Moreover, the country I knew and was born in actually did not exist. Yugoslavia was no more. No more Yugoslavs either.

The sense of animosity around me started burning again, reopening a painful wound. Refugees were more and more often accused of 'crowding our space', 'using our services', 'taking our jobs', 'behaving in an uncivilized manner', 'speaking with a strange accent' and so on and so forth. And I was one of them. It was not only disappointing, but also difficult to accept. Unbearable actually.

The thought of ever going back to Sarajevo at the end of the war was equally, if not more, unimaginable. Not only because of the painful memories of events past, but also because it was obvious that the future would be strongly influenced by the deep-seated antagonisms and binary divisions. Sarajevo had changed beyond recognition. I learned that 'back home' I was seen as a traitor: I would probably be asked to somehow prove my loyalty to the new country. In addition, the fact that I chose to flee to Belgrade, with a predominantly Serbian population, immediately labelled me a 'Chetnik', which insinuated my affiliation with the Serbian military that was shelling Sarajevo from the mountains: I was seen as the enemy.

It was all reminiscent of the animosities of the Second World War and post-war suspicions that were only anecdotally familiar to me. The apparent fact, though, was that none of the newly formed nation states had yet established even a minimal level of tolerance; they were still flooded with passions and negative emotions. So, actually, I believed I did not belong in Bosnia any more than I belonged in Serbia (also a new nation state). These states might change, but who knows when, I thought. I certainly could not wait for the change.

Having been in denial during the Bosnian civil war, I could not afford further denials. The atmosphere in Belgrade was tense. Rumour had it that some radically nationalistic men spent weekends in Bosnia fighting on the side of the Serbian army. However, it was not just rumours: actually, a physiotherapist

Sanja had managed to get for my father not long before he died happened to have been one of them. He offered to bring a computer for me as I had told him I did not have one. I stupidly assumed he meant the one from my home in Sarajevo. He only laughed and said that he meant the one from the pile of computers they had looted in Bosnia. He could not understand why I refused it. All three of us froze when, while treating my father, he explained his views and described the atrocious, horrific things he and his group did in Bosnia.

I feared that the war might spill over. Sida and Sanja were less pessimistic, but I just could not shed the fear. I did not want to leave it too late. Now that my father was gone, I could not use his health as an excuse. On top of that, my mother was all for leaving and joining the Sarajevo family in London. She believed London would be the best solution. After all, my BA in English language and literature had turned me into an anglophile, my mother argued, and the culture was familiar to me. I was hesitant. I found it difficult to leave behind another group of friends and the profession that meant so much to me. I felt that would mean losing a major 'ingredient' of my identity and the last vestiges of my previous life.

My UK friends strongly advised coming to the UK. I was in two minds about it. I could not hope to get a lectureship anywhere in the UK (especially at my age), I knew. To be on the dole was hard to imagine – handouts and charity again! I weighed the pros and cons and eventually decided to take a risk. I felt it was better for my sanity. So, gradually, immigrating to the UK seemed more and more feasible and attractive.

Finally, we both decided, my mother and I. Before leaving for the UK, we had a general health check-up. 'Just in case' again! We wanted to make sure everything was under control. We certainly did not want to have to see a doctor or a dentist as soon as we arrived. All other necessary preparations, administrative and otherwise, were made. There was only one more painful task left: to arrange and pay for my father's gravestone to be laid in our absence. Sad, but we did not have much choice. Finally, our suitcases were packed yet again. This time, we could take as many suitcases as we wanted, provided we could pay for the overweight luggage. However, with limited funds the issue of weight did weigh heavily upon us. After all, we were carrying with us all our earthly possessions (although significantly reduced). We bought the plane tickets for London and mustered all our courage.

Chapter 5

Recovery

London

My mother and I arrived in London, on 26 August 1995, this time with more than one suitcase per person. We brought family photographs and some books, paintings and personal items, and even a few household items, probably just out of the irrational need for a sense of continuity. Most of it we had managed to gather during the previous three years.

We were again invited to move in with the family, temporarily; this time with Ella, Moni and their family. Their London home was not as spacious as the one our Belgrade family had. Yet again, we disrupted the life of another family, crammed their space and felt a nuisance. Yet again, we appreciated the family's sacrifice. Yet again, we felt grateful, but still, it did not make us feel any more comfortable.

Before we arrived, Henika and Tanja had brought their parents from Zagreb and they all lived together. Their daughters, however, did not live with them. Henika's daughter, Tamara, who graduated from medical school in Sarajevo, in the spring of 1992, always an independent person, lived on her own. Tanja's daughter, Ivana, younger than Tamara, was at university in another city, supported by one of several Bosnian aid organizations. She only occasionally visited.

On the day we arrived, Henika and I had another vigorous emotional outburst; we could not stop crying. We had missed each other; we could not accept the fact that there had been so many difficult, sad moments we could not share. Tanja again disapproved of such outbursts. Tanja had always seemed more controlled. Henika and I ended up drowning our sorrows in a glass or two of gin and tonic and a big hug (the universal panacea!). The next day meant the next set of worries and existential matters to resolve for my mother and me. I felt the full weight of the pressure. I did not feel up to the job. I found it increasingly hard to cope with our predicament.

In London, I felt very strange. It was not the same place I knew and loved from the days when I visited. I had spent a considerable amount of time in London while working on my PhD dissertation, for instance, or just visiting. Now I was neither a tourist nor a visitor, but neither was I a resident. It was very hard to get one's head around the new situation. Who and where was I? My identity was quite unclear. Was I a former Yugoslav? But there was no Yugoslavia as such anymore! Certainly not British, not yet, but with the hope of becoming that. Did I have any idea what that entailed? Probably not. I certainly was not a sociolinguist or a university lecturer any more. However, unemployed was not how I was willing to define myself. A hugely challenging situation.

Our first step in the process of rehoming was to go to the CBF[1] (Central British Fund) offices for support with the immigration procedure, as the family advised us. That had been the procedure every refugee within Sarajevo Jewish Community in London (including my family) had gone through and the CBF helped all the members of the Community,[2] regardless of whether they were Jewish or not. Many of the Sarajevo refugees had arrived a few years before us. They exchanged experiences and advice with each other and advised me, too. Word of mouth as a source of information worked efficiently.

They were an unusual mixture of people, Jews as well as other Bosnian ethnic groups, of different ages, interests and professions but equally desperate. The group all lived in the same area of London. They were well organized; they had their own society, premises where they met and they had their bilingual journal *SaLon*,[3] all thanks to the support of the Jewish Care organization. Unexpectedly, I found myself again mostly among Jews, just like in Pirovac and partly in Belgrade, and hoping to be supported by a Jewish organization, as in Sarajevo. I realized I had increasingly been in contact with Jewish tradition and customs.

I prepared all the necessary documents for my mother and myself and made an appointment at the CBF a few days after we arrived. It was not that I did not worry, but the experience of our predecessors had been positive, so no need for anxiety, I thought. Leaving home on our way there, we met Tanja coming back from the CBF where she had been for a different reason. Both mother and I were rather apprehensive: not your everyday task asking for support in starting a new life, especially at a rather mature age. On top of that, Tanja told us that she had a message for us from the CBF official who, according to Tanja, was not best pleased with the way we had initially gone about contacting them. The official allegedly said that the route to apply for support was not via the directors, but through the regular channels, i.e. an interview with her.[4] That immediately made me uncomfortable. Was I being paranoid or was my gut telling me something? However, I managed to ignore it; I could not afford to dwell on it. I needed to be prepared to answer all sorts of possibly painful questions.

Once we arrived at the CBF, my worst nightmare started unravelling. The official, who represented all the refugees within Sarajevo Jewish Community in London at the Home Office, received us in her office. She was unfriendly, which already made me feel more apprehensive. She bluntly told us that the CBF could not represent us, that we were to be deported immediately back to Belgrade. The reasons she gave were rather convincing, albeit somewhat cruel. Since I had been in the UK in 1994, on a lecture tour, I was supposed to have sought asylum then. The fact that my father was dying at the time and I could not abandon him and my mother was apparently of no concern to either the CBF or the Home Office, for that matter, the young woman said.

I was devastated. I had certainly not expected this. Being deported back to Belgrade was unimaginable. I had not left because I wanted a change or a better life or anything like that. I left because staying there had become untenable. I had consciously taken a risk of losing my only connection with my peacetime life, my profession/vocation, as well as my friends. To be told now to go back! Nothing could be worse.

We managed somehow to return to the family's home, but I broke down, both physically and mentally. I was paralysed, distraught, hopeless, stuck. I just could not see a way out, or any point in further struggle. My mother panicked. She herself was distraught too. The entire family gathered round to think of a way to help. Ivana (who was there at the time) immediately rang her friend who worked for an immigration solicitor and arranged a meeting. Henika was asked to come home from work as soon as possible and she immediately 'administered' a glass of gin and tonic and a hug. Gradually, I collected myself and eventually went to sleep.

The next day, my mother and I visited the solicitor. He checked all the necessary details and saw no problem with my previous visit to the UK. We went to the Home Office. It was another stressful event, eased a bit by the presence of Ivana's friend. There we had our fingerprints taken, a somewhat humiliating procedure,[5] and we officially applied for asylum. In the Home Office register we were recorded as 'Bosnian Jews'. A new category for me to think about. By then, I had accepted my Jewishness, but Bosnian I did not feel. Yet, this was neither the place nor the time to dwell on issues of identity.

Once the Home Office had accepted our asylum application, the CBF accepted my mother and included her on the list of people for support. As for me, they never accepted or included me. Was I not Jewish enough for them? That could not have been the explanation as, not only my family members who were 'equally Jewish', but also all the non-Jews in the Sarajevo Jewish refugee community in London were included and supported. I have never managed to find out the reason. It remains a mystery. Why was everybody, including every other member of my family, accepted except for me?

It was not the first time I felt excluded. What was so different about me? It was one of those things I had never managed to grasp. My parents, especially my father, always encouraged me to be true to myself. And I was, but, probably as a consequence, I had always been the odd one out in the family. My eccentricity – I was seen as bonkers – possibly made it difficult for them to fully connect with me. Although the lives of our two Sarajevo families had always been intertwined to a great degree and although I felt very close to them, especially Ella and Henika, I was actually on the outside. I was the one who did not conform to the family 'codes of conduct'. I was headstrong and wayward, they would say. As children, the three cousins – Henika, Tanja and I – had spent a lot of time together. Tanja and I were very close in age and we looked alike, so as preteenagers, we would proudly lie to people that we were sisters, or twins even. However, the connection between Tanja and me became quite tentative in our teens. We followed a different path in life, so the bond, although still present, was not as strong as it once was.

While students, Tanja and I dated the same chap, but not at the same time. Soon after our brief encounter, he met Tanja and their relationship turned serious. She married him. It was almost a precursor of what Sanja would do many years later.

Much later, though, fact that Tanja and I looked alike played a strange trick on us. It was in the summer of 1995. Tanja was a guest at a party in central London where a friend from my Sarajevo student days was present. He worked for the BBC World Service. He noticed the resemblance and, knowing that Tanja came from Sarajevo, allegedly inquired after my whereabouts. Tanja, the story goes, said that I was arriving in London soon, sometime in August. He asked Tanja to tell me to get in touch because there was an opening in the Yugoslav (or whatever it was then called) division in Reading. Tanja never told me about it. I learned about it, far too late, from a mutual friend who was also present at the party and who reported that the BBC friend was annoyed by me. He was understandably hurt and, after I contacted him too late, he never got in touch with me again. I confronted Tanja, but she denied the story and always had done. Yet another mystery.

During the time my mother and I stayed with the family, Tanja and I had several rows, sometimes due to her jealousy, mostly of Henika. Admittedly, my emotional bond with Henika had been stronger than with Tanja. Hence some of my friends knew of Henika and not of Tanja. However, I found it difficult to admit it to myself, let alone to Tanja. At one occasion, Nancy rang and Tanja answered the telephone. Judging by Nancy's reaction, Tanja realized that Nancy knew all about Henika, but not her. It understandably hurt her feelings and she confronted me. Although I was a strong proponent of the 'whole truth, and nothing but', I did not have the courage to tell her the truth and came up with the most ludicrous explanation, which rightly infuriated her.

Our threshold of patience and tolerance under the circumstances was again significantly reduced. A minor thing would trigger aggravation. The fact is that existential crises change people for the worse. They affect even those who are close, maybe more so. In our case families seem to have been the first victims. Generally speaking, every conflict inevitably unveils some unpleasant truths about the parties involved. It is often the case that when one holds the 'mirror' to the other and if either does not like what they see, they readily and unreservedly blame the 'mirror holder' while failing to examine the image itself. That happened to me with the Belgrade family and now again with the Sarajevo family in London. Subjectivity replaced objectivity, resentment replaced acceptance and jealousy replaced empathy. Patience, tolerance and goodwill disappeared. Sad, but true. That must have particularly been true about Tanja and me.

Whatever the rows had been about, before and after the BBC incident, the consequences were serious for me. Tanja excommunicated me from the family which lasted for about fifteen years. Tanja had always denied that she had anything to do with my excommunication, yet it was at her behest that the family excluded me from their lives, a fact that my mother, who was close both with me and the rest of the family, confirmed. My mother tried to support me as much as she could, but she was between the rock and a hard place.

Henika, on the other hand, kept some contact with me, but it was difficult. (She lived with the parents and Tanja until my aunt's death.) Although Henika had a separate phone line, for instance, she asked me not to ring her because Tanja would sometimes answer and get upset. Tanja claimed that even mentioning my name caused additional stress to her already frail emotional state.

I was excluded from all the family gatherings, both happy and sad – be it Christmas and birthday parties, Tamara's wedding, the birth of Tamara's children, my uncle's gravestone setting[6] etc. (Surprisingly though, during the time of my excommunication, my aunt broke ranks, rang me while I was at Ned's funeral and left a message telling me how sorry she was.)

With time the attitude towards me got fiercer, so much so that in 2002 when Ella, my aunt, died, I received a painful blow. The message was passed onto me which in no uncertain terms stated that I was not allowed to attend her funeral. I found it difficult to believe, so I contacted Henika and she confirmed it. Hence, I had no choice but to respect that. Yet, rather indicatively, it was at Tanja's invitation, sometime around

2010, that I was reinstated into the family when, apparently, the death of a mutual friend made her see how preposterous situation between the two of us was. Although deeply hurt, I accepted it for the sake of our erstwhile Sarajevo life.

My mother, on the other hand, was welcome and invited to all the dos, which created tension between us. She attended and appeared to enjoy all those events I was excluded from. Our relationship at the time was strained anyway, so this was an unwelcome addition. I perceived it as a kind of betrayal and craved her loyalty and support. I did not get much of it then. The situation only caused more grief for both of us. All of it added to the enormous pressure I was under at the beginning of our 'new life'. At the same time my mother, quite understandably, was less bothered with our 'new chapter'. She was approaching her mid-seventies, was long retired and was reunited with her sister-in-law, with whom she had spent most of her life. A cousin from Mostar and his family, who had come to London before us, lived nearby and she rekindled a relationship with them too. She also started learning English and her English teacher (a Jewish Care volunteer), in time, became a friend, so she actually had new and interesting activities or distractions. Therefore, for her it was not so much of a radical change. Admittedly, she lost her well-earned income[7] and was homeless, but the social benefit became a pension substitute,[8] hence, while it was not easy, it was less stressful and demeaning than it was for me. Her inherent optimism greatly helped.

I was in charge of our resettling, of the administrative and financial aspects. While I did not mind this, it felt too big a task for one tired, worn-out person. On top of being homeless, I was also jobless again, financially dependent on the state and consequently I felt inadequate and ultimately worthless. I was awarded social benefits, but I would have preferred to have been asked to mop the post office floor before receiving the money. Handouts and charity did not sit comfortably with me. I found it difficult to resign myself to a position of one forever in need, not ever in a position to give. My second bout of depression began.

Finding a flat to rent for the two us was a relief. At least we would be on our own. We depended on state support for that too, which I disliked, but we had no choice. Henika, who was then working, was our guarantor. Soon, we moved in. From there, we made frequent trips to the solicitor. I had to write various reports for him. I, again, did not have a typewriter, so I was grateful when Tamara lent me one.

We had to count our pennies. I loved cooking and was a gourmet cook, my mother much less so. Gourmet cooking had to be forgotten, but luckily we did not have to go hungry. We could afford inexpensive ingredients to cook with. I did miss some foods: prawns, for instance, or as many tomatoes as I wanted. Tomatoes again and sweets too! My food cravings had to be put on hold.

Now that my mother spent so much time with Ella, her sister-in-law, I felt abandoned, with no support from anywhere. The clash between Tanja and me had spilled over into the rest of the family, which made things more difficult. I felt pretty much on my own, deserted, isolated. Henika was worried about the state I was in and tried to help by regularly phoning. However nice that was, it did not help much. My depression deepened.

On top of that, there were some psychological remnants of the Sarajevo experiences. Even though it was more than three years since we had left the shelling and shooting, I still found the sound of thunder and fireworks upsetting. It was a struggle to ward off the fear. We had moved into our flat not long before Guy Fawkes Night. That certainly was reminiscent of our nightmarish memories. Our adverse reaction was in sharp contrast to the rather cheery reality of the outside world. Quite a discrepancy there, which was disturbing. In addition, we had the kind of a home that did not feel like a home. It took a while. I tried to give it a personal touch. I blue-tacked an improvised collage of photos on the wall and displayed our little ivory 'elephants for luck' we had brought from Sarajevo, to have some familiar objects around us. Eventually, it stopped being an impersonal ambience; we made it ours as far as we could.

We felt we had everything we needed, because we needed little. We bought some household items, new coffee mugs, for example. Yet again, we had somebody else's furniture, but we managed to ignore that fact. We both made an effort to make our new life work, to turn the flat into a home. Moreover, we had our privacy and safety, which was of utmost importance. We started feeling freedom within ourselves and freedom in the world around us. Although our lives were restricted by our refugee circumstances, both my mother and I felt less tense.

However, although the absence of tension was a welcome change, I still realized that I was unwell. Namely, I became aware that I was spending more and more time in bed. The feeling of uselessness, of isolation, a lack of meaning and direction, a lack of vision for the future of any shape or form took over. I had to do something about it. I remembered that, for me, work was the most effective 'antidepressant'; it had always been my way out of misery. Therefore, I started searching for any work I felt I could do. Not teaching, of course, I knew I could not hope to get that. I applied for a job as a receptionist at a nearby university, but was unsuccessful. I went to an interview for a nanny – not that

I felt highly qualified for it – but was turned down there, too. In desperation, I decided that I should at least try to volunteer somewhere. Having been saved by Jewish organizations, my feeling of guilt for ignoring my Jewish identity for so long increased. I felt I owed the Jewish organizations more than I could ever give back. The fact was that my family and I literally owed our lives to them was not a hyperbole, it was the truth. With that in mind, I went to the Jewish Care offices that were conveniently located in the same area of London. I offered to volunteer. I was given a task of leading weekly discussion groups in a day care centre and, importantly, I was given the opportunity to borrow books. I mostly chose books on Judaism which expanded my knowledge of the subject matter. Volunteering did give me something to do, but provided neither financial reward nor the self-affirmation I needed so much.

Admittedly, those discussions reminded me of teaching, so I mostly enjoyed them. Only occasionally, there were few unpleasant moments: I had people object to me (and other refugees) coming to the UK, for instance. It was not particularly personal, I knew, but it hurt. It revived the refugee stigma as well as my 'refugee complex'. At the same time, there were a few highly sympathetic people. One of them, approaching his nineties, desperately tried to help me. He would ask around for a 'proper job' for me, one that would suit me. There was nothing he could do about it, but his willingness to help was both touching and reassuring.

At about that time, I renewed my friendship with Stoja,[9] a Sarajevo schoolmate, who was among the Sarajevo Jewish refugee group that arrived in London before us. He helped me enrol on a computer course offered by a company where he had a part time job. The course was free and very skilfully done, by a volunteer, I believe. Access to a computer was provided to those who needed it, in a Jewish Care office, and I needed it. The course was not only interesting, but helpful too. It was a necessary skill, I felt. If I were to get a job anywhere, computer literacy was a requirement. On top of that, these activities kept me occupied one way or another.

I also joined La Benevolencija, a society the Sarajevo group of refugees had established. It was an offshoot of a Sarajevo Jewish humanitarian organization with the same name. The group organized various events, as well as publishing the journal *SaLon*. They asked me to join the editorial board, which I readily accepted. I felt that was another way I could repay my debt to Jewish organizations and, in a way, make amends for my previous 'non-Jewishness', which kept bothering me.

I continued working for **SaLon** *even when I got married and moved to Cambridge. My husband, Ned Goy, a 'goy' – in Hebrew and Yiddish 'goy' is a* *term for a gentile, a non-Jew – also took part in the work. We translated texts and he proofread texts others had translated. The collaboration lasted till our disagreement with the editorial board regarding an editorial decision which we believed represented censorship and was based on ethnic biases, replicating those of 1992 Sarajevo. We both strongly opposed censorship in principle, especially that based on any sort of bias or prejudice. So, it was with regret, that we stopped our cooperation with the journal.*

However helpful all that was, it was still not enough to keep me busy and give me a sense of purpose. Therefore, I thought, another way to help myself would be to take a TEFL[10] course. I loved teaching. Only with this course could I hope to get any teaching job in the new country.[11] Yet, even for that, I needed money that I did not have. At La Benevolencija, I was advised to apply for a grant. I did, and was told to go to a liberal synagogue where a rabbi[12] would interview me.

I was quite uncomfortable going there. I wondered how I, a person who only started a process of discovering her Jewishness, a person who had not identified with Judaism for so long, could ask for support from a rabbi. In order to alleviate my discomfort, I decided to come clean straightaway, I fear in a rather rude manner. Namely, as soon as I entered his office, I said that I had originally come from a Jewish family, but knew next to nothing about Judaism. I added that I had always considered myself a Yugoslav, at least while I was allowed to. I said I did not feel eligible for the grant. The rabbi was kind and empathetic. He told me that he saw no conflict there. He was Jewish and British too. The two were not mutually exclusive, so neither would my Yugoslav identity be with my Jewish one. I calmed down and spent some time talking to him. I felt heard and accepted. He invited me to the synagogue on Saturdays, not so much for the service, he said, but more for the social gathering afterwards, to start networking. Having seen my CV, he was hoping someone might have an idea where I could look for a job. I was desperate to find one, I admitted. (I was also awarded the grant.)

That Saturday I went to the synagogue. Yet again I did not know the customs, did not know what I was expected to do. I felt out of place. However, as predicted, I met various people. Most of them made me feel welcome and I continued going there almost every Saturday. With time, I felt very comfortable there. Some of the people I met were more traditional than observant. I could relate to them. They invited me to restaurants and their homes. I was grateful and delighted.

I completed my TEFL course. It was not difficult. Previously, both in my undergraduate programme as well as in my MA one, I had had several modules on the methodology of language teaching. The course actually felt somewhat pointless and redundant; there was nothing challenging or interesting there; nothing new to learn. The sense that the course was more a waste of time than anything else did not help, although it kept me occupied. I needed a diploma, so I did all the required work.

My feeling of exhaustion increased. Around that time, my mother broke her pelvis. Luckily, the fracture was not too bad, so she still could walk and carry on visiting her sister-in-law. I worried, but could not be there to help her much. I had to attend the course every day. I travelled in the morning from North to Central London and back home in the evening when I had to cook and prepare presentations for the next day's class. It certainly was not a happy time for me. I was not feeling well, so I found it fraught running a home on limited funds and doing all sorts of budgeting.

Soon after I completed my TEFL course, the rabbi engaged me to 'curate' an exhibition by an Austrian painter[13] at the synagogue and I was to be paid for it. Earning some money, albeit a small amount, meant a lot for my confidence. I knew it was my presence that was required, not my expertise. Still, it was yet further proof that I was perhaps accepted, trusted and even valued. I desperately needed that kind of boost, or any kind of boost for that matter, considering the state I was in.

By then, I had to admit to myself that my depression was getting the better of me. I felt stuck and helpless; I had no idea what to do about it. It was my second bout of depression and it seemed rather more serious. (It did not occur to me that I could go to a GP.) Some people at the synagogue noticed my state and offered to finance psychotherapy sessions for me. I refused. I felt I had already benefitted from their help; it was somebody else's turn to get their support now. My depression worsened and I was eventually advised to turn to my GP and ask for psychotherapy. I was put on the waiting list. In the meantime, in early 1996 yet again, just as in Belgrade, I was offered a job, which I happily accepted. It was a job of a lector at SSEES – School of Slavonic and East European Studies – at University College London and I did not need therapy any longer.

Finding Home

At the end of the spring semester in 1996, the lector at SSEES, a former Sarajevo colleague of mine,[14] left and they needed a replacement. Some lecturers at SSEES knew me professionally and, one way or another, I got a job. I loved my job. I was lucky again. I was among students again. I regained some of my identity. I was working again, I was useful, and my life gradually started gaining meaning.

At SSEES, I worked with Duško, who was teaching Yugoslav literature. I had met him previously, but we became closer while teaching the same students. We worked on the same days. He had been invited to the UK in the 1970s, stayed on in the country and taught at various universities. He had enormous empathy for Bosnian refugees and tried to help as much as he could. His selfless nature and kindness were exceptional. He and his wife Tilda often invited my mother and me (and many other Sarajevo refugees) to their house. When he was asked by the office of an extremely eminent VIP to recommend a Serbo-Croat language instructor, he recommended me, so I became a language tutor to a TRH[15] couple who needed Serbo-Croat lessons. I was now earning some money. No more post office, no more social benefits, no more handouts.

Summer came, and a long university holiday. I was not looking forward to it and Duško knew it. For me, it meant no work, but also no contact with Duško or the students. Duško was going on a longish trip with his wife. I did not have many friends in the country and I certainly could not travel abroad. I could not afford travelling in general, but also, I did not have a passport so it was out of the question. Duško was worried about me. I had recovered, but not fully. He could sense that.

At the same time, he was worried about Ned, a friend and a colleague in Cambridge. Ned had been compelled to take early retirement from Cambridge University because he was teaching Yugoslav studies and that, as a subject, had been abolished. It upset him. Not least because the country whose literature and culture he had spent so much time researching and teaching suddenly ceased to exist. Also, not long before that, Ned lost his wife. Consequently, he was not in a good place. That troubled Duško. Duško also believed that it was a pity to let Ned's enormous knowledge and expertise of Yugoslav literature go to waste. He gave Ned a tape-recorded and convinced him that it would be good to record his various lectures on Yugoslav literature. The plan was to have them transcribed and eventually published. So, the idea was born: Duško's two friends he was concerned about, Ned and I, would each have a task, which would make both of us feel useful and busy. Ned was to carry on recording his lectures and I was to transcribe them. Duško gave me a few finished tapes he already had and told me to get in touch with Ned to keep him in the loop. I accepted the task with pleasure. More work close to my interest.

Whether Duško had something more in mind, matchmaking maybe,[16] we never discovered, and not for the lack of asking. Duško never said either way. Undoubtedly, he did us a huge favour, in more than simply dealing with recording and transcribing, for which we were eternally grateful.

Be that as it may, other than transcribing the lectures, something more did happen. I turned the first tape to the 'wrong' side and listened to Ned's ruminations, which I found highly interesting. I also liked the deep baritone, the beautiful English, the masterly turn of phrase. People believe in love at first sight, but, with me, it was love at first sound. I was so intrigued and attracted by what I heard that I soon found an excuse to ring Ned. We had a long conversation and Ned asked if he could ring me back some time. He rang me a few days later. Then I rang him. And then he rang, and then …

That summer, Sida came to visit. To my delight, the relationship between the two of us seemed back to normal. No past grudges in sight. My mother was very happy to host Sida and the two of them spent a lot of time together. Sida stayed for about a month. They went shopping, visited acquaintances, invited people over and prepared food they both enjoyed. The visit seemed to improve my mother's mood, where the antidepressants did not. That was a relief. With this somewhat positive attitude, I started seriously transcribing the tapes Duško had given me.

In September that year, 1996, I celebrated my birthday in our new home.[17] It was not a big event, but I did not want to ignore it – birthday celebrations used to be big affairs in our family.[18] Around the time of my birthday the difficulties in the relationship with my mother came to a head. By then we had had several gruelling exchanges; neither capable of controlling her outbursts. She seemed angry all the time,[19] mostly with me, and showed it at my birthday as well. There was no gift, nor a cake for me. I was disappointed and hurt. As for the family, only Henika and Tamara came. The rest boycotted me because of the row with Tanja. In spite of all that, I made the day special with a few delicacies Nina had sent from Germany which I could not have afforded otherwise. It was not the happiest of occasions. Loneliness, depression, family rift, general predicament – all the reasons why nothing could cheer me up, not even my job that I liked. By then I had had several phone conversations with Ned and had complained to him about my miserable birthday. That surprised me as I was a rather private person; how come I had opened up to him, I wondered.

I managed to transcribe one tape, the 'right' side of it. I soon visited Ned in Cambridge with the transcript in my hands. However, we never got to looking at it. We talked, we flirted and, overall, enjoyed each other's company. Then, more phone calls followed, more visits to Cambridge, until a rainy night when allegedly Ned could not get a taxi to take me to the station. That night in mid-September 1996, I stayed over. And more or less never left.

Ned proposed. (Time and events again followed a very speedy trajectory.) I refused. My sentimental, naïve, schoolgirl-like idea was that I did not want to besmirch our lovely, pure relationship with any immigration advantage that might ensue. (I still had not had my immigration status resolved). Luckily, both my old friend Stephen[20] and Ned himself were convincing enough, and I finally 'succumbed'. I had not believed that a piece of paper meant anything. I realized only later how much it meant to me. So, it all made sense.

We applied at the registry office. I submitted my Belgrade divorce papers. Ned had suggested not complicating matters with my real marriage and the Sarajevo divorce. A few days later, we were stunned when the registrar informed us that the wedding could not be allowed since I was officially a bigamist. I had got married in one country in 1992, got divorced in another the same year, and neither my husband nor I were nationals of that particular country, it was argued. Ned was furious. He called his solicitor, who managed to find an interpretation of the law that overruled the registry's decision. In the meantime, I contacted my 'ex-husband', Saša, who sent me copies of his wedding certificates for his marriage with Cica. I thought if he could marry again and was not a bigamist, then neither was I. I hoped that might convince the registry officials. In any event, the documents were not needed. Everything was happily resolved with the help of Ned's solicitor. In February 1997, we had a very private ceremony with only witnesses present: Stephen and Duško, and Tilda too. We had lunch at a local restaurant and came home delighted. Unfortunately, it being a Friday, there were no photographers at the registry office and the wedding party did not have a camera. Therefore, we had no wedding photographs.

When I informed my London solicitor that I had got married, he suggested I applied for a different immigration status, the status of a spouse of a UK citizen.[21] Something I initially resented, but came to accept. Ned and I filled in all sorts of forms. We were asked for wedding photos. We had none, but it turned out that this was not a big obstacle. The questions in the form were mostly about Ned. It made him laugh, but also irritated him. In one of the questions, he was asked to state the year he came/immigrated to the UK. With tongue in cheek, he replied 'in the seventeenth century'.[22] The Home Office also wanted him to submit his building society passbook. He refused. The whole process made both of us quite nervous. What if the application was refused?

I was now living in Cambridge. My mother remained in London. She did not want to move to Cambridge, even though Ned and I suggested it. She moved into a smaller flat in the same area and Ned and I helped her move. She was then within walking distance of her sister-in-law. She was often still angry and resentful towards me although she kept taking the prescribed antidepressants. But Ned, on the other hand, could do nothing wrong. I liked that.

Eventually, a consultant prescribed a different antidepressant for my mother. That one suited her and her behaviour changed so much so that I had my old, loving mother back.[23] *She was finally ready to receive my love and give love back in abundance too.*

She and I were on the telephone daily. We sometimes had phone conversations twice a day. I was still in charge of my mother's administrative and financial affairs. She visited us from time to time and we visited her regularly. Henika would come to see us at my mother's. Ned and Henika grew fond of each other. Tamara also met Ned, while the rest of the family never met him, a fact that saddened me.

The first Christmas Ned and I spent together was something I enjoyed hugely, although Christmas did not mean much to either of us. But it was the right occasion for me to show Ned my culinary abilities, impress him and, at the same time, enjoy the good food I had missed for so long. However, on the evening I did not exactly impress him much! Yes, the food was very good. Yes, he was pleased. Nevertheless, I was a bit embarrassed. I over-ate and made myself sick. My craving for quality food and sweets was in full swing. I just could not control myself. We laughed about it later and referred to it as the 'fudge and figs' day.

'Refugee' remained a dirty word for me. I felt the weight of the stigma it carried. Luckily, Ned not only loved me, but he was in tune with me and determined to help me. He could grasp all my weaknesses and quirks; he simply knew how to be with me. Consequently, he sensed the depth of my discomfort with the burden of refugee status. It took hard work and quite some time for him to enable me to get rid of the sense of shame buried deep within me. He knew I had my reasons for it and recognized the manifestations. Often, they were pretty obvious. For instance, I was reluctant to take a taxi, arguing, 'Refugees do not take taxis'. I refused to go to Heffers, a famous Cambridge bookshop, because 'I do not belong there any more', because 'it remained in my past life' and so on and so forth. With Ned's support, I gradually started to get rid of these feelings. I went to Heffers to buy some books for Ned and engaged in, according to me, activities 'not appropriate' for refugees. Finally, one day, I came home and complained about 'those foreigners who jump taxi queues' (without being aware of what I had said). Ned just looked at me and only then did I realize what I had said. 'Those foreigners!' We laughed. We celebrated the occasion. I had finally arrived HOME!

Every time I went to London to visit my mother, Ned came with me. My mother adored him. He had saved her daughter, she would say. Saved her as well. He was our messiah, she told everybody. From the outset there was a strange affinity between the two of them. For my mother, he was not only a man who made her daughter happy, but also an Englishman who spoke her language fluently and understood her culture. He even liked Serbian bean soup! As for Ned, he liked her gentle manner and her kindness.

Having acquired my TEFL diploma, I felt I wanted to try it out in practice. Ned encouraged me. I found myself a job teaching at a language school during the first summer in Cambridge, in 1997. I proved to myself that I could do it. That was all I needed, a confidence boost.

The next summer, when the school again invited me to teach, I declined.

When Ned and I celebrated my first birthday together we celebrated it at my mother's. I had had one too many to drink and I accused Ned of disappointing me. He refused to go to a restaurant for supper that evening and I told him I thought he was perfect, yet he was only *nearly* perfect! He laughed and said that nobody had ever given him a bigger compliment. We hugely enjoyed being with each other.

Having seen that teaching English went well, I took up another challenge. I started interpreting for the immigration service, the police and the courts, places I barely knew. I enjoyed that. It was a completely new and exciting experience. It all seemed like a well-rehearsed theatre performance; everybody knew their roles and everybody stuck to them. I was fascinated; a new unfamiliar world opened up for me. In addition, I wanted to earn some money on my own account. Ned encouraged me again.

My life was running smoothly, so the invitation to teach at SSEES again was not that attractive. Frankly, the money was not enough to make commuting worthwhile and I did not need to prove anything to anybody anymore. Above all, I did not want to spend too much time away from Ned. Therefore, I declined. Interpreting, which I started doing less and less of, did not take so much time away from home anyway. Home actually meant work, leisure, comfort and safety; it offered all I needed.

Soon, after a short illness, my uncle Moni died in London. My mother had helped Ella look after him at home while he was ill. (Henika and Tanja were mostly not at home during the day.) However, it was too much for my frail mother and, after the funeral, I brought her to Cambridge to recover with us for a few days. It helped her. She liked Cambridge and enjoyed being pampered. I enjoyed pampering her.

I greatly enjoyed my Cambridge life. I felt rooted; I could again talk about 'my fishmonger', 'my greengrocer', 'my favourite shops and shop assistants'. Also, importantly, they knew me and were accommodating. Ned and I would go to our local most evenings and socialize. I felt I belonged. Many people visited us, both Ned's and my colleagues and friends from the UK, from the former Yugoslavia and elsewhere. One of those who came to visit was Richard, Ned's Cambridge acquaintance, who had taught English in Yugoslavia and had been married to a Yugoslav.

Richard had recently divorced his Yugoslav wife who happened to be my namesake. He had married her while working in Belgrade, where he also heard about Ned's work and came to visit him upon his return to the UK. Somehow, with me around, our bond with Richard grew stronger.

We would meet up with Richard from time to time. Soon he got together with Melanie, his new partner, and she and I clicked immediately. We started meeting up more often and we soon became closer. I was pleased to have a friend like Melanie. I was a bit apprehensive, though. If I got too close and lost the friendship for whatever reason, would I be hurt again? Nevertheless, I took a risk.

Unfortunately, my hunch was right: the friendship was short-lived.

Quite soon a new challenge presented itself. Ned suggested we translate Yugoslav novels and a number of other texts[24] together. Now we had a computer; no more typewriters. However, I had always suffered from scriptophobia. To prepare either articles or translations for publication had been an uphill struggle for me. Yet, working on anything together with Ned was hugely attractive. So, I agreed. As a consequence, interpreting went onto the backburner. (Anyway, it became repetitive and no longer attractive.) We decided on the novel, got all the permissions as well as the interested publisher and we started. Translating with Ned was the most enjoyable work I had ever done. It was one of the best times of my life. Such peace and happiness within myself I had never felt.

Both Ned and I believed that we inspired each other to work, to write and to express ourselves. We each had several articles published during our time together. But above all, we loved translating. It was extremely gratifying and meaningful work. 'The Levinger/Goy[25] workshop', as we referred to it, worked like a well-oiled machine. That was an additional bond we had.

I had eventually realized my lifelong dream: I had found love and my faith in the power of love was confirmed. I have always believed that love is essential and that it is a strong motivational force. It creates a sense of happiness and fulfilment; it has both healing and enriching qualities. Ned and I proved it; we could not have been happier together. We provided each other everything each needed individually. Most importantly, we were aware of our luck and happiness. We fully enjoyed the unhindered togetherness, closeness and love.

Among the many things that Ned and I had in common, there was one of lesser significance and rather odd: the way the fall of Yugoslavia had affected us. While I was compelled to leave home when the country ceased to exist,[26] Ned was compelled to leave his job at Cambridge University, his intellectual home. He was given early retirement when the module he taught ceased to exist.

We had our daily routine. In the morning, Ned would 'doodle', as he called it, while I was on the computer, emailing my friends now all over the world. After lunch, we would do the translating and early evenings we would be in our local. We were together day and night. We worked together, went shopping together, cooked together,[27] went to the pub, to restaurants, entertained and visited people, did more or less everything together. I loved to spend evenings watching TV with my head on his knees while he massaged my head with one hand, holding his pipe with the other. We rarely argued. Ned made it impossible for me to pick a row. He would very often dissipate my anger by making me laugh.

There was quite a big age difference between us; it bothered Ned more than me. He sometimes talked about his death, me being left on my own. I could not stand that topic. Somehow, I hoped we would end life together. My denial in action again! I tried to make him feel better about it, rather clumsily, mostly by refusing to talk about it, which probably had the opposite effect. He, however, wanted to prepare me. He said he wanted to find a boyfriend for me and instruct him how to deal with me. He even asked Richard to find somebody. I hated that with a passion (Although somehow somewhere I admired his selflessness.) I could not think about losing him. How could anyone ever be prepared for the ultimate loss?

He was not ill, but I wanted to keep it that way as long as possible. I tried to make him eat healthily and drink less whisky. He liked his tipple. Grudgingly, he succumbed. Actually, he liked the attention he was getting. He had not had too much of that in life. He had been married before, but not happily. I was his third wife. (Formally speaking, he was my third husband too, counting my bogus marriage.) Third time lucky, we used to say.

I enjoyed having my own home, the home where I was 'in charge', the one I adjusted to our individual needs. I was happy and proud to welcome friends into my home and to introduce Ned to people from my 'previous life', as I would refer to them. I realized I still had quite a few friends; starting with those from my early days, to those I met later: from Goran,[28] my Sarajevo friend since the age of 6, to Melanie whom I met in Cambridge in my 'third life'.[29] Contact with friends was about the only element of continuity in my life.

However, the reminder of my previous life came from unexpected quarters. It must have been in the second half of the 1990s that stories of privatization of the flats in which we used to live in Sarajevo reached us. We began inquiries, but it all seemed rather far-fetched. However, unexpectedly, my friend Pavle got in touch. He was back in Sarajevo. He and his friend had been to the block of flats where I used to live, opened my garage and found my car in it. I asked him to sell the garage for me.[30] He did. I happily received the money. Small satisfaction or compensation for all the losses? Pavle asked what I wanted to do with the car. Ned and I agreed to offer it to him. He was delighted and accepted the offer. The car had no windshield and the petrol tank was full of sugar. Obviously, for some Sarajevo people, it had not only been about looting, but about vandalism as well. Pavle had the car fixed and it served him well for quite a while.

As time went by, there was more and more talk about the need to go to Sarajevo in order to sort out property. I could not easily go there – I had no passport – nor did I want to. I did not want to be away from Ned for too long. But, equally importantly and understandably, I feared the animosity and hatred. The flat, in which various people lived during those years, had to be formally repossessed by the original resident, i.e. me (or my mother who was too frail to travel). The alternative was to authorize a solicitor to represent us, I was told. A solicitor was recommended. I rang him, and sent him a letter of power of attorney, authorizing him to evict the people illegally occupying my flat. He agreed, took the fee, but later rang me to say he could not do it: he felt sorry for those unfortunate people who wanted to stay there because of their children's education; they couldn't return to their nearby village, he said. He then added that, after all, he, the solicitor, had to carry on living in that same Sarajevo; it was easy for me – I was far away, he claimed. A strange way of pursuing the law. However, nothing could surprise me anymore. Had I not lived through a great number of absurdities?

Ned helped me with all the turmoil with my Sarajevo flat, with negotiating options and solutions. He could follow all the various telephone conversations in Serbo-Croat I had and he would make suggestions. There was a time, though, when I hastily did the opposite of what he suggested. He told me not to accept the first price the buyer offered, so, precipitate as I was and eager to get it over with, I right away lowered the price. We both laughed. Yet, all those negotiations proved futile for one reason or another.

It was only much later that I finally started serious proceedings for the 'repossession' and sale of my flat.

Although Ned's Serbo-Croat was excellent, I never spoke Serbo-Croat with him. He used it communicating with Henika and my mother. When we were together, the situation might have seemed awkward to some. Not to us. I interchangeably used both languages: Serbo-Croat with my mother or Henika and English with Ned. Ned used both languages, too: Serbo-Croat with his mother-in-law or with Henika, and English with me. Only my mother, who had minimal command of English, spoke only Serbo-Croat to both me and Ned. Henika also spoke mostly Serbo-Croat. An interesting subject for a sociolinguistic research, perhaps. Yet Ned and I sometimes had arguments over the right and wrong way of speaking Serbo-Croat. Ned claimed that I corrupted the language. He was right in a way, as more often than not, I used colloquial or slangy forms.

I catch myself these days feeling the same resentment about sloppy use of English, even in the media.

Serbo-Croat was present when we did our translations, of course. We would both have suggestions for English translations and always accepted the best one. There was no competition there; nuances in both languages were discussed. I only had a problem directly communicating with Ned in Serbo-Croat. A possible explanation was that Ned represented my new beginning, my new life, the life I loved, the life I had been hoping for all my life and achieved rather late, in the UK (albeit not naturalized yet). It was my life in English, my English life. Moreover, it became clear that I could deeply love in a 'foreign'[31] language, as well as, unfortunately, grieve in it.

As if I had not had enough shocking experiences, yet another incredible, unexpected and awful event was about to occur. In 1999, Ned and I watched with horror the NATO bombing[32] of Belgrade and Novi Sad. Aerial bombardment, and of civilian targets too, in the middle of Europe in the twentieth century! In a way, my fear while in Belgrade was justified, except it was not the conflict from Bosnia and Herzegovina that spilled over, as I had feared then. Both Ned and I were distressed. I was mostly worried about Igor. He was only 10. Not the experience one would want for somebody one loved. We arranged everything for him to come to the UK and stay with my mother until the bombing stopped. Sanja thought it was unnecessary. Whether he was traumatized by it remained unclear. However, other than psychological damage, the family did not suffer any other damage.

In early 2000, the long-awaited Home Office decision arrived. I was granted permission to stay in the country, and both Ned and I were relieved. We celebrated 'our success'. I was on my way to becoming a UK citizen. Ned always teased me about my Slavonic origin. He claimed that I had no more Slavonic blood than he. We both spoke the language,[33] which was the only Slavonic trait either of us had. Therefore, I was as much Slavonic as he was and consequently not rooted in the country. Mostly true, actually. In any case, I felt I was more than ready to become British. That was in fact truer than I could have predicted.

The Fateful Loss

One sunny day in March 2000, Ned asked me to take him to his old house where he had lived as a young man. We went there and, after that, had lunch in our favourite pub. We returned home and Ned told me he wanted me to know how happy I had made him and how much he loved me. It did sort of come out of the blue, but it was nice to hear. I assumed the 'time travel' to his old home had triggered it. In the evening, as he was setting the date for next day on his old clock, he mentioned that the only superstition he had was to do with the number 13. The next day was the 13th, so he referred to it as 12Bth! I thought nothing of it, just another witty remark. Later that evening, the evening prior to 12Bth, an aortic aneurysm struck. Did he have some premonition? Is there such a thing? I did not believe in it, but could not stop wondering.

That fateful day, we started translating our third novel.[34] We were very much looking forward to it. Sometime late that evening, while watching a movie, Ned suddenly doubled over in pain and told me that was it. I refused to believe it. The ambulance came quickly. I suspected it was a heart attack, as did the paramedics. However, in the emergency room I noticed red blotches on his stomach. I knew what it meant but could not remember. Panic struck; I had a weird feeling that if only I could remember what it was everything would be all right. Obviously not a heart attack. He was very quickly rolled through to the operating theatre. I kissed him and promised to be there when he came back. I was hopeful; I could not accept anything else. Ned did not share my optimism.

I was taken to a small room provided for family members. A doctor came with me and told me it was an aortic aneurysm and that they had decided to operate immediately. He tried to explain things, but I could not hear anything. The hours spent in that little room were, even taking everything I had lived through into consideration, the worst four hours of my life. Every shadow I could see through a curtained window overlooking the corridor meant some sort of news. I was overwhelmed with fear. Each hour meant hope that Ned was still alive and that the operation might be successful. However, I could not get his words 'That is it, darling' out of my head. I kept fluctuating between positive and negative. I tried to comfort myself by believing that the fact the operation was lasting so long ought to give me hope.

After four hours, at about 3 a.m. on the 13th (12Bth), the surgeon came and told me that the operation had been unsuccessful. Ned had passed away. I could not and did not ask anything. The kind surgeon gave me his card and told me to feel free to ask him anything I needed to know any time later. There was nothing I needed to know. I just knew that Ned was gone and that I was lost again. My world stopped; my life was over. I had reached the end of the road. While I was still in hospital I rang our suspected matchmaker, Duško, in London at the crack of dawn to tell him the awful news. He was shocked, and soon came to Cambridge to be with me. My 'new' friend, Melanie, came to the hospital. She took me to their home.[35] It was then that my nightmare started. My third and most serious bout of depression began then. It lasted for quite a long time.

The next morning, Sida was due to come to London for a visit. I was planning to pick her up at the airport. I did not, I could not. The most I could do was to organize a taxi to pick her up. The day after that, both my mother and Sida came to visit me. My friend, Stoja, the 'computer guru' from London, brought them. I was numb, functioning on autopilot.

At the registry office where I went to register Ned's death, I ran into the registrar who had married us not so long before. I turned to him and said, 'Do you remember me? You married us and now I've come to ask you to bury us.' That was what it felt like to me, burying my life. The registrar was bemused, but Melanie, who had accompanied me, apologized and explained. Melanie was helping me a lot.

Duško took over organizing the funeral. It was not easy to find an environmentally friendly cemetery near Cambridge at the time. We managed to find one in Bedford. That was what Ned had requested. The funeral itself was a private, non-religious ceremony – again as Ned had requested. (Arranging it I made sure they could bury me in the same grave when the time comes.) We asked that the chapel be emptied of any religious symbols. Yet with or without symbols it felt a cold, alien and unfriendly place. Milica,[36] our non-officially fostered granddaughter (who by then had moved from Cambridge to London), stayed in Cambridge with me, helped me get ready and held my hand both literally and metaphorically. At the funeral Duško and I decided to play a classic Russian song and a popular Serbian one,[37] both of which Ned used to sing to me in his warm, soft baritone. Duško and Richard spoke at the funeral, as well as Stephen (our wedding witnesses). I was there, but miles away at the same time. My legs started jerking uncontrollably, as if they were not attached to my body. Apparently, it was visible, something similar to restless legs syndrome, I was told later. Hugely unpleasant. Henika, who was sitting next to me put her hand on my knees. All I could see was the green cardboard box, the coffin I chose, in front of me and also the flowers I chose on top of it. But was I able to acknowledge that my Ned was in there? I did put a note under the flowers. A message for him. A promise of loving reunion. Did I believe in it? Probably not, but hope was there. I simply did not and could not accept the reality, so

I eventually drifted off. I had arranged a little get-together in our pub after the funeral. Only those closest to me came home afterwards. Allegedly, I had an enormous amount of Scotch that did not affect me at all.

Duško was a great support. He brought all the newspaper obituaries that had appeared both in the UK and in the former Yugoslavia. He also consulted me on the gathering organized later by University College London in celebration of Ned's work and life. A group of former students and colleagues talked about Ned, both his work and about him as a person. They said he was a unique personality at Cambridge University, sometimes ahead of his time. It filled me with pride. Duško also helped me with sorting out Ned's notes, bits and pieces of paper and finding forgotten manuscripts.[38] I wanted to carry on working on his manuscripts. That way I felt I was keeping Ned alive and was close to him.

My desire to be near Ned was so strong that I often expected to see him at the door. My mind was playing tricks on me. Denial in action again. Bereavement creates a bizarrely altered state of mind. The pain was so strong that it almost completely paralysed me. I could not sleep, I could not cry and I could not think. My brain waves were moving only to churn out senseless foam onto the surface. Nothing nice or ugly came to mind. Time assumed a curious ability to turn into a subjective impression; long or short both lost their meaning. There was only empty timeless now. As if there had been no past, present or even a glimpse at the future. The darkness within me was scary. How could one ever accept such profound all-encompassing loss? Ned had played several roles in my life. He was my husband and my son, he was my lover and my best friend, he was my work colleague and my psychotherapist. He was a generous source of a myriad of gifts for me, the source I could never stop craving. Sunny days started offending me; rainy ones I felt were in tune with the state I was in. They made me feel as if I had been 'at the bottom of the village pond' (the phrase Ned sometimes used to describe such days). Except I was so overwhelmed by the mud and mire that I eventually felt completely enveloped by it. Autopilot was working only partially.

Listening to 'our' Beethoven concertos lost its magic. Almost everything became meaningless. I disliked every activity, including eating, maybe primarily eating. Actually, life itself had much in common with eating; it resembled being force-fed. I was swallowing it without chewing in order to avoid sensing its taste. I was swallowing quickly so as to get it down as fast as possible. But then, just like being force-fed, digesting it became gruelling, painful and long lasting. It certainly was not what I wanted. The only activities that made any sense at the time were those that had anything to do with Ned. I bought a voice recognition programme in order to dictate Ned's old lectures on Russian and

Yugoslav literature. I felt that kept him alive, at least for me. I transcribed quite a few, but did not know what to do with them. I managed to transcribe one tape on verse translation[39] and sent it to my friend,[40] who was the editor-in-chief of a literary journal that published it in 2002. I prepared a manuscript about two Dubrovnik fifteenth-century poets, Menčetić and Držić,[41] which, thanks to Duško, a Belgrade publishing house published. After some time, I put together and edited the unfinished manuscript on the poet Momčilo Nastasijević[42] with both Ned's essays and his translation of poems. An American publisher eventually published the book.[43] I tried to have other manuscripts published, mostly old lectures and translations, but to no avail. I worked almost obsessively. I received galley proofs for our translation of the novel *The Banquet in Blitva*, checked them and returned them to the publisher.[44]

Being on my own was too painful, too overwhelming; the silence seemed deafening. Our bed and Ned's chair were waiting for him, but in vain. I refused to move any of the furniture because I needed my eyes to rest on the familiar arrangement and decor. When I was not working on Ned's manuscripts, I spent a lot of time on the sofa watching TV. Every day felt like an odd, unpleasant continuum, merging into the next. Days felt like one big stretch of nothingness. I was not actually engaged with or aware of anything around me. The TV was on because I had to have sound around me and moving images in front of my eyes. My favourite programmes were adaptations of Jane Austen's novels, which I knew well, so I could just stay with the slow, gentle action and landscapes. Alternatively, I would watch horse racing – I knew nothing about it, but there was sound, movement and colour too. Neither needed any concentration. It was hard to escape the stupor. I found it difficult to cope with, yet there was nothing I felt I could do about it.

Shortly, a conference at University College London entitled 'Language in the Former Yugoslav Lands'[45] came up. I had submitted my application for the conference before Ned's death and had started my research into the divisions of Serbo-Croat while I was working at SSEES. My paper was almost ready. I had done quite a lot of research.[46] Duty driven, as ever, I decided to attend, but reluctantly. I was still quite frail and shaken when I went to London. Duško had arranged with some people to keep an eye on me. I presented the paper[47] in a sort of daze. It was nice, though, to meet colleagues from my 'peacetime' in Yugoslavia, for instance my PhD mentor from Zagreb whom I was very fond of. A Belgrade colleague, my friend and a distinguished linguist who had worked with me in Novi Sad, was at the conference, too. She advised me to take some time off, to allow myself to be weak and vulnerable. There was no further need to put on a brave face on, she told me. How true and soothing those words sounded.

Yet, I was scared, distraught and half-alive. My GP, a caring, empathetic person, visited me weekly. He was worried. It was nice to see him and I was grateful for the visits, but I did not want any medical help; I did not want to live, to exist in this painful place. I was angry. Whatever happened to 'dying of a broken heart'? That was my hope. I told him off but he did not give up on me. My mother visited; she brought me chicken soup, a Jewish panacea. I was glad to see my mother but the soup did not help much.

I made sure to carry out Ned's wish and I planted an English oak sapling at his gravesite when the time came. It was to be our tree. I arranged a small tree-planting ceremony and played another one of the songs Ned used to sing to me. This time it was a jazz song.[48] I also handed out books with Ned's drawings and poems.[49] I liked both. I had framed the drawings he called his doodles and they covered most of the walls. For me, they were works of art. I also cherished his poetry. So, I collected poems, scanned the drawings and assembled them all in a booklet, with the help of my friend Stoja, my computer 'guru'. I then had Milica arrange printing of the book in Belgrade.

I regularly visited my mother in London, who had many a chicken soup prepared with a firm belief in its healing properties, but I was in a daze all the time. Neither my mother's concern nor her chicken soups helped. The fact that my mother herself was grieving did not help either. Ned represented some sort of anchor for her too. She had learned how to divide her loyalty between the two families: the London family of in-laws who kept away from me and Ned and me, her immediate family. It was not an easy task, but she managed with varying success. However, now one point of the 'family triangle' had become destabilized. Without Ned and shattered as I was, I was not much of a support. So, she felt lost and frightened too.

Milica, although she lived in London, by then started looking after me and became a huge support. She would bring me to stay with her for a day or two, took me to theatres, restaurants and even organized my birthday celebration, the first one without Ned, at a London restaurant. I appreciated it but felt Ned's absence even more painfully (if that were possible). She also came up from London to keep me company and took me out from time to time. She genuinely worried about me – she was trying to bring me back to life; whenever she sensed my mood was even darker than usual, she would come to Cambridge. She made my life more bearable, less solitary; without her it would have been much more of a nightmare. What she was doing meant the world to me, but still I was only half there.

Richard put me in touch with a Sarajevo couple in Cambridge, Goca and Senja. He hoped they could be of help, and they were. I had never met them before, but they took it upon themselves to support me in that awful hour of need and they did it so wholeheartedly. I was at their place for lunch every Sunday and spent time with Goca and their son on weekends, visiting sights around Cambridge. I valued their concern and support enormously. Life without them would have been frightfully difficult and lonelier but, in my state, engaging felt like a chore, too.

Eva, my Belgrade friend, now living in Israel, was also worried about me. When a few years before she came to the UK, she visited us and with her exceptional sensibility realized how deep the relationship between Ned and me was. So, when she learned I had lost him, she alerted some of her UK friends and asked them to check up on me. One of her friends, a linguist, I had met when Eva was in the UK, wanted more than just to check up on me. In my desperation I briefly hoped that he might help. I thought I would have somebody to have a glass or two of brandy with in the evening and with whom I could incessantly talk about Ned. But it simply didn't and couldn't work.

I resumed visiting my mother regularly. She needed me and I needed to feel our bond. Yet we were two lost souls sharing sadness and fear, unable to help each other. I often drove back home in tears and driving far too fast. However, on the whole, being with my mother slightly charged my depleted 'batteries'.

All this helped a little. By then, it was obvious that I was to be around for some time to come. Therefore, I was doing all I could to pull out of the debilitating depression, but with little success. I needed work again, I felt. I believed work would speed up my recovery. My interpreting work was not a bad solution, but I needed more of it. For that purpose, I decided to take a DPSI[50] exam at the Institute of Linguists. I applied, but was told I should take the interpreting course the institute offered. I thought that was pointless. I did not want to repeat my TEFL experience. I knew my abilities and knew I could just take the exam. I fought for it, and took the exam in 2001. I passed with flying colours. I needed this encouragement. (Later, I became their examiner.) I started getting some work from various police stations and courts. I was not too busy, but I had some work. At about the same time, my GP introduced me to the person in charge of the Cambridge Linguistic Society, a local branch of the Institute of Linguists, and I joined the society. I made friends there. They asked me to give a talk on the language divisions in former Yugoslavia and I did. I gradually started 'waking' from the unbearable nightmare that life had become.

In the summer of 2001, Igor, aged 12, arrived in the UK for a visit with his grandmother, Sida.[51] He was to stay with my mother and Sida in London, but he was bored with them. Therefore, I invited him to come to Cambridge, although I feared that he might remember the moment I had called the police to throw his father out, when he was about 3, and hold it against me. Children sometimes remember events from that age, especially traumatic ones. None of that. He agreed and I went to London to fetch him. We re-established the loving relationship we had had since almost the day he was born.

We used to have non-verbal telephone 'conversations' while I was still in Sarajevo: only the intonation would hint at the meaning of short exchanges. Later, in Belgrade in 1992, we carried out conversations that only the two of us understood.

He was a boy of few words, shy. Although grieving, I made an effort to make his stay bearable, if not nice. Although Goca's and Senja's son was a bit older, he was a good companion for Igor, so Goca, the two boys and I did things together. In addition, Cambridge and the surroundings had a lot to offer to a 12-year-old. We spent time punting, visiting the countryside, landmarks and museums. There were times when I could not hold back the tears and Igor would comfort me. I was not too happy to show my grief in front of him, but I could not help it and his tenderness was both touching and soothing. Overall, we did have a good time together. When the time came, I took Igor back to London to join Sida for the trip home. The next morning, while I was having a shower, I noticed on the bathroom mirror a message he had left for me (visible only when the steam clouded the mirror). The message read, 'Igor loves Jasna' in both languages and both scripts.[52]

Later that same year, I was naturalized and became a UK citizen. After all the transitions the family and I personally had endured, I felt I could now finally define my identity. I saw myself as a British Traditional Secular Jew of Yugoslav origin. Complicated maybe, but it felt right. I even surprised myself. Traditional and secular were relatively easy to explain, at least to myself. That was clear. Growing up surrounded by a Jewish family, it was inevitable one picked up traditional elements of Judaism. It was present in our daily functioning, starting with specific vocabulary, an occasional traditional Jewish dish to some attitudes and values. But we were certainly not practising Jews, not in terms of celebrating holidays or adhering to dietary restrictions. As for the secular aspect, that was even more obvious. The wider society as a whole advocated atheism, which my immediate family accepted, so 'by default' I could be nothing other than secular, albeit of the agnostic variant. The other three – British, Jewish, Yugoslav – were a bit more complicated. I knew I'd got it right by checking it against the rational arguments, but also through testing my visceral reactions to each element of the identity respectively.

My British identity was rooted in my early affiliation with the culture and my intellectual engagement with it. It was founded on familiarity with the language, literature and history of the country. Studying it, I developed an attachment and fondness of things British, so there was an emotional dimension to it as well.

After all, the language I taught was what was known as British English or Oxford English (with pointing to the differences with the US variant).[53] I had a sense of 'distant belonging' or 'belonging by proxy'. Added to that, at the university we would refer to the staff of each department collectively as 'the English', 'the French', 'the Russians' and so on, depending which department one was teaching at. So, my colleagues and I were referred to as 'the English'. Not hugely significant, but indicative maybe. On top of all that, frequent visits to the UK also made it closer and more familiar. Finally, my gratitude for the refuge the UK had offered was a significant factor, too. I had actually felt at home in Britain from rather early days in the country. However, above all and most importantly, my British or rather English identity was based deeply on the fact that, for me, Englishness was synonymous with Ned and I felt I truly belonged with him. He had unwittingly created a little 'English kingdom' of our own for the two of us.

Then Judaism. Firstly, and most importantly I was born into a family with Jewish history. Also, I could not deny the fact that I felt at home among most Jewish people, from the kind man of 90 at the day care centre, the rabbi who interviewed me and the people who befriended me in the synagogue in London, to the Hatzola[54] ambulance crew, Dr Noimark (who inadvertently became a powerful influence) and quite a few more. I felt an inexplicable closeness and fondness towards them. There was significant commonality among us. Somehow, it felt that we shared a kind of shorthand for communication. Gradually, one by one, they each activated in me the dormant molecules of my Jewishness. Then the way I perceived anti-Semitism was also indicative. I had long discussions with Ned about it and about my acute awareness of anti-Semitism. My criteria differed from his: after all, Ned was not Jewish, but there were other factors too. In exploring it, we both concluded that I might be slightly hypersensitive, but for a reason. It was obvious that, as a Jew, albeit a newly 'awakened' one, I had historically earned the right to hypersensitivity. He realized, though, that anti-Semitism was present around us more than he was aware and that he had not been alert enough to it.

The final ingredient in the mix of my identity was that of 'Yugoslav origin'. That was easier to analyse. After all, I was born in a country called Yugoslavia[55] and had lived there for most of my life. In addition, that was the identity my immediate family assumed sometime before I was born and most of my life I genuinely believed that it was my identity too. However absurd the sense of belonging to a non-existent entity – the entity that existed in my memory only – might seem, it was a genuine and recognizable sense of belonging. I retained my sense of belonging to Yugoslavia in spite of the fact that the geopolitical whole no longer existed. It ended up divided into several separate countries, the former constituent parts I also used to consider 'mine'. Yet since the nineties they all tried hard to distance themselves from the former entity of Yugoslavia. Admittedly, disregarding the existence of those countries, I held onto the concept of the previous whole, while at the same time I grieved for the disappearance of that entity. Naturally, since Bosnia was only a part of that whole (in my head), I did not and could not consider myself Bosnian. Bosnia for me became one small separate unit, too narrow and one-dimensional.

However, in spite of the fact that my identity had been sorted out, citizenship granted, that I had my passport in my pocket (sometime later), that I had my home and a source of income, i.e. most of my existential problems solved, I still constantly struggled with depression and anxiety, a state hard to manage. I was stuck. Stephen visited, did not like what he saw and suggested I needed psychotherapy. That sounded like a good idea and I asked my, now different but equally dedicated, GP[56] to refer me to a psychotherapist. The long journey of finding my true self under the rubble of misfortune and adversity began. Life started coming back, slowly, but safely.

In the first session, I told the therapist that I felt I had lived three different lives and all were over. The therapist asked me if I meant three different phases in one life. I was adamant: three separate, different, completed lives – each with its own happy and sad moments, with losses and achievements, each with its start and finish, each gone forever. I said I had had my organized, average middle-class, somewhat eccentric life, back in Sarajevo. I had had my achievements and failures, marriage and divorce, flings and affairs, friends and enemies. Then I had a completely different, refugee life I was not equipped for. Moreover, that one took place in two different countries, but with more or less similar implications, conditions and psychological effects. Friends and enemies again, fewer achievements, but losses, too. Finally, I had the life I had always dreamed about – the husband I adored, who loved me, with whom I shared everything, who helped me become strong again. We worked together, we loved together, we spent most of our time together. So, again, it was an ordinary, if somewhat eccentric, middle-class life with the extraordinary luck of two people finding each other, with happy and not so happy moments, with losses and achievements, hopes and expectations. Then, abruptly and cruelly, it was all taken away from me. I was left with nothing. Only grief. No hopes, no expectations, no desire to live. Would not anyone consider that as three separate lives, or at least too much for one person and one life?

I was still excluded from the London family. Somewhere around that time, Tamara, whom I had always been very fond of and with whom I had been close, also stopped communicating with me. She cut me off from her family and her life completely.

I hardly knew her firstborn, met her twins only when they were toddlers and was introduced to her husband even later, unfortunately, I felt, too late.[57]

Although Tamara and I had had no contact for some time, on one of my birthdays she wrote an angry letter to me accusing me of two things that made no sense. Namely, she took umbrage over something that was unfounded gossip involving Tanja. She also accused me of casting a spell on her or something silly like that! I was stunned. Luckily, it was only a temporary glitch which, if truth be told, lasted too long. Yet another 'what' and 'why' for me, another mystery.

That third life did not end then. However, I was not aware of it at the time or, better still, did not want to and could not accept or imagine it. Yet, I managed to build the rest of my life on and around that third life, life with Ned, desperately holding onto the strength Ned had given me. Not a particularly happy life, but a decent life and my own.

As life started coming back to me, I felt I wanted to travel again. My first trip abroad with my new UK passport was to Germany. I visited Nina,[58] with whom I had previously had endless conversations and crying 'sessions' over the phone. The two of us always had a lot of time for each other. Then she came to visit me and we started visiting each other quite often. That helped me get out of my shell, helped me feel less vulnerable.

My old resilience gradually returned. I was slowly engaging more with things and people; I was more alive. I was a work believer who did not have enough work, so I decided to help myself by starting voluntary work. That gave me yet again the satisfaction of fighting evil with good. I was helping refugees: I volunteered at the Cambridge Refugee Support Group.[59] I also clicked with the people I worked with and I became friends with a few. The sense of belonging returned. My therapy helped considerably. I could clearly see the benefits. So, eventually, I decided to qualify as a psychotherapist and slowly but surely reclaimed my life.

My life was once again organized – ordinary, still a somewhat eccentric, middle-class life, this time a bit quieter. Reserved too. I valued my privacy, yet was willing to share. I needed friends again. Out of depression, I engaged more with the world around me. I carried on supporting my mother in every way I could.[60] My life had some sort of routine. I needed routine because that gave me a sense of security and safety. Change of any sort was frightening. Most of the changes in those ten years of my life were generally not for the better.[61] There was only one, a great and precious 'change', the one that helped me recover, the one that showed me there was hope and happiness still to come. I knew I could not find a replacement for that kind of life, but

I tried to find some sense in my life, some meaning I could use to build on those firm foundations. Having gone through many a challenge in my life, I gradually realized that there was beauty and goodness in abundance around me but, blinded by evil and tragedy, I had found this difficult to register. Yet, when one does find a way of grasping it, one's life makes so much more sense. I started searching for beauty in the countryside, in music, anywhere. I turned to helping others, turned to working again. The dream of my youth to become a clinical psychologist, which I could not realize due to circumstances, was finally realized. As my mother pointed out, I came full circle. Circle or not, it was a long and turbulent journey with a satisfactory outcome. I became hopeful. I managed to find and define my place. What more could one want?

Yet, Božo's words never stopped puzzling me. 'It is all your fault! Had you, our parents, ever told us about your Second World War experiences, we might have been better prepared,' he had said. Would we have been? Would knowing have marred our perception of life around us? Would it have made us more cautious or more resilient? The civil war had not destroyed us, neither me and my family, nor most of my friends and relatives. One could even say it enriched our experience, widened our horizons. But it also had a significant negative effect on us: it wounded us. So many things were challenged – from the way we saw ourselves to grasping the world around us. We did survive the atrocious circumstances, but I still wonder whether it was our inherent resilience or just luck. I wonder whether the parents' untold (hi)story hindered or helped our survival, or whether, like everybody else for that matter, we just had to learn our own lessons. This has remained an open question.

Epilogue

This personal story is an attempt to show what can happen to ordinary, unsuspecting human beings caught up in the turmoil of a civil war. In the second half of the twentieth century my family lived a quiet, rather well-organized middle-class life of three professionals in a socialist country. We believed we were Yugoslavs of Jewish origin. We cherished our family values, felt comfortable within ourselves, and mostly knew (or thought we knew) who and what we were. Suddenly (at least for us) in the 1990s our country began falling apart. We were not prepared for the dramatic, overwhelming evil that was to come to Bosnia and Herzegovina in early 1992.

Identity did not loom large in our family. My parents readily associated with the identity they felt defined them to a high degree and the one with which they felt comfortable, i.e. Yugoslav identity. It epitomized everything they had hoped for during the Second World War. However, it turned out to have been just wishful thinking but they were too tired and old to dwell upon it in the 1990s. On the other hand, at the same time, I found myself unexpectedly compelled to deal with my own identity issues and rather late in life, at that. Yet, regardless of our individual perspective on identity, our mutual primary aim, during the Sarajevo civil war, was to survive and to retain our integrity and sanity as much as possible.

Over ten years after I had left Sarajevo, I eventually went back to my former hometown, in 2004. I went there with some trepidation and discomfort, but I was a UK citizen by then so I felt safer. The familiar resentments, divisions, animosities and hatreds were still palpable. There was a new division: patriot versus traitor. Traitors were all those who had fled the country and antagonism towards them was strong. And I was one of them.

The town had changed hugely. It scarcely bore any resemblance to the town where I was born and had lived for so many years. There were so many changes, too many to mention here. Yet, to my huge surprise, there was one bizarre reminder of the days gone by. I certainly did not expect to see a revival of a long-forgotten use of loudspeakers. I was astounded to be taken back to my childhood so many years later, suddenly and in the most unusual manner: during the day, loudspeakers scattered all over the town centre (and elsewhere) broadcast the muezzins'[1] calls to prayers, which could be heard far and wide. It was strangely reminiscent of my childhood. Namely, in the years after the Second World War, during national holidays, loudspeakers on the streets[2] would broadcast partisan songs celebrating Marshal Tito. That practice disappeared several years later, but now, I was bewildered to see almost the same practice, after so many years. It was undeniably a different kind of indoctrination but it used some of the same means. My parents had subscribed to the socialist ideology after the Second World War, but now, after the Bosnian civil war, I definitely could not and would not subscribe to this new 'ideology'.

I stayed at Henika's flat, which was quite well preserved thanks to a well-connected neighbour who had looked after it. I visited my own flat, previously inhabited by God knows how many different families. There was very little of what belonged to us left there. No surprise there since properties were regularly looted. But I did not expect to find only bare walls – no washbasin or bathtub in the bathroom, no sink or anything in the kitchen, even some internal walls inexplicably damaged. Only my big heavy desk (too heavy and purposeless for looters probably) and a few cupboards in the hall, fixed onto the wall above door level, were left. Lo and behold, my diplomas (which I failed to take when we fled) were there, as well as my parents' decorations and medals. Rather unusual, I was told: people allegedly enjoyed destroying documents of those who had fled, believing that they were destroying traces of their existence and identity by the gesture.

I went to several government offices to obtain various documents, because the ultimate aim of the visit was to sell the flat. Although some offices had been refurbished, transformed into modern, shiny spaces, all marble, glass and bronze, the gloss would be wiped away in an instance by a rude and officious official. The rudeness assumed new levels, to the point of offensiveness. Impolite behaviour was not particularly new, but the open aggression and resentment, especially towards those who had fled the country, was. Officials blatantly refused to help and did their best to embarrass you. For instance, in the registry office, when I asked the official where the public loos were, she not only refused to direct me to them, but also purposely embarrassed me by loudly announcing to all willing to listen what my 'shameful' intentions were, in a surprisingly crude choice of words.[3] At another department, it was suggested to me that I was expected to bribe the counter clerk in Deutsche Marks. I tried to give it discreetly half-hidden in the wrapper of the box of chocolate, but he took the money openly and unashamedly, with no sense of propriety. I was embarrassed again: the tradition of bribery had evolved; it had always been popular, but less widespread and done more discreetly.

New types of black market had emerged out on the streets. The most popular place to buy foreign currency and 'certificates' was next to the memorial to the victims of the Second World War known as the 'Eternal Flame'. Cynical, unbelievable, but true. Repulsive too. I needed more certificates for the flat, but I did not turn to them. I chose to pay the missing amount in real money, Deutsche Marks of course, rather than use the black-market 'certificates'.

The entire Sarajevo experience was deeply painful, distressing and disappointing, in spite of the efforts of several friends who helped me out. Some came from Belgrade, some from Pale and some were living in Sarajevo. They did all they could to make my stay less stressful. I was hugely grateful, but nothing could prevent old wounds from opening or alleviate the anguish I felt all the time and everywhere.

I began the administrative process in order first to buy the flat off the institution that had allocated it to my father and then to sell it. Bane took me from one government office to the other, where I spent a lot of time applying for various documents. It was tiring, but worth it. Luckily, I already had a solicitor who had earlier (when the first solicitor refused) agreed to evict the people illegally occupying my flat and he now represented me again. With my authorization, and on my behalf, he went through the legal process of repossession of the flat, after I had left. He then bought the flat for me at a very agreeable price, i.e. using both my mother's 'certificates' and my own, as well as the Deutsche Marks. (For some reason, I could not access my late father's 'certificates' – hurtful and offensive – as if he had never worked or, for all intents and purposes, had never existed.)[4] The dealings with the flat turned out to be more complicated and took longer than expected. However, the solicitor eventually, much later, sold the flat for Deutsche Marks for me.

During my visit, I visited my friend Tatjana's family home. Both her parents had stayed in Sarajevo. By sheer chance, and to our mutual delight, Tatjana, her husband and all the children were visiting at the same time. (They had all been abroad during the war.) Tatjana and I had been schoolmates in primary school. Although of different sensibility and temperament – or maybe because of it, we gradually became close friends and were in frequent contact. Now we had not seen each other for over ten years. It was an emotional moment for all involved, especially the adults. We, the adults, were recognizable, the younger children[5] almost not at all. They were not kids anymore; they were teenagers.

All of my books were there. Tatjana's mother had kept them for me. I was by then living in Cambridge, living a different life, both privately and professionally, therefore I took only a few, for me, significant books. I donated the rest to the library of the Faculty of Philosophy.

The photographs I already had. My Belgrade student days' friend had brought them to me.

I also went to the bank to withdraw my foreign currency savings. 'Oh, no! That is not possible. It is the old foreign currency savings account,' I was told. What did that mean? What was the adjective 'old' supposed to imply? I did not understand, but could do nothing. I have never ever managed to access my or my parents' foreign currency savings. I realized how much of what belonged to my past, both materially and otherwise, was lost and I noticed that it did not bother me much. Loss must have been engraved into my DNA and in my collective memory. No wonder, with Jewish history as well as all the wars and regime changes in the area.

My visit in 2004 was the first and the last time I went back to Sarajevo. I felt there was no place for me there. On top of that, none of my family, not even distant relatives, were still there and very few friends. Most of the Department of English colleagues had gone too. Sarajevo had turned into an alien, unfamiliar environment, a place I could not relate to. My final farewell to Sarajevo, I realized, had been that one quick glance at the Faculty of Philosophy, once *my* Faculty of Philosophy, through the window of a bus speeding down the so-called 'sniper alley' on that fateful summer morning in 1992.

Addendum

Yugoslavia in the Second World War

The whole set-up of Yugoslavia (and consequently Bosnia and Herzegovina) has always been complicated. Therefore, I feel that highlighting a few historical and political facts, especially those relating to the Second World War, might shed some light on a number of references and connotations in the text. Although the events of the 1990s occurred quite some time after the Second World War, they still carried a certain echo. Hence, a brief overview of Yugoslavia in the Second World War, based on various reliable sources and summarized for the purpose of this book, is offered below.

The Axis allies – Germany backed by Italian, Romanian, Hungarian and Bulgarian forces – invaded the Kingdom of Yugoslavia on 6 April 1941 which heralded the beginning of the Second World War in Yugoslavia. The population of Yugoslavia was a mixture of a number of ethnic groups, which complicated the situation. According to Stephen A. Hart on the BBC History website,[1] broadly speaking there were two main ethnic groups, mostly characterized by a specific religion: the Serbs who are Orthodox Christian and the Croats who are Catholic. However, smaller ethnic groups such as Macedonians and Slovenes lived in Yugoslavia too. Macedonians were mostly Orthodox Christians and Slovenes were mostly Catholic. On top of that there were minority groups such as Jews and Roma[2] and others, Hungarians and Italians, for instance. There was a significant Muslim[3] population, mostly, but not only, in Bosnia and Herzegovina and Croatia. Hart claims that, 'many Bosnians were Muslims ("Bosnians" are the descendants of Serbs who converted to Islam many centuries ago, and lived in Bosnia-Hercegovina)'.[4] A considerable number of Muslims lived in Serbia too, especially the southern parts. Although estimates of the number of Muslims vary, it is safe to say that about 30 per cent of the population in Bosnia and Herzegovina, before the Second World War, were Muslims. Prior to the war, tensions between ethnic groups in Yugoslavia were evident and as Hart states, 'Hitler was able to profit from the tension between these ethnic groups, particularly that between the Serbs and Croats.'[5] Yugoslavia had capitulated by 17 April 1941 and Hart writes: 'in the aftermath of the conflict, the Axis victors claimed the spoils of conquest and dismembered the country.'[6]

At the beginning of the occupation the new pro-Axis state, called NDH – the Independent State of Croatia – was formed, covering both Croatian territory and Bosnia and Herzegovina. The state was ruled by the anti-Semitic and anti-Serbian fascist–nationalist formation called Ustashi. According to a US Holocaust Memorial Museum document, 'the Ustaša authorities erected numerous concentration camps in Croatia between 1941 and 1945.'[7] The largest and most notorious extermination camp was Jasenovac where, as in other camps, Ustashi isolated and murdered Jews, Serbs, Roma and other non-Catholic minorities, as well as those Croats who opposed NDH authorities, their political system and/or religion. There were no gas chambers in Jasenovac, but the violence and brutality were widespread so that, according to the Holocaust Education & Archive Research Team, General von Horstenau, Hitler's representative in Zagreb, wrote: 'The Ustaša camps in the NDH are the "epitome of horror".'[8 & 9]

The rest of Yugoslavia was occupied, with parts of Slovenia and Serbia occupied by the Germans, and the other parts by their allies. For instance, Fascist Italy occupied the Dalmatian coast, parts of Slovenia, Herzegovina and Montenegro. They established their own concentration (but not extermination) camp on the Adriatic island of Rab in July 1942, interning Jews and Slavs (mostly Slovenes and Croats). According to the European Observatory on Memories, the camp 'held 10,000–15,000 people until it was disbanded in September 1943. Rab was notorious for having the worst sanitary and living conditions of all the Fascist camps'.[10]

From the outset Axis forces were faced with fierce resistance from both the Partisans and the Chetniks. The Chetniks served the Yugoslav Royalist government in exile,[11] led by a former Yugoslav Army colonel, Dragoljub ('Draža') Mihailović. The first Chetnik troops were formed out of ethnic Serb soldiers in the Yugoslav Army who had evaded capture and were mostly scattered in the hills of Bosnia, Montenegro and Serbia. Serb peasants who had fled Croatia, where Serbs were persecuted, later joined the Chetniks (but no non-Serbs could join). Atrocities against Serbs in the NDH were so terrible that, as Hart states: 'The latter [i.e. Ustase atrocities][12] were so brutal that they even drew protests from the Germans – not on humanitarian grounds, but because Ustase ethnic cleansing was fuelling the resistance movements.'[13]

Another resistance movement, the Partisans, was led by Communist Party of Yugoslavia leader Josip Broz 'Tito'. It was an underground movement supported by Stalin's Soviet Union, the aim of which was to form a Socialist state through advancing socialist revolution. In order to promote their ideals, they appealed to all ethnic groups, including Muslims, throughout the country. Partisans were also joined by a number of Serbs, Jews and others whose objective was to fight Fascism, rather than supporting the Partisans' political aim.

The two resistance groups, the Chetniks and the Partisans, had a complicated relationship and fought their battles separately, as Hart mentions. The fact that the Chetniks were not a homogenous group reinforced division within the resistance, but was not the true cause of the division. The ultimate aim of the Chetniks, according to Hart, was 'to forge an ethnically pure Greater Serbia by violently 'cleansing' these areas of Croats and Muslims'.[14] What was common in all the Chetniks was their effort to fight for the survival of Serbian population, as well as being loyal to the royalist regime. In general, Chetniks were divided into two groups: anti-German and anti-Partisan. Yet even the anti-German ones were reluctant to attack Axis troops for fear of retribution against the Serbian population.

The relationship between the Chetniks and the Partisans soured further in the autumn of 1941 and developed into a full-scale conflict. According to Hart: 'To the Chetniks, Tito's pan-ethnic policies seemed anti-Serbian, whereas the Chetniks' Royalism was anathema to the Communists.'[15] As the war progressed, the Chetniks began openly collaborating with the Axis forces.

On 8 May 1945, at the time of German surrender, Partisan forces, together with the Red Army, embarked on the final battle of the war, driving the enemy north-westward in an attempt to gain control over the country. Axis forces and their Chetnik sympathizers intended to surrender to Allied forces in Austria, but failed. As a consequence, Hart notes: 'The days that followed the end of the war led to one last round of vengeful bloodletting. Tito's Partisans executed at least 30,000 Croat Ustase troops, plus many civilian refugees.'[16]

The Second World War had devastating consequences for Yugoslavia, the total death toll between 1941 and 1945 exceeding 1.7 million. (According to some estimates the population of the Kingdom of Yugoslavia in 1939 was around 15,400,000.) The unfortunate fact, according to Hart, is that out of this 1.7 million, around one million were 'caused by Yugoslav killing Yugoslav, whether it was Croat Ustase against Jews, Muslims, Serbs, Chetniks and Partisans; or Partisans against Chetniks and Ustase; or Chetniks against Ustase, Muslims, and Partisans.'[17]

Appendix A

2021 Update of Family Members and the People from Sarajevo Mentioned in the Text

My husband, Edward Dennis Goy (Ned), died in March 2000 in Cambridge.

My father, Mirko-Imre Levinger, died in Belgrade in March 1995, and was buried there.

My mother Sara-Beba Levinger née Danon, died in London in December 2017. Her ashes were laid in Belgrade, at her husband's (my father's) grave.

Maternal Family
Sida (Levi) lived and died in Belgrade in 2002.

Sanja (Marković), now retired, lives in Belgrade with her partner.

Igor (Marković) lives in Belgrade with his partner.

Teo (Levi) – Sanja's brother – and his wife, Renata, live in Belgrade; their daughter, Laura, lives in France, married, with one son.

Gorana-Goga (Kušić-Uzelac), my second cousin who lived in Germany, died in 1994, and was buried in Belgrade.

Sladjana (Levi-Mendicino), retired, lives in Belgrade with her husband, Peppe-Giuseppe (Mendicino).

Dušanka (Levi), Sladjana's mother, lived and died in Belgrade in 2003.

Paternal Family
Ella and Salamon-Moni (Konforti) died in London, Moni in 1997, Ella in 2002.

Henika (Konforti) is retired and lives in London

Tanja (Konforti) lived in London and died there in 2017.

2021 Update of Family Members and the People from Sarajevo Mentioned in the Text   145

Željko (Djuretić), Henika's son, lives in Rotterdam with his family.

Tamara (Janjić), Henika's daughter, lives in London with three children. Her husband, Predrag-Šagi (Janjić), died in London in 2016.

Ivana (Ružić), Tanja's daughter, lives in London with two children and her partner.

Tomica (Levinger), the son of my cousin, Zvonko, from Lošinj, went to Israel and returned to Lošinj, where he now lives.

Friends, Colleagues and Others from Sarajevo

A colleague and friend, Eja, who was my lecturer in my student days, the one who offered to take me in after the war, never left Sarajevo. She died there in 2018.

A colleague with a small child whom I referred to the Jewish Community at the outset, left Sarajevo with her entire family, went to Belgrade and to London from there. The entire extended family now lives in London.

A friend who brought me a jar of beetroot now lives in Croatia. His children, both married, live in Italy.

A friend who pleaded with me to leave on a Jewish convoy immigrated with his wife and children, via Mauritius, to Canada. Their daughter lives in Australia and their son died in Canada.

A librarian who suggested I went to my 'spare homeland' never left Sarajevo and died there.

A literary theory professor who talked about genetic codes during the Sarajevo war and who told me off for crying, taught at various universities abroad, including SSEES, and returned to Sarajevo, where he died in 2018.

A painter acquaintance, who offered me a drink and saved my life, stayed on in Sarajevo and died there in 2015.

A Sarajevo couple who had a room next to ours in Pirovac, live in France. Their son also lives in France, is married, as is their daughter who lives in the UK.

A Sarajevo neuropsychiatrist who examined my mother and then spent the night in the Jewish Community Centre with us, now lives in Zagreb.

A young neighbour who was wounded in Sarajevo, lives in Australia.

Avdo, my father's friend, stayed in Sarajevo and was killed while queueing for water in 1993.

Benko, who helped organize convoys and escorted them, lives in Dubrovnik, Croatia, with his wife.

Boris, the official in charge of convoy lists in the Jewish Community Centre, lives in Sarajevo and is still engaged with the Jewish Community Centre.

Cveja, Henika's partner, fled to Belgrade in 1992 and died there in 1999.

David, the university professor and a policeman from the Jewish Community Centre, after a short diplomatic service abroad, returned to Sarajevo where he died in 2021.

Gliga-Igor, my ex-husband, left Sarajevo in 1992, lived in Stockholm, Sweden, with his third wife and died there in 2010.

Goran, my childhood friend, temporarily left Sarajevo for Israel for work experience in 1998, but stayed on and lives there with his wife, daughter and granddaughter.

Ivica, President of the Jewish Community Centre, eventually immigrated to Israel where he lives with his family; in 1994, he was awarded the Légion d'Honneur for non-sectarian humanitarian relief work during the Bosnian war.

Jaki, a Jewish Community Centre representative with whom I discussed Sveto's departure from Sarajevo, returned to Sarajevo after a diplomatic career abroad and is still involved with the Jewish Community. He lives there with his wife.

Klara, my mother's friend, immigrated to Canada straight from Pirovac in 1992. She is now in her nineties and lives there with her daughter and granddaughter, who married and has her own family.

Lala, my Sarajevo housebound friend, left Sarajevo in 1992 and died in Split, Croatia, and was buried there in 1993.

Marina, my writer friend, left for Poland before the civil war, lived and worked there, retired and returned to Sarajevo, where she died in 2011.

Mima and Božo, friends and neighbours, fled to Belgrade and then immigrated to Denmark. Much later they moved to Barcelona, Spain, where they now live; both their children live there too and are married with children. Bennie, the dog, had to be put down in Copenhagen in 2004.

2021 Update of Family Members and the People from Sarajevo Mentioned in the Text 147

Mima's sister fled to Belgrade and died there in 1993.

Minja, my bogus marriage mother-in-law, never left Sarajevo, and died there after the war, in 1995; her sons managed to visit her.

Mrs S., the old neighbour, I know nothing about.

My father's childhood playmate left Sarajevo and spent some time in a Zagreb Jewish residential care home, where she died.

My father's Sarajevo doctor, Zlatko, remained in Sarajevo where he died in 2021.

My former university lecturer and a friend, Ljubica, once Chair of Language Department, who saved me from political minders and to whom I sent some food from Novi Sad, never left Sarajevo, where she died in 2005.

Nikola, my long-time married 'boyfriend', left Sarajevo early on in the civil war and, having lived and worked abroad in the diplomatic service, returned to the University of Sarajevo; he died there in 2007.

Nina, my close friend, now retired, has lived in Germany since the late 1970s.

Omer, my friend and colleague immigrated to the US, where he died in 2016. His wife and two daughters live in the US.

Pavle, my friend, a Sarajevo refugee in Belgrade, returned to Sarajevo after the war and died there in 2018.

Saša, my bogus husband, fled to Belgrade and then immigrated to Denmark where he now lives with his wife, Cica, and two sons.

Sveto, my friend, ex-professor and colleague fled to Novi Sad with his wife, where they both died, the wife in 2014 and Sveto in 2016.

Taša, who brought her ill mother, Mima's sister, from Sarajevo to Belgrade, immigrated to Denmark. She lives in Copenhagen with her husband, also a former Yugoslav. They met and got married in Copenhagen.

Taša's brother, who immigrated to Denmark with Mima and Božo, lives in Copenhagen and is married with two children.

Tatjana, my childhood friend went to Libya in 1991. Her husband was in Libya on business so she and the children joined him. After the war they briefly returned to Sarajevo and immigrated to Canada with their twins. They all now live in Canada. Tatjana's older son (from her first marriage), Alen, left for Germany before the civil war broke out and still lives there.

Tatjana's mother who saved my books and photos, never left Sarajevo and died there in 2011. Her husband, Tatjana's father, died there before her.

The acquaintance with greenery in his carrier bag who ignored me I know nothing about.

The engineer who told me about a secret greengrocer's I lost track of.

The hospital doctor who checked my thyroid in Sarajevo during the war, now lives in London with his wife.

The Sarajevo doctor friend, my ex-husband's colleague who examined my father in Pirovac and later in Belgrade, although not Jewish, immigrated to Israel with his wife where he died.

The surgeon who would not break Saša's leg, spent time in various places in the former Yugoslavia and now lives in Sarajevo.

The woman who gave me the fan on the coach joined her husband and they stayed on in Dalmatia; after that, I lost track of them, but they were both quite elderly in 1992.

Zora and Bane, my 'Chetnik' friend and his wife who stayed in Sarajevo almost until the end of the war, are now retired and live in a mountain cottage previously owned by Zora's family in Pale, the Republic of Srpska; their daughter, married with two children, lives in Subotica, Serbia, and their son lives in Belgrade.

Zora's niece and nephew to whom I taught English in Sarajevo both live in Belgrade.

Zvonko, my friend and colleague, never left Sarajevo where he died in 2021. One of his two sons lives in Sarajevo, another with his family in Zagreb.

Appendix B

Excerpt from a Story by Ivo Andrić

A story 'Letter from 1920'[1] one of Ivo Andrić's short stories, in translation, was published in the collection *The Damned Yard and Other Stories*.[2] For those interested in finding out more about Sarajevo and its multicultural or multi-religious dispensation, this excerpt might be of interest. Although it was written long before the period described in this memoir, it nevertheless poignantly illustrates some aspects of life in Sarajevo which have been at the root of the issues mentioned throughout the text.

> *Whoever lies awake at night in Sarajevo hears the voices of the Sarajevo night. The clock on the Catholic cathedral strikes the hour with weighty confidence: 2 a.m. More than a minute passes (to be exact, seventy-five seconds – I counted) and only then with a rather weaker, but piercing sound does the Orthodox church announce the hour, and chime its own 2 a.m. A moment after it the tower clock on the Beys' Mosque strikes the hour in a hoarse, faraway voice, and that strikes 11, the ghostly Turkish hour, by the strange calculation of distant and alien parts of the world. The Jews have no clock to sound their hour, so God alone knows what time it is for them by the Sephardic reckoning or the Ashkenazy.*
>
> *Thus, at night, while everyone is sleeping, division keeps vigil in the counting of the late, small hours, and separates these sleeping people who, awake, rejoice and mourn, feast and fast by four different and antagonistic calendars, and send all their prayers and wishes to one heaven in four different ecclesiastical languages. And this difference, sometimes visible and open, sometimes invisible and hidden, is always similar to hatred, and often completely identical with it. This uniquely Bosnian hatred should be studied and eradicated like some pernicious, deeply-rooted disease.*

Endnotes

Dedication

1. E. D. Goy, *The Sabre and the Song*, Serbian P.E.N. Publications, 1995, (rough translation) p. 45.
2. D. Vušović, redakcija, *Cjelokupna djela Petra Petrovića Njegoša*, Narodna kultura, Beograd 1936, '*Gorski vijenac*', L137–138, p. 12

Author's Note

1. Although the term 'civil war' has not been accepted by all, the conflict actually had all the hallmarks of a civil war.
2. One of the six republics constituting Yugoslavia, the country that ceased to exist.
3. For those interested in the turbulent history of Yugoslavia in the Second World War a brief summary is offered at the end of the book.
4. Her hometown was Gacko.
5. Popularly known as independent Bosnia since it passed the 'Memorandum on the Sovereignty of Bosnia-Herzegovina' accepted by the current leading nationalist parties except Bosnian Serbs (they boycotted the referendum).
6. In 1992, the Bosnian Serbs seceded and proclaimed the 'Republic of the Serbian People in Bosnia-Herzegovina' (later Republika Srpska, the Republic of Srpska). It eventually (verified by the Dayton Accords, 1995) became one of the two entities of Bosnia and Herzegovina, the other being the Federation of Bosnia and Herzegovina.
7. I. D. Yalom, *Becoming Myself*, Basic Books, New York, p. 50.
8. However, the subsequent COVID-19 pandemic in 2020, which came when the manuscript was completed, often caused behavioural patterns reminiscent of and comparable with my Sarajevo war experience. Author's article describing this was published in www.contemporarypsychotherapy.org in 2020.
9. www.britannica.com/

Chapter 1: Prelude to the Events to Come

1. At the beginning of the period described, still one of the republics of Yugoslavia.

Endnotes 151

2. 'Josip Broz Tito ... a Yugoslav revolutionary and statesman ... Tito was the chief architect of the "Second Yugoslavia", a socialist federation that lasted from the Second World War until 1991.' www.britannica.com/biography/Josip-Broz-Tito. Tito was at the helm of the country from 19945 until 1980.
3. My maternal family were Sephardic Jews who came to the Balkans when they were expelled from the Iberian Peninsula, at the end of the fifteenth/early sixteenth century. My paternal family were Ashkenazy Jews. The paternal grandparents came to Bosnia during the Austro-Hungarian reign, from Budapest.
4. At the very outset of the war, Germans shot the child's father, just as the aunt finally fell pregnant after seven years of trying.
5. 'Croatian fascist movement ...[of] the Independent State of Croatia during World War II ... [They] formed the government of a Croatian state ... to include some of Serbia and ... Bosnia and Herzegovina.' www.britannica.com/topic/Ustasa
6. Capital of the region of Herzegovina.
7. An island in the northern Adriatic.
8. Partisans, members of the Communist Party of Yugoslavia guerrilla force during the Second World War against the Axis power and collaborators and a rival resistance force, to the royalist Chetniks. www.britannica.com /topic/Partisan-Yugoslavian-military-force
9. In multi-ethnic areas villages were mostly ethnically exclusive; only one ethnic group in each village, often not far from each other.
10. Henika was born as a refugee in Mostar in 1942.
11. Officially, as Britannica states, the Socialist Yugoslavia was formed in 1946 after Josip Broz Tito and his communist-led Partisans had helped liberate the country from German rule in 1944–45. www.britannica.com/place/Yugoslavia-former-federated-nation-1929-2003
12. My father's family (parents and sister) remained in Sarajevo. Ella remarried after the war and with her husband Salamon-Moni had another daughter, Tanja. My mother's family (parents and sister) also stayed in Sarajevo (except for her sister Sida who left Sarajevo in the 1950s and ended up living in Belgrade). However, my father's older half-brother Ferdo-Feri Levinger left Sarajevo before the Second World War and in the 1990s he and his family lived in Lošinj, an island in the Adriatic. Also, my mother's older brother Iso Danon, a sea captain, left Sarajevo in his youth and lived in the US from 1940 until his death in the1980s.
13. A German-based variant of language used by Ashkenazy Jews.
14. At school we were officially asked by teachers to declare our ethnicity from time to time. I am not sure whether it was census time or something else.
15. Miljenko Jergovic, a writer born in Sarajevo, now living in Croatia.
16. www.6yka.com/novosti/miljenko-jergovic-kratka-povijest-holokausta-kroz-dva-telefonska-imenika (author's translation)

17. It was during the spate of imprisonments related to the Yugoslav–Soviet split (Tito–Stalin split), a conflict between the leaders of the two countries, which resulted in Yugoslavia's expulsion from the Communist Information Bureau (Cominform) in 1948. Soon afterwards my father was exculpated.
18. J. Bauman, *A Dream of Belonging*, Virago, London, 1988, p. 88.
19. R. M. Hayden, 'From Yugoslavia to the Western Balkans, Studies of a European Disunion, 1991–2011', Leiden, p. ix.
20. It has been customary in towns and cities for people to live in blocks of flats rather than in individual houses.
21. Immediately after the war, those who had big flats were made to share them with those who needed accommodation.
22. The official policy was actually anti-religious, emphasizing the negative aspects of religious influences.
23. He died in 1953.
24. One could not simply purchase a flat. The only way to get a flat, according to the socialist practice, was to be allocated one by one's employer. One needed a certain number of points depending on the number of years one had worked there, marital status, number of children, the type of accommodation one lived in and various other social factors. It was not social housing; it was actually the only way to get a place to live in.
25. MA at Georgetown University, Washington DC, US.
26. It must have been about that time that I learned of the devastating political ordeal my parents went through.
27. With time, the wording changed, but not the sentiment among Communist Party members.
28. However, I disliked the statement. It could have cost my maternal grandfather his life. He had refused to flee Sarajevo in the Second World War, professing the same statement. Eventually the family pressurized him to leave.
29. It was the one-party (communist) totalitarian regime, i.e. a system of government that is centralized and requires complete subservience to the state.
30. I was aware of the fact that, unlike in the homes of my friends, both in my paternal and maternal grandparents' homes a different, 'secret' language was used among the adults when they wanted not to be understood by the children or those outside the family. My paternal Ashkenazy family used Hungarian or German and/or Yiddish while the maternal family, who were Sephardi, used Ladino (a form of old Spanish used by the Sephardi Jews).
31. Dr Dean Noimark was well known in the area as an exceptionally dedicated, caring and selfless doctor, full of empathy. Nevertheless, I believe our common 'Jewish roots' (for him much more than just roots) eased us into a more straightforward communication.
32. A brimless cap traditionally worn by Jewish males to fulfil the customary requirement.

33. Michael Grant Ignatieff is a Canadian author, academic and former politician.
34. It was also the birthplace of my parents.
35. The assassination of the Archduke Franz Ferdinand, the heir to the throne of Austria and his wife, in Sarajevo in 1914, by members of the movement *Mlada Bosna*, the Young Bosnia, was widely considered critical in setting off the chain of events that led to the First World War.
36. That was one of the factors for Sarajevo to have been chosen for 1984 Winter Olympic Games.
37. Yugoslav airline known as *Jugoslavenski aero transport* or JAT.
38. By today's standards it would hardly be considered a skyscraper; it is 12 storeys high.
39. Some of the newly built housing developments contained only high-rises.
40. Significantly damaged during the civil war.
41. Those were among the early casualties of civil war, burning menacingly one next to the other.
42. The mountain south-east of Sarajevo, 1,627 metres (5,338 feet) above sea level.
43. There were many mixed ethnicity marriages. Our family was an example; none of my cousins, nor I married a Jew.
44. If I remember correctly those were the official administrative names given to those boroughs.
45. The Ottoman Empire, according to most sources, ruled in Bosnia and Herzegovina from fifteenth century to late nineteenth century, when the Austro-Hungarian monarchy took control, although, nominally, Bosnia and Herzegovina remained under Turkish sovereignty till the early twentieth century.
46. The Austro-Hungarian monarchy ruled from 1878, with nominal Turkish sovereignty till 1918 when the Kingdom of Serbs, Croats, and Slovenes was formed. The new kingdom included the previously independent kingdoms of Serbia and Montenegro and the South Slav territories in areas formerly subject to the Austro-Hungarian Empire: Dalmatia, Croatia-Slavonia, Slovenia, Bosnia and Herzegovina and the Vojvodina.
47. The socialist government (using different names) ruled the area from 1945–91/2.
48. An Ottoman-style wooden fountain originally built in 1753 and relocated in 1891.
49. Since the late 1960s, the term Muslim (spelled with a capital 'M') officially referred to ethnicity.
50. Even in 2014 one subtitle in *The Guardian* newspaper referring to the Bosnian seventh general election in October read: 'Since the end of the war, political allegiance has been usually based on ethnic identity, and divisions are still enshrined in what is possibly the world's most complicated institutional set up.' www.theguardian.com/news/datablog/2014/oct/08/bosnia-herzegovina-elections-the-worlds-most-complicated-system-of-government

51. Croats, Muslims and Serbs, each of different religion: Croats mostly Catholics, Muslims mostly Islam, Serbs mostly Serbian Orthodox (author's comment).
52. A term denoting inhabitants of Bosnia of Muslim religion, replacing the previous capital 'M' Muslims. The word Bosnian refers to all the inhabitants in the geographical region of Bosnia.
53. www.britannica.com/place/Bosnia-and-Herzegovina/Bosnia-and-Herzegovina-in-communist-Yugoslavia#ref223952
54. The second largest city in Bosnia and Herzegovina.
55. Term used to refer to *Republika Srpska* in the West in the 1990s. (author's comment).
56. www.radiosarajevo.ba/kolumne/miljenko-jergovic/moze-li-covjek-biti-bosanac/310805 (author's translation).
57. Spring-cleaning often included taking big rugs out into the garden, hanging them on contraptions made for the purpose and beating them with a raffia utensil.
58. The children of my father's late half-brother.
59. A Croatian island in the northern Adriatic Sea.
60. A term used to denote channels or connections made through knowing someone or someone who knew someone. A way of getting things done, a form of corruption, perhaps slightly more sophisticated one.

Chapter 2: Blind Denial

1. They lived in the same block of flats where we lived. His mother was my parents' generation.
2. Hannah Arendt, 'We Refugees' in *The Jewish Writings*, eds: J. Kohn and R. F. Feldman, New York, p. 265 (online). www.jus.uio.no/smr/om/aktuelt/arrangementer/2015/arendt-we-refugees.pdf
3. A type of lecturer, especially one employed in a foreign university to teach in their native language.
4. Georgetown University in Washington DC we both attended in the late 1970s.
5. Nina had lived in Germany since the 1970s.
6. Not counting the children, the two families consisted of my immediate family i.e. my mother, father and myself, on the one hand and my father's sister Ella, her husband Moni and their two daughters, Henika and Tanja, on the other. Both Henika and Tanja were long divorced by then too.
7. I do not think we ever saw that rifle.
8. Most people had had back-up savings in Deutsche Marks, often some in cash 'under the mattress' and some in the foreign currency accounts in the bank. The dinar had not been stable enough for some time.

9. They moved into the apartment block we had lived in a fair few years before the war and we rekindled our friendship.
10. In the early days of the conflict the Jewish Community hired planes to take people to Belgrade.
11. Grbavica, new part of town south-west of the town centre, ethnically mixed too, which was under the jurisdiction of Serbian authorities. Yet there were Bosnian military formations in action on some of the hills north-west of Sarajevo, such as Žuč and Hum, shooting down on Grbavica, which meant at Bosniaks as well.
12. During the Second World War the Chetniks fought against the Axis, but also fought a civil war against the Yugoslav communists, the Partisans. www.britannica.com/topic/Chetnik
13. A small mountain town east of Sarajevo, where some of the government offices of the Republic of Srpska were located.
14. By then, together with paramilitary troops, most of the Bosnian army was in action, in the town and positioned mostly on the south-western hills around Sarajevo.
15. A river on the border between Bosnia and Herzegovina and Serbia.
16. Still the name of the language, which later was relabelled into Bosnian, Croatian and Serbian respectively.
17. Name of a Muslim charitable organization.
18. At the time that seemed the only safe option to leave the besieged town.
19. It was only after I had finished writing this book that I realized this had been a convenient delusion. In March 2021, I learned of a number of incidents one could class as anti-Semitic, particularly in relation to the old Jewish cemetery. The cemetery dates from sixteenth century when the Sephardi Jews arrived in Bosnia and Herzegovina, having been expelled from the Iberian Peninsula. Burials at the cemetery ceased in around 1966 and it remains registered as a monument of national interest. Jews, firstly Sephardi and later Ashkenazy, had been active participants in the life of the country (during the Ottoman rule to the extent they were allowed). They seemingly integrated into society, especially in the twentieth century (of course, excluding the period of the Second World War) and appeared respected. Unfortunately, primarily in the second half of the twentieth century, numerous incidents relating to the devastation of the cemetery – not publicized at the time and not widely known – point to the contrary. It transpired that every few years, closely tied with the political 'trends' (be it wars between Israel and its neighbours or neo-fascist incidents, for instance) a huge number of graves and other objects were vandalized or destroyed. Apparently the first major destructive incident was recorded in 1967 (Israeli–Egyptian war) and the last in 2000 – altogether eight significant incidents (excluding the 1992–5 civil war) all reflecting the anti-Jewish sentiments. These details can be found at www.centar.ba/stranica/536, the webpage of the Council

of the Municipality of Sarajevo *Centar* which states that as of March 2021, about 95 per cent of tombstones are registered as damaged, in spite of the fact that, as the same source states, (in author's translation)*:* 'the old Jewish cemetery ... represents, after the cemetery in Prague, the largest Jewish sepulchral complex in Europe' and as such is 'classed a listed monument'. (Author's article on The Old Jewish Cemetery was published both in Serbo-Croat and English on various internet platforms in 2021.)

20. She was offensively anti-Semitic and opposed her son's decision to marry me.
21. A candlestick used in Jewish worship, especially one with eight branches and a central socket used at Hanukkah.
22. Mishnah, Sanhedrin 4:5.
23. Due to their devastating Second World War experiences, a number of Jews refused to be included on any list of those of Jewish origin and often even the idea of being recognized as Jewish felt sinister.
24. '*ć*' sound as 't' in English 'culture'
25. '*dobro*' meaning good in Serbo-Croat, a translation of German '*gut*'.
26. Civil war this time. But she had died before that.
27. As Hayden stated: '[It was] during the 1991–95 war [that] these conflicts introduced the term "ethnic cleansing" into the international lexicon.' R. M. Hayden, *From Yugoslavia to the Western Balkans, Studies of a European Disunion, 1991–2011*, Leiden, p. ix.
28. Tatjana and her family were abroad at the time.
29. They later all immigrated to the US. I never found out how they had managed it.
30. They left later and went first to Mauritius and then moved to Canada.
31. Some friends told me that he considered me an enemy, due to the fact that I went to Belgrade (albeit not via Pale!). But after a long period of no contact, we resumed our friendly relationship. Who knows how true the gossip had been.
32. 'All of us' meant my parents and me and Ella, her husband Moni, Henika and Tanja. Both Henika's and Tanja's adult children were abroad at the time.
33. By then the airlifts had stopped.
34. A small coastal town in Croatia, near Šibenik, where a summer resort of the Yugoslav Association of Jewish Communities had been for years, prior to the fall of Yugoslavia.
35. A mountain in Herzegovina on one of the convoy routes.
36. Serbian Democratic Party.
37. We needed somebody we could trust with our lives.
38. 'The Jewish Writings', eds: J. Kohn, R. F. Feldman, Hannah Arendt, *We Refugees*, New York, p. 265 (online). www.jus.uio.no/smr/om/aktuelt/arrangementer/2015/arendt-we-refugees.pdf

39. The facsimile of Saša's signature on the document indicating the surname he chose upon the marriage.

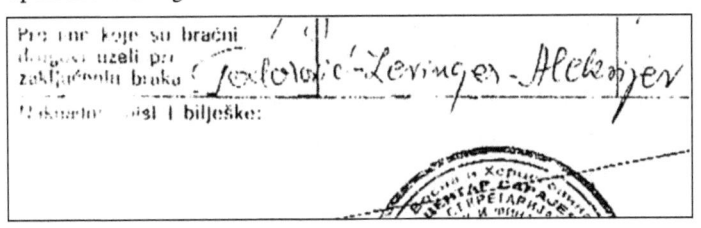

40. Very soon, he was thrown out and somebody else moved in. And several more moved in and out after that, I was told. Who and why I never found out.
41. We carried those paintings with us and had them framed as soon as we could afford it and continued cherishing them.
42. The capital of Croatia.
43. A Sarajevo suburb on the western side of town.

Chapter 3: Reluctant Recognition

1. Croats were predominantly Catholic.
2. The unsubstantiated rumour was that Benko was instrumental in organizing the convoys.
3. A Sarajevo suburb on the western side of town.
4. The villa was nationalized by the state in 1945 and divided into separate units, given to those who needed accommodation.
5. She survived the Second World War and died when I was about 10 years old.
6. She hurt me with overt anti-Semitism.
7. A town next to the hydroelectric power station.
8. A river in Herzegovina.
9. A small town in the Dalmatian hinterland, Croatia.
10. A town on the Adriatic coast.
11. The journey used to take about five hours in peacetime.
12. A contraceptive intrauterine device.
13. The procedure was done in Belgrade probably due to the fact that the Chief Rabbi of Yugoslavia was stationed there, within the Association of Jewish Communities of Yugoslavia – possibly the only one authorized to verify the conversion. However, this is just a guess.
14. Ivo Andrić was a Yugoslav novelist, poet and short-story writer who won the Nobel Prize for Literature in 1961. As the Nobel Prize website states: 'The author describes the life of this region in which East and West have for centuries clashed … a region

with [a] population composed of different nationalities and religions.' In many of his works, there was a hint at potential conflict. www.nobelprize.org/prizes/literature/1961/andric/biographical/
15. For those interested, a relevant excerpt from the story is included at the end of the book.
16. There were no phone lines operational in their part of town.
17. Although Nikola did not want to leave Sarajevo, I felt I had deserted him. Not a pleasant feeling.
18. The nickname she had for her uncle; from the German *onkel*, or uncle.
19. Since she was born posthumously, the *onkel* took on the role of father substitute for the first few years.
20. Henika would not see her first granddaughter for far too long. They had to come to visit her in London. Henika waited for her immigration status to be decided upon for a long time.
21. In particular Mr Yechiel Bar-Chaim, who worked for the American Jewish Joint Distribution Committee (JDC) and Mr Tomi Shosberger from Israel.
22. The Croatian–Serbian border could not be crossed because of bitter military battles along that border.
23. Their passports had expired and they had not applied for the new ones, because they did not intend to travel anywhere any more.
24. I never found out who the female was. It was a bit unsettling. She might have been his girlfriend, who was there to keep him company.
25. German for 'Return to Zagreb'.
26. Serbia kept the name Yugoslavia at the time.
27. One of the examples was the bread queue mentioned earlier and a few more.
28. The actual name of the bank was Dafiment Bank, effectively a pyramid scheme.

Chapter 4: Rude Awakening

1. I enrolled to read psychology as an 18-year-old, but I had to give it up after the first semester.
2. The same one my parents were in.
3. Teo and Renata who lived in Belgrade with their daughter, Laura, of the same age as Igor.
4. Although the situation might have exacerbated Sida's state, the fact was that, in her late forties, she had been diagnosed and treated (unfortunately not successfully) for bipolar disorder.
5. Italian neorealist films were popular in Yugoslavia in the 1950s and 1960s.
6. My mother did not teach there. She then worked in the administration while attending her French and Serbo-Croat teaching course.

Endnotes 159

7. Brian Friel, *Dancing at Lughnasa* (translated as *Lunasa*), Theatre Atelje 212, Belgrade, 1994.
8. There was no civil war in the area, but the economic crisis had started with all accompanying nastiness.
9. The war lasted for about three years, but we left after less than five months into the war.
10. When I rang Sveto's daughter from Pirovac she suggested we split the list. She would get in touch with those in the US and elsewhere, and I with those in Belgrade.
11. Dobrica Ćosić who was also a well-known writer.
12. Patrick Early
13. Sida's son Teo from Belgrade (Serbia), Henika's son Željko from Sarajevo (Bosnia and Herzegovina) and Tomica, my cousin Zvonko's son, from Lošinj (Croatia).
14. United Nations High Commissioner for Refugees
15. One of those who we actually knew was not Jewish, ironically, still lives in Israel.
16. Adventist Church's charitable organization, among the first to organize delivery of parcels and letters to and from Sarajevo.
17. Washing machines were commonly kept in bathrooms.
18. Apparently, the US had specific quotas with specific requirements. As far as I know, she was told that the quota included Bosnian Muslims and Russian Jews.
19. E. Hoffman, *Lost in Translation*, Vintage Books, London, 1989.
20. My Sarajevo friend Jadranka secured the interview for me through some of her Belgrade relatives.
21. The Yugoslav economic (as well as political) crisis actually started in the 1980s.
22. Chicken soup is well-known among Jews as a universal remedy and comfort food.
23. Sveto, who arrived in Serbia after me, was one of them; the other one was Branko O. with whom I was less close.
24. Vesna, happened to be a sister of my Belgrade student days' friend, who later brought to me a bag full of my photographs from Sarajevo.
25. En route to Belgrade he picked up Cica who remained in the Republic of Srpska.
26. That bond, created under such horrendous circumstances, both with Mima and Božo and Taša, as well as with Zora and Bane, made me finally fathom what my parents meant when they talked about their 'war friends' – the pre-existing friendship reinforced and tested through adversities.
27. Saša was 18 years younger than me.
28. Two of their children, who were in Belgrade previously, and the son of Mima's ill sister.
29. Pepe was an 'adopted' Yugoslav. He worked in the embassy of his home country.
30. Although, we were seen as speaking a 'different language' due to the regional dialect we used.
31. In general, there was no private ownership or even private practice/enterprise in socialism, especially before the 1970s. Only few who retained their property from

before the Second World War or villagers had their own small property. Also, very few doctors, dentists or tradesmen had their own private practice. It was later, probably from the 1970s onwards that people started owning property or small business as well as building holiday homes.
32. They kept increasing the rent with time but, due to our circumstances, even if we wanted to, we would not have been able to move to a cheaper flat (even if we could find one).
33. A member of the Communist Party of Yugoslavia who was a member of the administrative system, a communist bureaucrat.
34. He allegedly went to a Middle Eastern country temporarily to join his sister who lived there, while his wife lived in Belgrade in another flat, with her mother. We were paying the rent to her.
35. The Director of the Institute for Philosophy and Social Theory (*Institut za filozofiju i društvenu teoriju*) with whom I became friends almost as soon as we arrived.
36. The name of Serbia and Montenegro until 2003.
37. If they could not get one or two items for my father, a friend of mine living in France then sent them to me.
38. They still regularly send me the magazine, which I appreciate.
39. She read English language and literature at Belgrade University in the post-Second World War years.
40. My former university colleagues.
41. The part of town under the jurisdiction of Serbian authorities which could be reached via the Serbian-held territories of Pale and Trebević.
42. Published in *Language Sciences 16/2*: pp. 229–36, 1994.
43. That evening both a Belgrade linguist friend and I presented our talks.
44. Yet another example of the absurdity of the times we were living in. The two proxy marriage options were: 1) she was to obtain the boyfriend's authorization for Saša's brother, who lived in Belgrade, to marry her there on the boyfriend's behalf. She would leave for Denmark afterwards and the boyfriend would then join her as her husband, in Denmark; 2) in case the boyfriend's authorization did not reach her in time, I was to marry him on her behalf. He would have to get to Belgrade first and after the wedding by proxy proceed to Denmark to join his wife. She gave me a certified authorization to represent her. To my relief it was the first version that worked.
45. 'Premostiti most ili srušiti ćupriju' (Bridging the Gap or Making it Larger), published in *Interculturality in Multiethnic Societies*, Beograd, 1995, pp. 165–85.
46. The talk was entitled 'Metaporuka – kako i zašto' (Metamessage – How and Why), published in *Towards a Language of Peace*, Beograd, 1996, pp. 63–71.
47. With time Pavle, his wife and I became close.
48. A small bite-sized confectionery.

49. *rakija*, a strong local spirit made from plums.
50. However, that did not last. As the economic situation became dire, so did the general atmosphere. Resentment towards refugees was the first sign of the deterioration.
51. Yet the Sarajevo department had changed hugely by then. More than half of my colleagues had left Sarajevo and Bosnia and Herzegovina. The 'brain drain' was in full swing. Also, the middle classes in general were disappearing as mentioned in Z. Radeljković, *Intelektualna staza do zelene grane*, (*Intellectual path to pastures green*) Lettre International, No. 14, Zima '96, p.14.
52. I remain friends with most of them to this very day.
53. I was paid in Deutsche Marks at the Jewish Community Centre and for private tuition, while at other places I was paid in dinars.
54. By then almost nothing could be bought for dinars, not even at farmers' markets.
55. The money was being devalued so steadily and rapidly that, sometimes in a matter of a month, it would lose a huge percentage of value.
56. International delegations were gladly allowed into Sarajevo because most of those would either promise some form of support or help with media coverage of the horrendous situation in the city.
57. Unfortunately, he could not bring any books.
58. My weight then was hardly over forty kilos.
59. Vlado and Nada who had lived in Serbia since after the Second World War.
60. Dušanka who was the wife of Sanja's paternal uncle and Sladjana's mother.
61. It was called *Jugobanka* then, which implied it was a Yugoslav bank as before, but it transpired it was not.
62. School of Slavonic and East European Studies at University College London.
63. Željko, Henika's son, with his wife and daughter immigrated to Holland shortly before the outbreak of the war and the entire extended family gave them both moral and financial support, as much as we could.
64. The saying that Jews always have a suitcase packed 'just in case' is well known among the Jews.
65. The original is in French: '*une valise dans la tête, une valise dans le couloir*' (the English translation Mazower's). M. Mazower, *What You Did Not Tell*, Penguin Books, UK, 2018, p. 179.
66. It was even called Yugoslavia at the time.
67. A. Towles, *A Gentleman in Moscow*, Windmill Books, 2016, p.164, talks about the Soviet exile of Russians to Siberia (italics in the original).
68. We always had a big New Year's Eve celebration, which actually had all the hallmarks of Christmas (tree, gifts, dinner, even a Santa Claus named 'Grandpa Frost', without the religious attributes. One could say it was a 'socialist religion's' replacement for Christmas.
69. I managed to organize a dignified secular ceremony for my mother some 22 years later.

Chapter 5: Recovery

1. Central British Fund for German Jewry was the original name of World Jewish Relief. In the 1990s, they were helping Bosnian refugees.
2. It was a relatively big group gathered at La Benevolencia and Friends society.
3. A combination of the words Sarajevo and London indicating the connections.
4. Apparently, the fact that Henika had mentioned earlier to one of the directors at CBF (with whom Henika was friendly) that we would be applying for asylum, was seen as unacceptable by the person we had an appointment with. On such a serious matter both Henika and I thought a little nudge, a semblance of *veza*, would do no harm. Old habits die hard.
5. In our minds, fingerprints were taken from criminals only.
6. However, when my uncle died in 1997, I was allowed to attend his funeral. The excommunication occurred a bit later.
7. She never got her well-deserved Bosnian pension.
8. It was even called 'pension credit' at some point.
9. I later nicknamed him 'my computer guru' because he was helping me with my computer in Cambridge.
10. Teaching English as a Foreign Language.
11. My previous education and training did not count.
12. Rabbi David Goldberg at St John's Wood synagogue in London.
13. Georg Chaimowitz, an Austrian post-war and contemporary artist.
14. Ironically, it was the literary theory professor who in Sarajevo disappointed me with his reactions. He inadvertently did me a favour by accepting a job elsewhere.
15. Their Royal Highnesses.
16. That would not have been surprising since he introduced me to his divorced poet friend, earlier in London, but that did not work out.
17. My first birthday in the UK was several days after we arrived, so I was not up for any sort of celebration.
18. Having not been religious, along with the New Year's Eve celebration, all our birthdays and wedding anniversaries were big family celebrations when the entire family would get together – our substitute for religious holidays.
19. She had been diagnosed with depression and her GP prescribed her first antidepressants. Unfortunately, they did not help much.
20. He was my student days UK lector and a friend who warned me about the imminent civil war in Bosnia and who then visited me several times when I arrived in London and was the first of my friends to meet Ned.
21. He also further represented my mother who was then naturalized in 2004.

22. He was English born and bred. His Huguenot family came to the UK in the seventeenth century.
23. He even suggested that my mother might have suffered from PTSD (Post-Traumatic Stress Disorder).
24. We translated into English: a) M. Selimović, *The Fortress*, Northwestern University Press, Illinois, 1999; b) M. Krleža, *The Banquet in Blitva*, Northwestern University Press, Illinois, 2004, novels; and also, into English: P. Finci *Applause, and then Silence*, Style Writers Now, 2012, essays; and into Serbo-Croat: E. D. Goy, *Sablja i pjesna*, (a book on 'Gorski vijenac') OKTOIH, Podgorica, 2000, essays.
25. We decided I would keep my maiden name in signing translations. For some reason we felt our relationship was of no concern for readers. However, once Ned was gone, I insisted on using double-barrelled surname – with obligatory Goy part – as my only signature.
26. Admittedly, it was my choice, but out of necessity.
27. We used to refer to it as 'cabbaging' because our culinary cooperation started with cabbage cutting for a stew which Ned used to make.
28. Unfortunately, Goran only visited Cambridge after Ned's death. I badly wanted him to meet Ned, but it was not to be.
29. Interestingly, mostly by chance I believe, a small minority of my friends have ever been Jewish.
30. Unlike flats, it was common to own a garage. And I did.
31. The quotation marks are used because, by then, English did not feel like a foreign language any more and it is a reference to my earlier conviction.
32. The bombing of Yugoslavia was the North Atlantic Treaty Organization's military operation against the Federal Republic of Yugoslavia during the Kosovo War. The air strikes lasted from 24 March 1999 to 10 June 1999.
33. We both referred to it as Serbo-Croat.
34. Miloš Crnjanski, *Roman o Londonu*.
35. The home where she and Richard lived and Ned and I visited often.
36. The granddaughter of Ned's Belgrade friend who took her PhD at Cambridge. Coming from Serbia she needed Ned's support to accomplish it and he was happy to help her both financially and otherwise. In order to get the lower university fees, i.e. not those for overseas students, he requested that she be treated as his granddaughter. So both Ned and, later I, became her 'foster' grandparents.
37. The Russian one was *Stenka Razin* and the Serbian *Gde si, dušo, gde si, 'rano* with lyrics by the poet Branko Radičević. Radičević (1824–53) is considered the founder of Serbian lyrical Romanticism. Ned translated his poems and wrote about him.
38. Ned kept some in a big chest of drawers in the garage.

39. E. D Goy, 'Starina Novak and Chieftain Bogosav: Theory and Practice of Verse Translation', *Serbian Studies*, Vol. 16, 2002, No. 1, pp. 17–27.
40. Bogdan Rakić, my Sarajevo English department colleague and friend who was in the US then.
41. E. D Goy, *Love and Death in the Poetry of Šiško Menčetić and Džore Držić*, Akademija nova, Beograd 2001.
42. Momčilo Nastasijević (1894–1938) was a Serbian poet, writer and thinker, who had been at the forefront of Ned's interest for a long time.
43. E. D Goy, *The Escaped Mystery*, Slavica, Bloomington, 2010.
44. The novel by Miroslav Krleža that we translated together and submitted to Northwestern University Press, Evanston, Illinois, United States. The book was published in 2004.
45. Held in September 2000.
46. I had been analysing the language, mostly in the press, from the different parts of the former Yugoslavia. Before I met Ned, I received financial help from the Ian Karten Charitable Trust in obtaining the necessary material.
47. For some reason unknown to me the paper was not included in the collection published by the organizers, but was published in *The South Slav Journal*, Vol. 25, Nos 1–2 (95–6), Spring–Summer 2004, pp. 59–62, London 2004, as 'Serbo-Croat or Bosnian, Croatian or Serbian'.
48. 'The Darktown Poker Club'. He loved the lyrics.
49. J. Levinger-Goy, ed., *The Game*, Cambridge 2000.
50. Diploma in Public Service Interpreting.
51. Sanja, Igor's mother, visited us in the UK a few years later.
52. English, Roman script and Serbian, Cyrillic script.
53. We always had two lectors, a British one and an American one.
54. Hatzola Trust, in North London, is a non-profit organization primarily set up to provide a free 24-hour First Responder and Ambulance Service for medical emergencies.
55. The official name at the time was the Federal People's Republic of Yugoslavia.
56. My old GP had by then retired.
57. Her husband sadly died not too long after I had the pleasure of getting to know him.
58. She was also in a bad place at the time.
59. It was organized by Cambridge Voluntary Services.
60. My mother died in London in 2017 and I took her ashes to Belgrade to lay them with her husband/my father, as was her wish.
61. As I was finalizing the manuscript, the Covid-19 pandemic was in full swing. Yet another change, a radical one with the lockdown, and definitely not for the better!

Endnotes

Epilogue

1. A man who calls Muslims to prayer from the minaret of a mosque. In previous years, I remembered, calls for prayers were common, but they used to emanate from minarets without the help of any electronic equipment. So, the calls could not be heard far from the mosque.
2. The loudspeakers were located mostly along the main street and those around, especially during the 1st of May parades, for instance.
3. She announced my physiological need as an unreasonable demand using the unacceptable vocabulary.
4. Unlike my mother who took an early retirement, my father even worked post-retirement age, as long as he was capable.
5. Except for Alen, her older son who was an adult too.

Addendum: Yugoslavia in the Second World War

1. Dr Stephen A. Hart. www.bbc.co.uk/history/worldwars/wwtwo/partisan_fighters_01.shtml
2. Also often referred to as Gypsies, a pejorative term.
3. Muslims were recognized as a separate ethnic group/nation (as well as a religious one) only in the late 1960s in Socialist Yugoslavia and recorded as a separate ethnic group in the 1971 census. The distinction was then made between Muslim with a capital 'M' and with a lower case 'm', the former being ethnicity, the latter religion. Yet another confusing phenomenon. In the 1990s, this group was relabelled. Previous Muslims (earlier capital 'M') were referred to as Bosniaks, denoting ethnicity now; Muslim (previously lower case 'm') now with capital 'M' denoted religion, while the term Bosnians referred to the entire population (all ethnicities) of the country called Bosnia. Difficult and confusing maybe, but true (author's explanation).
4. Dr Stephen A. Hart. www.bbc.co.uk/history/worldwars/wwtwo/partisan_fighters_01.shtml
5. Ibid.
6. Ibid.
7. https://encyclopedia.ushmm.org/content/en/article/jasenovac
8. italics in the original.
9. www.holocaustresearchproject.org/othercamps/jasenovac.html
10. https://europeanmemories.net/memorial-heritage/rab-concentration-camp/
11. The king and the government fled to the UK.
12. The reference in brackets by J. Levinger-Goy.

13. Dr Stephen A. Hart. www.bbc.co.uk/history/worldwars/wwtwo/partisan_fighters_01.shtml
14. Ibid.
15. Ibid.
16. Ibid.
17. Ibid.

Appendix B: Excerpt from a Story by Ivo Andrić

1. Copyright permission both for the story and the translation obtained.
2. 'A Letter from 1920', translated by L. Grenoble, in C. Hawkesworth ed., *Ivo Andrić, The Damned Yard and Other Stories*, London and Boston: Forest Books, 1992, pp. 117–18.